CAMP & TRAIL
COOKING
TECHNIQUES

PRACTICAL OUTDOOR GUIDE BOOKS
by Jim Capossela

How to Catch Crabs by the Bushel!

Part Time Cash for the Sportsman

How to Write for the Outdoor Magazines

Good Fishing Close to New York City

Good Fishing in the Catskills
(with other contributors)

Northeast Hunting Guide
(with other contributors)

Northeast Upland Hunting Guide
(with other contributors)

Trophy Trout Streams of the Northeast
(editor)

Ice Fishing

Camp & Trail Cooking Techniques

A JIM CAPOSSELA OUTDOOR BOOK

CAMP & TRAIL COOKING TECHNIQUES

by Jim Capossela

Drawings by John Wright

The Countryman Press
Woodstock, Vermont

The Countryman Press, Inc.
Post Office Box 175
Woodstock, Vermont 05091

©1994 by James P. Capossela
Line drawings ©1994 by John Wright

All rights reserved. No part of this book may be reproduced in any form or by any electronic or mechanical means, including information storage or retrieval systems, without permission in writing from the publisher, except by a reviewer who may quote brief passages.

Library of Congress Cataloging-in-Publication Data
Capossela, Jim.
    Camp and trail cooking techniques: a treasury of skills and
    recipes for all outdoor chefs / Jim Capossela; drawings by John Wright.
        p.   cm.
      "A Jim Capossela outdoor book."
    Includes bibliographical references and index.
    ISBN 0-88150-282-0 ;
    1. Outdoor cookery.   I. Title
TX823.C295   1994
641.5'782--dc20   93-46139
                                                                             CIP

Cover art and design by Karen Savary
Text design by Sue Lobel and Harry Wirtz
All photographs by the author except as noted
Cast-iron artwork on chapter title pages courtesy Lodge Mfr. Co.

Printed in the United States of America

5 4 3 2 1

In memory of "Nana"

We'll always remember her warm little kitchen and her wonderful cooking

Rose Holicky Zajicek
1896 – 1989

Daughter of Izidor and Anna Holicky
Wife of Louis Zajicek
Sister of Helena, Maria, Matilda, and Emery
Mother of Josephine, Louis and Joan
Grandmother of Carolee, Karen, Jimmy, Ronald, Bobby, Timothy, Sharon, Patty, and John
Great-grandmother of Andrew, Laura, Breana, Kira, Megan Robbie, Billy, Christopher and ...

Rose was born in Nahač, a small town near Prague in what was then Austria-Hungary and is now Czechoslovakia. Seeking a better life, she bravely left her family in 1912 at the age of 16 and boarded a boat for the United States. She would never again see her mother or father or two of her four brothers and sisters.

Along with her brother Emery and her sister Matilda, she settled in the Tarrytowns, pleasant hamlets along the Hudson River in southern New York. In 1917 she married Louis Zajicek, also an immigrant from Austria-Hungary.

Rose had a great capacity for work and in some years earned more than her husband, who was a laborer at the famous Sleepy Hollow Cemetery, where Washington Irving is buried. In the hard depression years, she worked where she could, but housekeeping was her main enterprise. She worked until her mid-eighties, and enjoyed reasonably good health until ninety.

Rose took great delight in cooking for the family, especially on holidays. Everything she made was good, including—in the early years—her Slovakian specialties like genuine apple strudel, poppy seed cakes, and stuffed cabbage. She had an equally good touch outdoors, and perennially had beautiful flowers ablaze on her property. Always the strongest one in the family, she lived alone in her comfortable home until the age of 92. In the summer of 1988 I helped her put in a garden of tomatoes, beans, and peppers. It was her last garden, and she tended it proudly and well.

CONTENTS

Recipe notes and listing

Only those recipes set off from the text are included in the list that follows these notes. Dozens more recipes, or general cooking formulas, are woven through the text but are not listed here.

Abbreviations have been kept to a minimum, but a few are used repeatedly: tsp. = teaspoon; T. = tablespoon; opt. = optional (means that satisfactory results can be expected even if that ingredient is omitted); lb. = pound; oz. = ounce and, with only a couple of exceptions, refers to volume measure, not weight.

I have not been a milk drinker since childhood but I do use it in cooking. I now use skim milk very often, and find that it rarely degrades a recipe to any degree. When a recipe says "milk or skim milk," it means I have tested the recipe both ways and in each case the results were satisfactory.

I use margarine about half the time, and the kind I prefer is soy margarine purchased at the health food store. When margarine is listed as an option to butter, it does not necessarily mean that I also tested the recipe with margarine; however, acceptable (if not ideal) results can usually be expected with margarine when butter is called for.

I almost always use sweet, unsalted butter. In the couple of instances where I use salted butter, that is stated.

All the recipes specifying "powdered milk" were tested with "nonfat dry milk," of various brands. There are other types of powdered milk but I have not used them.

I detest "table syrups" and would rather skip breakfast. Any time maple syrup is specified, it is the real stuff I am referring to.

I used "low sodium salt" in many of these recipes with no detectable ill effect. Many people are, of course, greatly concerned with reducing salt intake. In most of the recipes, the salt can be reduced or eliminated. Some of the baked goods, though, will taste strangely flat without the salt.

Whenever mustard is specified, it is the familiar prepared mustard that I am referring to. In the few instances when dry (powdered) mustard is called for, that is specifically stated.

Campers, especially backpackers, often cook for only one or two. Most of the recipes in this book can be halved with satisfactory results. When halving a recipe calling for one egg, it's usually advisable to beat the egg and use only half in the smaller recipe.

I personally tested every recipe in this book. They will work with an extremely high degree of accuracy. I am all too familiar with recipes that do not communicate their messages clearly and completely. I believe the ones in this book do.

A great many of the recipes in this book are original. Some—like my Easy White Chowder and Easy Red Chowder—I created expressly for this book. In those instances when a credit line was appropriate, I placed it right beneath the recipe title as opposed to burying it somewhere in the back of the book. Those recipes taken from other sources but changed in any substantive way were considered to be new recipes and no credit was given. In many cases, when a recipe was changed, it was to simplify it for camp use. But I discovered that most recipes simply did not work as stated, proof positive to me that many cookbook authors never test their recipes at all.

Each recipe that follows is listed under only one category—the most logical one—although, clearly, some recipes do overlap categories.

The general index, at the back of the book, will be very useful in helping you locate not only specific types of foods but other areas of interest as well.

Although sometimes a recipe is introduced by the text that precedes it, more often this is not the case. The recipes are set in a smaller and bolder typeface and should be easily distinguished from the text proper. To some extent, the recipes are randomly scattered through the text, although most have been placed in what seemed to be a logical chapter and section.

TO BUILD A FIRE

Anyone who has read Jack London's compelling story of that title will have little trouble imagining that, down through the long march of history, more than a few lives have hung on the ability to make a fire. But should modern-day recreational campers even be making campfires in this age when there is so much rightful concern with preserving what's left of the wild places?

The most controversial aspect of this book is apt to be the rather substantial discussions of and references to wood fires. It is difficult to deny the premise that campers who foray more than a mile from the road should know how to make a wood fire—the life-saving thing it certainly can be. But when a fire isn't really needed, then what? Let's look at the objections to wood fires one by one.

Air pollution should not be a genuine concern. All the campfires burning in one evening in any given state are not likely to produce as much smoke as one good working factory with multiple smokestacks. And of course, wood fires burn cleaner.

Consumption of wood is a factor. The forest keeps on generating new wood, but in heavily-used camping areas—typically either close to the road or well off the road and very popular—supply can exceed demand. Cutting of live trees is always taboo, of course, and cutting of standing dead wood—if done to excess—can change the character of a place. In these heavy-use areas, fires should be as small and of as short duration as possible. You want to change the appearance of the location as minimally as possible while also leaving a little wood for the next fellow.

The actual impact of the fire and fireplace on the earth is really the center of the discussion. Next to footsteps, no camper's activity affects the land more than fires.

Much of this book has to do with campground-type settings. Here, you make your fire in an existing fireplace and often, burn wood you purchase from the campground. You don't come expecting wilderness and of course you don't get wilderness.

In near-the-road picnic/camping areas, and close-to-civilization backpacking areas you might arrive with somewhat higher expectations of beauty. Still, in such camping areas, there will almost invariably be existing fireplaces—ones put there by the municipality or ad hoc ones created by campers. The best thing you can do is use what you find as opposed to expanding the diameter of the fire area. It's too bad that, in these types of areas, campers have to construct such large fireplaces. I often find myself tidying them, making them smaller. I also try to pack out what garbage others have left behind. But you won't be doing the woods a favor by removing the fireplace in a heavy-use area. Another one will just spring up in its place.

In the true backcountry, your expectations will be higher, and so will everyone else's. In the deep woods, stoves should be used for all cooking, and campfires—if they're made at all—should only be enjoyed if they are made in such a way that the area of the fire can be returned to a completely natural state. In very sensitive areas, like alpine zones, no fires should be made.

Keep campfires small in the backcountry. Use only a couple of rocks for containment or none at all. Make only one campfire on a three-day trip. Burn small wood so ugly, half-burned logs do not remain behind. Scatter to the woods any rocks you do use before you go.

Do your camping in the less-visited places. Not only will you help take the pressure off the most popular areas, but you may be startled at the solitude and beauty you find—even if you do miss the famous peak or the renowned lake or river.

Perhaps most importantly, read some of the books on no-trace camping that discuss these measures in much greater detail.

PREFACE

One day I was sitting next to the campfire along my beloved Delaware River and decided that if ever I was going to own a camp cookbook that had all the information I wanted, I was going to have to write it myself.

Six years, dozens of campfires, and 642,196 bits of data later, here it is.

Camp cooking is as rich in lore as the outdoors itself. But now, much of that lore is being forgotten or, in some quarters, even denounced. Almost all the old-time camp cookbooks, like this cookbook, were written by sportsmen: fishermen and hunters. Their pages were rich with game and fish recipes, with anecdotes of glorious days afield with rod and gun, with now-quaint pictures of nuclear families grilling hot dogs in front of simonized Chevies and canvas tents. To modern-day sportsmen they are cherished windows back to a time that seemed much friendlier to their interests. To modern-day nonsportsmen they may seem not only obsolete but perhaps environmentally unfriendly, or something even worse.

There is no need to express my views here on the old camping ways versus the new; you cannot put down 115,000 words without painting a pretty good portrait of yourself and your views. It is fair, though, to state the aims of this book, and then to have you hold me up to them after you've finished reading it.

This is, first and foremost, a technique-oriented cookbook. Even in the old-time camp cookbooks, where technique was given somewhat more space than today, the real intricacies of reflector-oven cooking, of cast-iron cooking, of the whole range of outdoor cooking techniques was given too little attention. But "technique" in this book goes well beyond correct manipulation of the various implements and kinds of fires being used. It goes right to the core of the cooking itself.

How do you make a quick fish stock in camp? Or, how do you churn out a fast, foolproof gravy? For that matter, what goes into a gravy, and how can you make-do (in making one) with what you have hanging around camp? What are the underlying principles of a braise, and why exactly is it so versatile? What about deep-frying, or making soups, always under the constraints of a camp environment? How can you offer fresh, raw fruits and vegetables in such a way that people will unfailingly eat them? Since camp cooking almost always has to be reduced in complexity, knowing the underlying principles and formulas is ever so important. Such primary knowledge allows you to vary, to substitute, to work with what you have. Knowing the underlying technique places in your hand that magic wand of camp cooks: adaptability!

Second, and just as important, this is a camp cookbook designed to bridge the old and the new. No generation is so illuminated that all its ideas will endure the long scrutiny of time; new generations keep proving that. This book looks fondly over its shoulder to what Brad Angier, a great outdoorsman, liked to call "a younger continent," and attempts to preserve not only the old-time camping techniques but their spirit as well. At the same time, it looks just as cheerfully ahead on the trail, to not only bespeak but actively promote what's best of the new camp ways, and to capture their spirit too.

Camp & Trail Cooking Techniques, in that sense at least, is for every camper.

Third, this cookbook is a celebration of good eating. There are more than 180 recipes presented in the usual formats plus dozens more either woven through the text or suggested by the underlying principles from which so much variation is possible. To find a type of recipe quickly, just turn back a few pages to the recipe list.

You'd be as hard pressed to find a hash 'n' egg recipe in a modern-day, health-oriented camp cookbook as you would be to find kasha-stuffed tomatoes in an old-time one. You will find both in this book! Do you need to smell that bacon sizzling, to hear those burgers chirping, to see that portly 16-ounce steak smothered in a rich onion gravy? I've tried to see to these needs. But you also have dishes aplenty made without meat, some of them my very favorites and composed with hearty and nutty-tasting grains and potatoes and all kinds of vegetables and spices—both general and lightweight recipes. Not only does this book participate in the movement towards healthier food, but also in the one towards more interesting food. Ingredients and international flavors never even heard of by the old-time campers are being carried to camp more and more, and many will be found in these pages.

As for philosophy—to get back to it for a moment—I think I capped it pretty well in these pages. Moreover, I'm the kind of person who, after everyone in camp is well fed, likes to fade into the woodwork and listen to everyone else philosophize: about what constitutes healthy food, about what a trout could possibly see in a Royal Coachman, and—most frequently—about why in hell they allow those transistor radios in campgrounds.

ACKNOWLEDGMENTS

The author would like to thank the following individuals and companies for their generous assistance in the preparation of this book: Angela Aiello, Mike Bleech, Larry Boutis, Per Brandin, Campmor, The Coleman Company, The Color Group, Robin Dutcher-Bayer, Eastern Mountain Sports, Tom Fegeley, Murray Gruber, Peter Lewis, Sue Lobel, Lodge Manufacturing, Christopher Merce, Jim Merce, Dick Michaud, George Milite, Bob Morrison,. Bud Murray, The Original Image, Christine Ponte, REI, Tom and Tina Schlichter, Dwight Shuh, *Sports Afield,* Robert Titterton, Alice Vera, Jim and Nancy Walsh, Harry Wirtz, John Wright, and John and Loretta Zelyez.

More than half of the recipes in this book are originals, created by the author or adapted by him for camp use. Many others are old favorites that have been in the family recipe box for two or three generations, their origins unknown. Still others were donated by friends and associates. The author would here like to thank those individuals and companies who granted permission to use certain previously published recipes. Please also see the full bibliographical citations near the back of the book:

Gerald and Chauna Duffin, for Paradise Potatoes, p. 89; Celestial Seasonings Inc., for Strawberry Yogurt Swirl, p. 114 and Sleepytime® Nightcap, p. 131; Wolff's Buckwheat Products (a division of Birkett Mills, Inc.), for Kasha-Stuffed Tomatoes, p. 130, and Call of the Wild Kasha, p. 230, which appeared in *Wolff's Buckwheat Cookbook;* Gibbs Wild Rice, for North Country Stuffed Peppers, p. 130; Tom and Tina Schlichter, for Deep Sea Parmagiana, p. 155, Tom's Spicy Cocktail Sauce, p. 157, and Half-Shell Mussel Delight, p. 157, which appeared in *How to Catch Clams By The Bushel!;* Gunnings Crab House, Baltimore, MD, for Gunnings Famous Crab Cakes, p 156; Stephen Kaminski, for Marinated Duck, p. 168, which appeared in *The North American Hunting Club Wild Game Cookbook;* and Sierra Club Books, for Whole Wheat Soy Pancakes, p. 228, which appeared in *Simple Foods for the Pack,* by Axcell, Cooke and Kinmont.

Very minor changes have been made by the author to some of these recipes. Also, some of the recipe titles may have been changed to be more in keeping with the spirit of this book.

Part One
GENERAL CAMP COOKERY

If home is where you hang your hat, then just maybe camp is where you hang your heart. For the weary city dweller or suburban commuter, camp is as much a place to long for as be at. A little cabin, sitting there in that small clearing, the sun dappling through the maples, is a reverie that can shrink a 52-week corporate work year down to 2, but make the whole 52 seem bearable. Camp, today, takes many physical forms, but almost always it is a place of rivers or mountains or trees, where the clutter of modern existence is reduced to the point that you really can put things into perspective.

As generously as I define camp in this book, there still are two types of camp-cooking situations. I call these general and lightweight. There are always some limitations when cooking outdoors, but in general camp situations—covered here in part 1—the assumption is that the weight or bulk of one's equipment is not of paramount importance. Nonetheless, even in part 1 a careful eye has been paid to simplifying procedures and recipes whenever possible.

A great deal of information in this first part will have substantial application to the lightweight camps part 2 is dedicated to. For example, most of the discussion in chapter 9 on reflector ovens would be of use to go-light campers, since small, packable reflector ovens are made, and since on-the-trail baking procedures can often be simplified. Then, too, a great many of the recipes found here in part 1 can be judiciously trimmed (with careful substitutions made) and imported with great effect to the backcountry.

Part 1, then, is the real meat 'n' potatoes of the book—even when (as just mentioned in the Preface) it's more like kasha and tomatoes.

Chapter 1
CHECKLISTS FOR
THE CAMPGROUND CHEF

One of my good camping buddies has suggested that my idea of roughing it is arriving at the campsite without the julienne blade to my Cuisinart. I'm not that bad, but sometimes I come pretty close.

One time at a river's-edge campground I was laboring cheerfully over my stove, whipping up some sourdough bread and fresh fish chowder—two of my camp favorites. At the site next to me, a young couple was grilling hot dogs and hamburgers on a home-type barbecue unit. The female half of that couple at some point walked over to me and asked if I had any mustard. I pulled out the condiment tray from my camp kitchen and said, "Sure, what kind?"

With a perfect blend of ridicule and admiration she looked at my camp kitchen, glanced over to the fireplace where a two-crust pie was baking, and asked, "You carry more than one kind of mustard on a camping trip?"

"Sure—doesn't everyone?" I said, and then recommended an herbed green peppercorn.

In the Boy Scouts they told me, "Be prepared." Being only 12 at the time, and already loving food to a fault, I took it literally. A zip-locking bag of fresh cilantro and a teak pepper mill? Alas, both have made their way into my camp kitchen. As far as the Cuisinart goes, I wanted to bring that on a canoe trip once but the hundred-mile extension cord would not fit into my Isuzu Trooper.

For the types of camping situations discussed in part 1, you will not be restricted by weight but by how much you can fit into your vehicle or are willing to bring. Of course you can choose to keep it simple, making do with just your backpacking cookset and perhaps a few added items. But from what I've seen at most campgrounds, I draw a clear conclusion: In an away-from-home situation, most people like to bring as many comforts, culinary or otherwise, as they feasibly can.

Even if you're among those Spartan exceptions, I think you'll agree that, at the

My camp kitchen (right) and my tool box, described ahead and in chapter 2. These two boxes transport all my camp cooking gear except my dutch oven.

least, you want to get to the campsite with all the things you really did want to have. The simple solution? Checklists. Every year I see people at campgrounds rummaging furiously through their gear and their car for a simple can opener, for a pack of matches, for a knife that actually cuts, for something to use as a pot holder. Without checklists you will forget these things, and others that are even more important.

In this chapter, we'll discuss a rather complete camp-cook's checklist without much regard to organizing and transporting it. Those two concerns will be highlighted in the next chapter.

A complete checklist would seem to be a foolproof way of getting to camp with everything you wanted to have along. Yet it's amazing how many ways people find to screw up this simple procedure.

Some check off an item in anticipation of actually packing it. This is a big mistake. You must discipline yourself not to check off the item until it goes into its container, or, in the case of large objects (such as tents), into the vehicle that will get you to where you're going.

Some people have the nervous habit of packing, unpacking, and repacking. Usually, such double-checking stems from uncertainty about whether an item was really packed, and it defeats the whole purpose of the checklist. Better to pack each container once and leave it alone.

Think in terms of "ultimate containers," a phrase I'm afraid I will have to take the blame for coining. Try to leave home with as few ultimate containers as possible. For example, try to have all cooking equipment in one or two boxes, all clothing in one duffel, all tools in one box. Pack these up to several days in advance of your trip. Use a list for each and don't check off the item until it's actually in the container. Resist the urge to check it off 10 minutes or even 10 seconds before it's packed. Use your checklist literally! On the morning of your departure, you should be down to your master list. I like to leave home with only 15 to 20

The entire contents of my camp kitchen, spread out before it.

separate items to put into the car. Now let your mind drift back to that summer day when you left home with spouse, kids, dogs, and dozens of loose items all yelling, banging, clinking, clanging, barking, bouncing, gouging, scraping, bulging, and protruding out of the station wagon.

I know spontaneity is fun, but which scenario would you honestly prefer? If the answer is the groaning station wagon, please return this book for a full refund—if the store will give it to you.

Presented on the following pages is the checklist I used for a recent nine-day camping trip to Maine. The master list lists all ultimate containers except the special gear. As you can see, the tent, folding table, and so forth are considered ultimate containers even though they each comprise only one object. An asterisk is next to each ultimate container that has its own checklist. In this case, the following had their own list: car box, camp kitchen, toolbox, clothes bag, and special gear.

The car box is nothing but a cardboard box that I keep in the truck at all times. All I need do is quickly check that everything is still there. Naturally, if I go in someone else's vehicle the items in this box related to camping will have to be fit into other containers, if the person I'm traveling with doesn't have them along.

My camp kitchen (see chapter 2) contains most of my cooking gear and is

Camping checklist

Trip _Maine - Baxter_____ Date 6/10-6/19

Master List

✔ Tent
✔ Folding table
NO Chair
✔ Cooler/water bottle
✔ Sleeping bag
✔ Clothing*
✔ Dutch oven
✔ Coleman lantern
___
___

✔ Tool box*
NO Food pack
✔ Water jug
✔ Camp kitchen*
✔ Mattress
✔ Car box*
✔ Camera bag
✔ Special gear*
___
___

Camp Kitchen

✔ Nesting cook set
✔ Reflector oven
✔ Cutting boards
NO Griddle
✔ Potholders
✔ Two canopeners
✔ Large slotted spoon
✔ Spatula
✔ Skewers
✔ 2 biscuit cutters
✔ Flat grater
NO Sharpening steel
✔ Wooden matches
✔ Plastic bags & ties
✔ Silverware pouch
✔ Mirror
✔ Baking tins
✔ Mixing bowls
___
___

✔ Baking tray
✔ Measuring cups
✔ Recipe cards
NO Large spoon
✔ Vegetable peeler
✔ Measuring spoons
✔ Large fork
✔ Rubber spatula
✔ Two whisks
✔ Aluminum foil
✔ Claw cracker
✔ Coffee pot
✔ Knives
✔ Tongs
✔ Spices per menu
✔ CORKSCREW
✔ Wooden Spoon
___

Car Box

✔ Rubber patch kits
✔ Whisk broom
✔ Rain gear
✔ Basic tools
✔ Flares
✔ Rope
✔ Waterproof matches
✔ Glass cleaner
✔ Laundry detergent

✔ Paper towels
✔ Duct tape
NO Lantern
✔ Toilet paper
✔ Asst. plastic bags
✔ String
✔ Rags
NO Blanket
✔ Lug wrench

Tool Box

NO Axe   ✔ Rope with hooks
✔ Stove   ✔ Tablecloth and clamps
✔ Fuel   ✔ Small shovel
✔ 2 Wash Basins   ✔ Wire lifter
NO Tarp   ✔ Box with odds n' ends
✔ Folding saw   ✔ Fly spray
✔ Grill   ✔ Candle lantern
✔ Canteen   ✔ Funnels
✔ Cast iron skillet   ✔ Dish soap
NO Stove stand   ✔ Plastic containers
✔ Stove starter

——   ——
——   ——
——   ——

Clothing

✔ Sweatshirt   ✔ 2 light socks
✔ 1 light socks   ✔ Ditty bag
✔ Jeans   NO Shorts
NO Bathing suit   ✔ Underwear 3
✔ 2 flannel shirts   ✔ 2 t-shirts
✔ Wool jacket   ✔ Sweat pants
✔ Mocassins   ✔ Laundry bag
✔ Belt   ✔ Towel
✔ Sewing kit   ✔ Hat, headband
NO Old sneakers   NO Beach towel
✔ Pillow   ✔ Paper material
NO Camera   ✔ Blue parka
✔ Wading shoes

——   ——
——   ——

Special Gear

✔ Rod case
✔ Vest/net
✔ Waders   ——
✔ Kit bag   ——
——   ——
——   ——

Author's campground checklist, this and facing page. This list and the items on it are discussed fully in the text.

A cutting board is one of the most useful, yet most frequently forgotten camp cooking implements.

used exclusively for camping. Relatively little was bought new. These are hand-me-downs, items bought in flea markets, and so on. All of it stays all the time in my camp kitchen. I really shouldn't have to check this box, since nothing is ever removed, but I do a couple of times a year anyway in case some item was lost on a previous trip. I always check it at the beginning of the camping season.

Like the camp kitchen, the toolbox is a handmade wooden box. I describe how to construct both boxes in the next chapter. I do use some of the things in this ultimate container for purposes other than camping. Still, I'm usually able to pack this box, using the checklist shown, days ahead of any camping trip.

The clothes bag is nothing but a tough, canvas suitcase. Use what you will, but try to keep it to one suitcase or duffel. Any more than that and you're probably bringing too much clothing.

The special gear is just that: fishing or hunting gear, photographic equipment, or perhaps objects used for water sports in summer. It could also be things related to boating. Unfortunately, this type of stuff often comprises quite a number of ultimate containers and can really add to your bulk. On the Maine trip, though, it consisted of just four items: rod case with rods, vest with net, waders, and kit bag. There was no room for these objects in any of my other ultimate containers. Thus, add four more objects to the total number brought on the trip.

What did I have left to do on the morning of this trip? I did have to pack a few items of fresh food into the cooler. That took about five minutes. As far as the rest of the food, no checklist was made by the group as we'd decided to pick and choose at the supermarket near our destination. In other circumstances, I might make up a separate, hand-written checklist for food either to be brought along or purchased en route. I don't use any kind of formal checklist for food, unless it's a wilderness trip where stores are nonexistent. Then I would make up a detailed food list.

After putting those few items in the cooler, I made a cup of coffee, relaxed for half an hour and read a magazine. The truck had been fully packed the night before and I really had nothing else to do. I wasn't agonizing over what I might have forgotten. I knew I had everything I wanted in the truck. I like leaving home with that peace of mind, and I have to say that this particular excursion went very smoothly, until the blackflies came along and carried us over into New Brunswick.

What you want to do, then, is use a series of lists. The minor lists can and should be checked off in the days leading up to your trip, as you pack your ultimate containers. On the day you leave, you should be down to your master list. Check off the 15 to 20 items (sometimes only 12 to 14 for me, on shorter trips) and you're off.

Don't think I go through the trouble of typing up a separate list for each trip.

I have a master copy for road-type camping (two pages as shown) and a separate, much shorter (one page) one for backpacking (see p. 188). Before each season, I run off copies of each and keep them in folders. For each trip, I put the date and place of the trip, and then I add the special gear needed. I always save old lists for future reference. I also adjust the clothing and other gear by writing in, longhand, items that I've left blank spaces for, and by writing "No" next to items I won't need on that particular trip. I never take everything—I pick and choose depending on circumstances. But I always use a checklist, and I never check off an item until it goes into either its ultimate container or the vehicle.

For group camping, we usually get together and decide what the community gear is to be. We decide who brings what, and then I add to or subtract things from my lists prior to the checking-off process.

Since this book is focussed on camp cookery, we'll now look in detail at just the two ultimate containers that I use to transport cooking equipment. Anything and everything pertaining to the cooking goes into these two boxes except the dutch oven, which is so heavy it has its own box (and I only bring this implement sometimes).

Camp Kitchen

NESTING COOK SET. As discussed, all my camp cooking gear goes into just two boxes. I could not accomplish this with a variety of random pots, pans, cups, and plates, none of which nest together. My set includes the following:
- 6-quart pot with lid and this lid also serves as an excellent 10-inch frypan
- 3-quart pot with lid
- 1-quart pot with lid

This is what came with this stainless-steel set, which cost around $60. I added a set of four nesting, rigid plastic dinner plates that fit inside the pot set. I did not add plastic cups since each person usually brings his or her own drinking cup. I do bring a few paper "hot cups" in case someone has nothing at all to drink out of. I also usually recommend that each person bring a dinner plate, so my four good ones are almost always enough.

My nesting camp cookset, photographed when brand new. It's rugged stainless steel and should easily last a lifetime.

As shown in the photo, the flexible steel handle on each pot folds down so it hugs the pot, for compactness. The lids have small fold-down handles on top. The set comes with a handle which attaches (with difficulty) to the skillet/top. A more deluxe set than mine comes not only with cups and plates but also a 10-quart pot. For larger groups, this big pot can be essential for certain cooking chores and for heating dishwater.

REFLECTOR OVEN. Mine is 18 inches long by about 8 inches wide. Since baking has its own chapter, we'll wait until then to discuss it.

CUTTING BOARDS. Believe it or not I have two: a square wooden one (nine inches on a side) and a folding, hard plastic one that measures 14½ by 3¾ inches when folded. Either you have one along or you cut up the plate or the picnic table, or dull your knife by cutting on some even harder surface.

GRIDDLE. Available in cast iron, which is ideal, but mine is made of heavy aluminum with a no-stick surface and fits perfectly over the two burners of my camp stove. It measures 18¼ by 9⅝ inches. I can make pancakes perfectly well in my cast-iron skillet, but it only makes three at a time. The griddle makes six, which really speeds up the process. Good for French toast, and many other things too.

POT HOLDERS. I bring two thick ones. One of the items you're most likely to forget to bring camping. A fireproof mitt is nice to have along for reflector-oven cooking.

TWO TYPES OF CAN OPENERS. The regular two-ended "church key," and the revolving type. For the latter, get a good one as the cheapies are about worthless and most frustrating to use.

LARGE SLOTTED SPOON. You can get by without this item, but it comes in handy.

SPATULA. I do not bring the oversized spatulas and forks that are often seen in the hands of backyard barbecuers. My spatula (pancake flipper) is just a normal-sized one, but it is needed. For dutch-oven cookery, the long-handled implements are highly desirable.

SKEWERS. If you want to make shish kebab. I bought a set of six.

TWO BISCUIT CUTTERS. Technically, these are flan rings. Each measures three inches in diameter. You can make a perfect egg inside one, and I also use them to cut biscuit or scone dough. Can be used to make tasty crumpets for breakfast (photo next page).

FLAT GRATER. The typical four-sided one is too bulky, but this flat, two-sided model is only 2½ ounces and comes in handy.

SHARPENING STEEL. A small one that folds into a leather case. Made just for outdoor use.

WOODEN MATCHES. Paper matches are worthless in camp, where dampness is rampant. Keep the wooden ones in a waterproof case.

PLASTIC BAGS AND TIES. The uses are endless. I usually buy a box of one-gallon bags and they last the camping season. Bags of other sizes are always in my car box.

SILVERWARE. I have about eight each stainless-steel spoons and forks, plus some oversized soup spoons. All these stay in a cloth silverware pouch, discussed in the next chapter.

MIRROR. A small model with a plastic frame. (I made a protective case for mine out of an old hand towel.) Mainly for shaving, but very important on occasion for dealing with medical calamities. I feel it's better protected in the camp kitchen than anywhere else in my camping gear.

A flan ring is useful for cutting biscuits or scones. The laminated inner surface of the camp kitchen door is my main food preparation area.

BAKING TINS. I realize that many campers will never bake in camp. That's a shame, but for those who will, the three tins I have and recommend are:

- Square, 8 inches on a side
- Round cake pan, 10 inches in diameter
- Small bread pan, 9 by 5 inches

These are discussed further in chapter 9. Also see photo on page 103.

MIXING BOWLS. Three nesting ones, made of plastic. Mine are white, which shows the dirt. I wish I bought beige or some other color. They have a tremendous number of secondary uses, for example shaving, teeth brushing, and food storage.

BAKING TRAY. Goes inside my reflector oven. Discussed in chapter 9.

MEASURING CUPS. Made of plastic, in the standard increments: ⅛ cup, ¼ cup, ⅓ cup, ½ cup, and 1 cup. I wired the three small ones together and the two larger ones together, to help keep them from getting lost. You could get by with just a one-cup plastic cup as long as the key increments are plainly marked. Again, most useful for camp bakers.

RECIPE CARDS. See chapter 2.

LARGE SPOON. Not a humongous one, just a large kitchen spoon.

VEGETABLE PEELER. Either bring one or waste half of your potatoes.

MEASURING SPOONS. Mine are stainless steel, in the usual increments. Make sure they're wired together or they'll get lost, I guarantee it.

LARGE FORK. Just a little larger than normal. Mine is an antique, with four indented prongs extending out from the hilt.

RUBBER SPATULA. A very small one, only six inches long and a half-ounce in weight. Lets you scrape the bowl or pot to minimize waste of food.

TWO WHISKS. A very small one and a larger one. Admittedly, for the more serious camp cook. Can save the day when you lack an eggbeater.

ALUMINUM FOIL. A 75-foot roll of the heavy duty stuff lasts me the camping season.

CLAW CRACKER. For shellfish, if you plan to eat any. Add a clam knife if you camp near the shore.

COFFEEPOT. Mine is an eight-cup baked enamel pot. It makes six cups OK but does not perk fewer than that too well. Seriously consider getting a smaller pot if your group is not too large. I have a four-cup stainless steel pot for when group size is small.

KNIVES. This will be a very personal decision. For the past 20 years I have always brought along my folding German-made Puma, which goes on my belt and was a 21st birthday present from my father. It has a 3¼-inch blade and I could get by with it alone. However, I bring two others: a folding Opinel "French Country Knife" and a small fillet knife for fish. Sharpen them on a good whetstone before leaving home and bring the previously mentioned steel to touch them up in camp.

TONGS. For turning meat, especially on the grill.

SPICES PER MENU. It really doesn't pay to try to transfer minute quantities of spices into tiny containers for transportation to camp. Unless you have a trailer, pop-

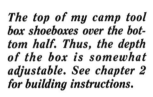

The top of my camp tool box shoeboxes over the bottom half. Thus, the depth of the box is somewhat adjustable. See chapter 2 for building instructions.

up, or some other kind of semipermanent camp, you might just as well take the spices you need from home and then simply return them to the cupboard at the end of your trip. On my kitchen shelf at home I have an empty cardboard box that I cut and taped together so it fits the upper right shelf in my camp kitchen. When I leave home, I simply put into this box all the spices I want. It holds about 20. I also stick in things like dry yeast, baking soda, and chicken or beef bouillon packets.

Toolbox

Although I call this a toolbox, many of the things I carry in it relate directly to cooking. We'll discuss only those that do.

STOVE. Mine is the standard (not heavy-duty) two-burner Coleman stove (Model 428B) that is so commonly seen in camp. I find this serves perfectly fine for a group of up to about 10. If your group is routinely larger than that, consider a three-burner model or get a second stove. Mine is at least 35 years old.

GRILL. Mine is 24 by 12 inches and it has folding legs so its height above the fire can be adjusted. With this item along, I don't have to worry about whether there will be an adequate cooking grill at the campsite.

WIRE LIFTER FOR DUTCH OVEN. As discussed in another chapter, this is necessary. Use it to remove the dutch oven's lid, or to move the entire oven into or out of the coals. Commercially made ones are available. More on dutch-oven accessories in chapter 8.

FUEL. I bring a gallon of Coleman fuel on most trips and I close the cap very tightly so fumes can't get into the other things in this box. Don't vent the other side of the can!

FUNNELS. Essential for fueling the camp appliances. I like to have a spare along with me. The little filters are replaceable, and should be replaced periodically.

STOVE STAND. A folding metal stand on which you place your camp stove. Costs about $20 and is worth it as it frees up the picnic table for eating.

SKILLET WITH TOP. This 10½-inch cast-iron skillet is my real workhorse cooking implement, and it has a surface like a baby's skin. I probably do half of all my camp cooking in it. It must have a top—without a top, its usefulness will be halved.

STOVE STARTER. You just can't beat this little spark-producing gadget. Mine is called a Piezoelectric Starter. You just place the tip of it right next to your stove's burner, open the stove's valve and press the little button on the starter. It is supposed to be good for 100,000 lights. This gadget will save much time searching for and fiddling with matches. It will also save a lot of burnt fingers.

PLASTIC CONTAINERS. I notice that a great deal of food goes to waste at campgrounds. Often, this stems from the belief that it will be just too much trouble to store leftovers. I once was also somewhat guilty of this attitude. Now I bring three plastic containers between one-half pint and one quart in size. They nest together for compactness. I keep the set in a plastic bag so they won't get dirty. Usually by the middle of the trip they're all in the cooler, filled with leftovers.

Several of the other items listed under Toolbox also relate to cooking in one way or another. Some of these are obvious, while others will be discussed further in other chapters.

It took me about 10 years to really get my camping gear together. My primary boxes are quite full now on most trips and I'm trying not to add more to my master list. So if I add an item now, it's only after considerable thought. Nonetheless, here are a few things that I've been bringing lately and, alas, one or more may sneak its way onto my permanent list next season.

SMALL STRAINER. This is only eight inches long, with a basket section that measures just three inches in diameter. Strainers have several purposes, for example straining sauces or gravies that turn out a little lumpy.

WOODEN SPOON. The large metal spoon will suffice, but wood is better for sourdough, and it never gets hot if left in the pot. Still, it's an optional item.

POTGRABBER. I've always managed without one, but they do make life easier since compact camp cookware often lacks true handles. Put it on your permanent list.

PAPER PLATE HOLDERS. I bought four, made of some kind of wicker, and I guess I like them enough to make them a fixture in my camp kitchen. They're flat to nest together, and very light.

That's it, the new toys I've been playing around with in camp this year. Now here are a few other optional items that some campers will feel they have to have along.

COLANDER. Big, bulky, and extremely useful for any type of noodles. If life for you is dreary without spaghetti three times a week, better bring one. As for me, I can usually tip the pot carefully and eventually get the noodles drained. I might drill holes in one of my three mixing bowls, but I just don't have room for a colander.

FIREPOT. For heating dishwater, I am satisfied with the largest pot in my camp cookset: the 6-quart pot. However, I'll be fast to admit that a larger pot of 10 to 16 quarts is very useful when group size exceeds six or eight persons. An oversized pot is sometimes a real blessing when cooking corn, crabs, or lobster. If you don't have a large pot on your permanent list, at least consider it from trip to trip, especially when you have a large group.

There is one more category of camp cookware: the "sometimes" items. These are not new possibilities, nor are they part of my permanent list. Rather, they are items I occasionally bring to have a little fun with or to do something different.

Note that on all my lists, there are blank spaces left for items to be added for a particular trip. These "sometimes items" would be written into these blanks.

FOLDING CAMP-STOVE OVEN. Does things a reflector oven can't handily do. See chapter 9.

OTHER BAKING TINS. Once in a while, I'll bring along a six-muffin tin. Recently, I inherited a cast-iron corn-stick pan and I plan to bring that on occasion to make corn sticks in camp.

Without doubt, some bare-bones fanatics or some rugged backpackers who have read this far may be having a good raucous laugh at all this cooking equipment. Well I backpack too, and I also take trips where an in-between amount of gear can be taken. However, my response to any such criticism is twofold: One, it's easier to delete from an existing list than to spend 20 years camping to find out what constitutes a good list; and two, bringing the amount of gear listed is not a problem if it's all organized into a couple of functional boxes and remains in those boxes for camping only. To me it's much more of a problem not having something you need when you get to camp.

Make your choices, and your deletions and additions, but by all means make up a checklist and use it correctly. Camp—wherever that is for you—is a special place. If you're prepared, you can enjoy what you came for all the better, you won't have to borrow constantly from other campers, and you'll have the satisfaction that comes from being self-sufficient out there in the great outdoors.

Chapter 2

A Homemade Camp Kitchen & Other Ingenuities

No matter how complete a checklist you compose, and no matter how fastidiously you use it, unless you come up with a logical way of transporting and storing your camp cooking gear confusion will still reign.

The average campground chef heads out for the destination (usually without any checklist) with his various pots, pans, and utensils all thrown into a couple of cardboard boxes. The cardboard gets wet the first day and disintegrates and then the several dozen items end up, for the duration of the trip, scattered about picnic table, clean-up area, tent, and the back seat of the car.

The somewhat more organized camp chef puts his stuff into some kind of a rigid box. This is a step up, but still far from ideal. With items all piled on top of each other the gear is still not organized, although it may at least be centralized.

If you're a trailer camper, the solution will be readily at hand. You'll have cabinets and drawers and, hopefully, everything properly put away in them. But if your camp is a mobile one, what you really need is a specialized box to both store and organize your cooking equipment. I call mine "Cappy's Camp Kitchen," and because I'm proud of it I have those words stenciled on both sides of the box.

As shown in the accompanying illustrations, the box serves three main functions: It keeps most of my camp cooking gear (including all the small stuff) together, it organizes it via adjustable shelves, and it serves as a table when the front door is folded down. It's also a pantry, storing all my spices and staples. This latter feature is important. It saves having to constantly dash in and out of the tent or vehicle for often-used items.

The sidebar within this chapter shows the box from various angles and gives all the important dimensions. Of course you will likely modify it to fit your particular gear, and it is most important to measure your gear before you do your sketching.

It is worth saying a few more things about the box that are not covered in the sidebar. Of primary importance is strength. You don't want to go through all the

MAKING THE CAMP KITCHEN

Front view, top door up, lower door/table removed. The sides and middle vertical divider are ½" plywood. The top, bottom, back, and top door are ¼" plywood. The shelves are ⅜" plywood. The lower door is ½" plywood laminated with formica on the inside. The piece labelled 4½" x ¼" is nothing but a separate strip of ¼" plywood glued to the inside of the top door for strength and rigidity. The entire outside of the box (prior to the doors being mounted) is fiberglassed for strength and for waterproofing.

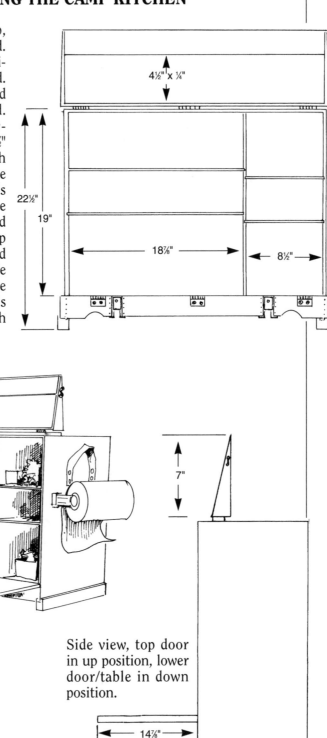

Side view, top door in up position, lower door/table in down position.

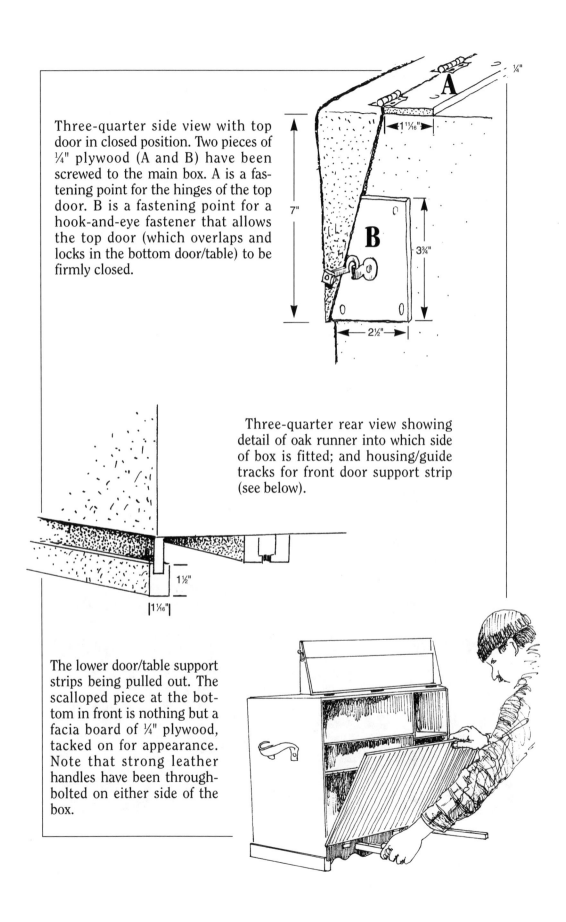

Three-quarter side view with top door in closed position. Two pieces of ¼" plywood (A and B) have been screwed to the main box. A is a fastening point for the hinges of the top door. B is a fastening point for a hook-and-eye fastener that allows the top door (which overlaps and locks in the bottom door/table) to be firmly closed.

Three-quarter rear view showing detail of oak runner into which side of box is fitted; and housing/guide tracks for front door support strip (see below).

The lower door/table support strips being pulled out. The scalloped piece at the bottom in front is nothing but a facia board of ¼" plywood, tacked on for appearance. Note that strong leather handles have been through-bolted on either side of the box.

trouble of making your box only to have it fall apart in a few years. However you might modify my design, keep strength uppermost in mind. The primary components of the box are ¼" plywood. This is for lightness. The entire outside of the box, prior to the doors being mounted, is fiberglassed. Fiberglassing is a bit tricky, and you should try and enlist the help of someone who has done it before if this is your first attempt. You will need fiberglass cloth, polyester resin, and some throwaway paint brushes. At the local hobby shop you can obtain all of these, as well as some useful advice. If you elect to skip the fiberglassing, you will need to use at least ⅝" plywood for the main frame of the box. You would lose, though, the complete waterproofing that the fiberglass provides.

My box is designed to be placed on the end of a picnic table. I could make legs or some kind of stand for it, but when filled it is quite heavy and any such legs would have to be very strong. That would add yet more weight and bulk to my gear. Virtually all commercial campgrounds and even many wilderness campgrounds have picnic tables, but if I got to a place that didn't have one I'd still be prepared because I bring a sturdy, folding table that seats four. I usually set this up within my wall tent but I can use it outdoors when needed. I also could set up the box on the end of the truck with the tailgate open.

As you've probably observed, the picnic table very quickly gets crowded with all kinds of things at a campground. True, the camp kitchen takes up about 18 inches at one end of the table, but since things can be placed on top of it, it really doesn't kill any space. In fact, because of the hardwood runners I have on the box, the bottom of the box proper is actually 1¾ inches off the table, and so I can even place a few things underneath. Usually, I stick my silverware pouch under there so it's always readily available.

In any event, the last thing you want to do is try to cook on the always-crowded picnic table. After all, someone has to set the table, and that usually takes place

when the cooking is still in progress. Some people bring a small, folding table for food preparation, and that's a good idea. However, I find that the table provided by the open door of my camp kitchen suffices. I have it laminated with formica, and I do most of my mixing and measuring on it.

I could put my camp stove on the box's table, but I don't. Rather, I use a standard stove stand. The sum total of all this? Well, the picnic table stays mainly free for eating, drinking, card playing, and the like. Also, my cooking area is isolated and ample, rather than being crowded into some little corner of the picnic table; it's also just a bit higher, which helps. Further, it is more sanitary, since I only perform cooking chores on the box's table. When you work on the picnic table there are usually all kinds of undesirable substances that can work their way into the food being prepared.

The top photo shows how the shelves in the camp kitchen pull out, for easier access to items in the back. Pictured just below are the simple cardboard boxes I fashioned to contain (left) small cooking implements and (right) spices. Bottom photo shows the wooden strip that sits on top of the door support strips and thus levels the table.

Toolbox

The better part of my camp cooking gear, including almost all the small gear, goes into my camp kitchen. But this box didn't quite cover it, so I built a large wooden toolbox to house large items, cooking-related and otherwise. While I always set my camp kitchen up on the end of the picnic table, I set my toolbox up on the ground and under the overhang of the picnic table—opposite side from the camp kitchen. With the cooler, water can, and stove also right at hand, every bit of my camp cooking gear is within five feet of me.

This box was another item inspired by my friend and Allagash canoe guide, Gil Gilpatrick. All his "boxes" are really packs, with backstraps for portaging. I have not yet put backpack straps on my toolbox, but in the essential design features the box mimics Gil's packs.

Shown in the photo on page 12, the bottom part of my toolbox is 31 by 19¼ by 9¼ inches deep. The top part slips over the bottom part and measures 32 by 21½ by 6 inches. On the bottom of the bottom part are two solid-oak runners, each two inches high. They are screwed to the box with wood screws from the inside. The entire box is made of quarter-inch plywood, for lightness. It is then completely fiberglassed on the outside for strength. Empty, this large box weighs a remarkable five pounds. When full, it probably pushes the scale to the 40-pound mark, and it's strong enough to carry that much. Leather carry straps are through-bolted on either side. The straps must be set way down low on the bottom part of the box, since the top "shoeboxes" over the bottom. Exactly where the top sits depends on the load. In this sense, the overall depth of the box is somewhat adjustable.

If I ever wanted to canoe-camp with this box, I could add straps and a back pad just as Gil does with his packs. In that instance, I'd also have to add closure straps, not necessary now because the box is never tipped on its end or turned upside down.

I used solid-brass screws, bolts, nuts, and washers. Besides half-inch brads used to construct the box prior to fiberglassing, no other hardware is needed. There is no partition inside the box. It is, in short, a very simple yet lightweight and functional container. The hardwood runners on the bottom are, I feel, important for keeping the box up out of the mud and wet. But essentially, the outside of the box is completely waterproof because of the fiberglassing. It doesn't even have to be painted, although for appearance I did paint it the same Forest Green as my camp kitchen. I treated the inside of both the top and bottom with two coats of semigloss polyurethane. Since the inside is not fiberglassed, some protection is called for.

Camp Recipe File

This is another invention that I've gotten a lot of use out of. I spend many days each year camping, and I cook a wide variety of things in the course of a season. I have a fair memory for recipes and, beyond that, do a lot of improvising. But since I don't have the exceptional memory that characterizes the best chefs, I write some recipes down.

When I first started to camp seriously, I used to scribble down the recipes of a few dishes I wanted to make on any given trip. But at the campground, these little scraps of paper would get lost, tattered, or wet. Then I went through a phase of bringing along my favorite outdoor cookbooks: Marshall, Bates, Angier, Weiss—I'd have a small library along with me on every excursion. This wasn't very practical, though, and my books started getting messed up.

Then I began thinking: How could I create a little waterproof cookbook? I

Rear view of camp kitchen. Things can be placed both below it and on top of it, so no picnic table space is really lost.

On the left is my first camp recipe file, unlaminated. Dampness caused some blurring, but the recipes can still be read. On the right is the laminated version.

started with a dozen 3 by 5 file cards and wrote some recipes down on them—my top favorites. Then I affixed to them, each side, some clear, plastic shelf liner. At the edges I left a quarter-inch where the liner attaches to itself beyond the perimeter of the card. Then I punched holes in the ends and bound them with little bead chains. I knew that as the number of cards increased, I could simply snap on more little chains.

It seemed nice, but dampness started to very slowly seep in between the two layers of plastic. The result was that many of the recipes became blurry even though I used what I thought was a waterproof ink; perhaps with true waterproof ink there would not have been this problem. In any case, while a bit blurry all these cards can still be read.

I was up to about 40 cards when I decided to go one step further. I sought out a friend who had access to a lamination machine. When I retyped the cards prior to getting them laminated, I punched the holes before I typed in the recipes. This way I couldn't punch out some of the writing as I'd erringly done on the first go-round. Naturally, after the laminating I had to repunch all the holes but at least I had the underlying holes to go by.

A good carrier for silverware: an old terry cloth towel (above) sewn at each end to form pouches. The author's folding Puma knife (below) will—if necessary—perform all the cutting chores in a camp kitchen. Shown next to the knife is the rolled up silverware pouch.

Silverware Pouch

Another very useful item is my silverware pouch. It's just a regular terry cloth towel sewn to form a pouch at one end. Just put in the washed and thoroughly cleaned silverware and the pouch not only holds it but dries it! If you use stainless, there will be no fear of rusting.

A simple but very useful gadget relating to the cooking chores is my rope with hooks. It sounds simple, and it is, and is described fully in chapter 3.

A Dining Canopy Add-On

Smart campers who frequent commercial campgrounds come to rely heavily on their dining canopy. Almost always, the canopy or "fly" as it is often called, is set up directly over the picnic table. There are four poles at the corners well out beyond the table, and a fifth, shorter pole that sits in the middle of the

picnic table and supports the middle of the fly so it's a comfortable distance above people sitting or working at the table. I decided to make my dining fly work a little harder.

Dinner in camp has a way of not being quite over when the sun goes down. And of course, campers don't always hit the sleeping bag right after supper. Thus, a light source at the table can be most important. A couple of candles provide a little light but not enough to do much by. A step up is a candle lantern, a wonderfully simple and inexpensive gadget that just might be the ticket when the bright light of a gasoline lantern would be just too much or would draw too many bugs.

The question is, where do you place the candle lantern? I drilled a few holes in the middle pole of the dining fly and through any one of these holes I can place a seven-inch metal pin. The pin exactly matches the diameter of the holes I drilled, so it doesn't slide out too easily. Nonetheless, I bent one end of the pin to prevent whatever is hung on it from simply sliding off.

I have three of these pins, one for each of the three holes I drilled in the fly's middle pole. From them I can hang any of a number of things: stove starter, camp recipe file, pot holder, personal drinking cup, larger lantern if the candle lantern isn't enough (but keep it a safe distance from the canopy), mirror, and the list goes on.

Camp cooking is a game of gadgets. If you're a gadgeteer like me who loves to solve little problems and make things yourself, you should be able to come up with other ingenuities that will keep you better organized and better able to handle the camp cooking chores.

Chapter 3
ABOUT THE COOKING AREA

Now you have along all the cooking gear you need and that gear is organized in some kind of logical way. But you still have an important consideration: the cooking area. How well you choose and set up this site will have a lot to do with how well things fall together when it comes time to ring the dinner bell.

Let's return to the original checklists. The main things relevant to the cooking area are the dining canopy, or fly as many call it, and rope with hooks. The rope I use is ³⁄₁₆-inch cotton and is 13 feet long. It has a loop on each end so I can just droop it over the top tips of any two parallel poles of the dining canopy. To the rope I affixed a dozen 1½-inch S hooks, available at hardware stores. After attaching each hook, I crimped it closed at one end so it can't fall off the rope. The other end stays open and serves as a hook from which to hang things.

As you can well imagine, the rope will sag when things are hung from it. This causes the hooks and thus the gizmos on the hooks to slide together. To thwart this, I made overhand knots at four-inch intervals near each end of the rope. Each hook snugs up against a knot and does not slide past it.

On the first day, the most often used cooking implements will start collecting on my rope where they're likely to stay to the trip's end. Vegetable peeler, measuring spoons, whisk, large slotted spoon, spatula, personal drinking cup—it's nice to just look behind me when I'm cooking and see all these essentials close at hand.

It's hard to place too much value on a dining fly. Virtually all pop-ups and camping trailers have awnings that pull out from the vehicle, but even the owners of these rigs often use a separate dining fly. A tenter camping where it might rain really should have one. It saves the day when it rains, letting you cook and letting people out of their tents. Twelve feet square is a commonly sold size; 11 by 12 feet is another. As for the larger sizes, they should only be necessary when a large group is involved and only one dining fly is to be brought along. These big

The rope with hooks discussed in the text. Overhand knots keep the implements hung on the rope from sliding all together.

Just the right mix of sun and shade can make for a happy camp. This river's-edge site was just as inviting as it looks, but we're prepared with a dining fly if bad weather sets in.

jobs are often called party canopies and some of the sizes you have to choose from (in feet) are 20 by 20, 20 by 30, and 20 by 40. In a current catalog, these range in price from $800 to $1300. Party canopies can also be rented.

Prices for a 12 by 12 fly average $29 to $89 at present. I strongly recommend that you avoid the true bottom-end canopies. They're often very brittle and not that strong. They have fewer grommets, too, and most significantly, the poles will be weaker than with a better fly (they may also be less adjustable).

The top-of-the-line flies often have eight grommets, four at the corners plus four more between the corners for extra guying in very windy weather. The good models also have very sturdy aluminum poles. In fact, if you go to a midprice fly, you may well get the same fabric as with the top of the line model only it will have less sturdy poles. By all means if you camp where high winds are common, go for the good fly with the very rugged poles.

If you don't have a dining fly and aren't inclined to buy one, a tarp will be better than nothing. It must have grommets, but even with grommets you still have to hope for the serendipitous encounter of trees all in the right places. Some campgrounds have ridgepoles over the picnic tables so a tarp can be stretched over. This certainly helps. In a pinch, you

At some campsites, ridgepoles have been installed and over these, tarps can be stretched in rainy weather.

can tie the tarp ends to a vehicle or whatever's available. Learn to tie a taut-line hitch if you're going to use a tarp.

A dining fly is prone to being badly tossed around in high winds. The smart camper will have stakes in different lengths and materials to keep the fly anchored in various ground conditions.

Where do you locate the dining fly? The primary criteria are the same ones applied to tent site selection: level ground, and high ground where water won't accumulate. At most campgrounds, sites are not too large and a tent, dining fly, and automobile will usually take up the better part of it. If you happen to be at a campground with more spacious sites, there are a few other things you might consider.

First, situate the fly in reasonable proximity to the fireplace. You may decide to cook or at least heat something on the grill. Second, erect the fly close to the site's water source, if in fact your site has its own water. Third, try to locate the fly in as much sun as possible. Fully shaded areas are damp, clammy, often buggier, and never seem to dry out after a rain. And after all, the dining fly provides its own shade.

More important than where to locate the fly within a given site is what site to choose in the first place. It can make all the difference in the world, so if the campground owner gives you a choice really look around carefully. In general, I feel that too much sun is better than too little. Try to estimate which way the sun is going to track across your site. This, of course, requires some qualification. If you're camping in a very hot region you may believe, correctly, that the more shade there is the better. I camp mainly north of the Mason-Dixon line and while I've camped in weather over 100°F, I still look for a sunny site. As an example, last summer I camped at a beautiful off-the-road campground in New York's Adirondacks. This is a cold region, and even though it was the end of August the temperature dipped down to near freezing at night. In the daytime it probably hit the high 60s, but the site was in full shade and I never seemed to shake the chill from my bones.

The right way to store your dining fly: First fold it so that the short side is the same length as the length of a pole. Then lay your sets of poles and stakes across the tarp at intervals. You can now roll it up tight, and none of the components will get lost. Store in the original box it came in.

It was almost an ideal site in every other way, located right near the edge of a picturesque lake and backed up by nothing but woods. If it had 50 percent sun, it would have been ideal.

In many campgrounds there is one common water spigot for a group of sites. You don't want to be too far from it, but on the other hand if you're right next to it you'll have people constantly trudging through your little piece of paradise. The same goes for showers, toilets, trash stations, and bathhouses. In particular, stay far enough away from toilets to avoid odors.

Set up your camp kitchen at the end of the picnic table. Have your cook stove on its stand off to one side and just near the edge of the dining fly. Keep your five-gallon water container and your cooler on your other side, but still under the canopy and in the shade. Make sure the fire in your fireplace is burning softly and is no more than 10 paces away. Now, with everything close at hand, you're ready to wash your hands and drum up a professional meal that your guests will remember for a long time to come.

One of the biggest benefits of the camp kitchen is that it gets things off the picnic table, so that precious space can be used for better purposes. Without some kind of organization, you'll end up with a table that looks like the one in the top photo.

Chapter 4
COOKING ON STOVES

I would like to have a 16-inch trout for every camp meal that's ever been prepared on a trusty old two-burner camp stove. But why even bring a stove when the woods are full of fuel and a wood fire seems so appropriate in a camp setting? I'm very enthusiastic about cooking over wood coals, as I hope chapter 5 conveys. But—and it's a big but—I almost always consider wood an alternative cooking fuel when I go camping. The reasons are many.

In some parts of the country wood may be scarce, or at least suitable burning wood may be scarce. Sometimes the campground owners or the park proprietors simply won't let you pick any wood. Or, they may only allow you to scrounge what's on the ground, dead wood that's likely to be wet. If the weather has been dry, there may well be a moratorium on open fires in the neck of the woods where you're camping.

If your hiking schedule is an ambitious one, there just may not be time in the morning to cook the decent breakfast you need over a wood fire. If it's wet weather, fire building may be very difficult, especially without an axe. Or, as discussed in other chapters, the fireplace at the campground you've chosen may be inadequate or missing altogether, and there may be no feasible or quick way of devising one.

The pioneers burned wood to cook on the trail because they had to. You have better choices. By all means, become an expert at fire building and cooking over coals. But bring along a modern, portable stove for those times when nature, or man's rules, make fire building untenable.

Whatever brand stove you elect to buy, you'll quickly find that you have two primary types to choose from: gasoline-fueled and propane-fueled. There are other types, but in general camp cooking they place a distant third. Gasoline and propane stoves cost about the same, but they are different in many ways. It's worth taking a look at those differences.

BOTH PHOTOS COURTESY COLEMAN, INC.

The traditional gasoline-fueled camp stove (this page) sitting on the convenient foldable stand made just for this purpose. Always fill the fuel canister away from the tent and eating area. An LPG camp stove (facing page), when hooked up to a bulk tank, is extremely economical to run.

Traditional gasoline-fueled stoves can operate on what was once called "white gas," sold at certain gas stations, and even (less ideally) on unleaded gasoline. However, makers of these stoves recommend that you use their own fuel, claiming it will provide better and more trouble-free performance. Although there are a couple of others, Coleman Fuel is the only one of these specialty fuels I've personally used. To quote the Coleman Company:

All fuels are not the same. While Coleman lanterns and stoves will perform well with ordinary white gasoline, they will perform better, last longer, and maintain greater efficiency with Coleman Fuel. That's because Coleman Fuel is specially blended for Coleman products and Coleman products are specially calibrated to burn Coleman Fuel. Unlike ordinary

COURTESY COLEMAN, INC.

A camp lantern designed to run on regular unleaded gasoline. Camp stoves are now made to run on this cheaper fuel, too.

fuels, the Coleman brand guards against clogging and corrosion and other damaging effects with extra high purity and special additives.

The most significant development in camp appliances in recent years is the introduction of stoves and lanterns that can run on ordinary unleaded gas. Because unleaded fuel is so much cheaper, these appliances should become very popular as time goes by. On the other hand, because traditional camp stoves last almost indefinitely, they aren't about to be replaced too quickly.

The biggest problem that can arise by using ordinary gas, assuming you have a traditional unit, is that the generator in your appliance will clog more quickly. On one trip I took with a professional guide, I was somewhat surprised to see him using Coleman Fuel as he was the frugal sort. I would have thought he'd take his chances with unleaded gas. But he explained to me that he felt the extra cost of the Coleman Fuel was compensated for by the time and money saved in replacing generators, each one of which can cost about 10 bucks.

If you choose to use fuel made just for camp appliances, keep in mind that the price can vary widely. At the campground it is likely to be marked way up. At a sporting goods store it might be just as high or a little less. At a big department store it is almost certain to cost less, and it will be found on sale at times.

Gasoline camp stoves of two burners or more usually have a detachable gas tank. When the stove is not in use, the tank is stored inside the appliance and the appliance then folds up into a box. When in use, the generator housing or long

A gasoline-fueled camp stove has to be pumped every so often. This procedure is not necessary with propane-fueled camp stoves.

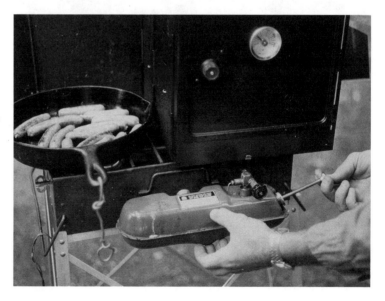

metal arm of the gas tank is inserted into the burner assembly which is permanently fixed to the stove. The tank is pressurized via a pump located on the end of the tank. Once under pressure, fuel from the tank is forced in a tiny liquid stream into the generator. Since the generator sits right over the flame, the fuel passing through the generator is vaporized, and that highly flammable gas then travels through the intake chamber and around to the burning port.

There are pluses and minuses to this design, but before we get to them let's look at the other main type of camp stove, the propane stove.

Propane is the familiar bottled gas still used as a cooking, heating, and refrigeration fuel source in rural areas and even in many suburban and urban areas. The type of camp stove that uses this fuel looks fairly similar to a gasoline stove, but contemporary models are sleeker and more compact. With a propane stove, neither pumping nor vaporization are necessary. That's because the burnable gas rises naturally from the liquid stored in the tank or canister, which is pressurized. With its simple design, many find propane easier to use than gas stoves.

Which of the two types of stoves is better for general campground use? Propane has a few minuses, but mostly it has it all over the gasoline models in my opinion. Thus, while I own a gasoline model I will probably switch one day to a propane model.

Advantages of Propane vs. Gasoline

1. No pumping necessary. Saves time and effort, and in general makes the cooking go more smoothly.
2. A constant heat source. Because the pressure is not user-regulated (yes, the flame is) propane stoves provide a much more constant heat level. Make sure the propane stove you buy is "regulated," in that it provides constant pressure.
3. Cleaner and easier to refuel. Instead of adding a liquid gasoline which could overflow onto your hands or something else, with a propane stove you merely change a coupling.
4. Can be hooked up to a bulk system. There is no convenient way to do this with a gasoline-fueled stove.
5. No changing generators. With a propane stove, there is never any generator to change; if the generator goes on your gasoline stove you better have a spare, and the tools to change it. (However, generators last a long time.)

Disadvantages of Propane vs. Gasoline

1. Greater fuel bulk. Propane is typically sold in disposable canisters, and these canisters—regardless of their size—take up more room per hour of cooking time yielded than does liquid gasoline fuel. This should only be a problem in wilderness or backpacking situations where most professional outdoor people do use the gasoline models.
2. Higher cost per hour. Propane is more expensive to run per hour. However, if you camp only a few times a year, the overall convenience should over-

shadow the small extra cost. Then, too, if you hook up a bulk propane system, the running cost becomes considerably less than with gasoline. In fact, it becomes extremely economical.

3. Poorer fuel availability in rural areas. You will find it easier to buy a gallon of Coleman Fuel than a two-pound canister of propane in most rural areas. Also, the sizes of the coupling that join gas canister to stove are not universal among all manufacturers.

Perhaps the foregoing will help you choose a camp stove if you don't already have one. But if you do already own a stove, here are some tips for using it.

With a gasoline stove, more attention must be paid to safety. This is mainly because of the possibilities of spilled fuel and flare-ups. If the generator is good and you know how to use your gasoline stove perfectly, flare-ups should not occur. But the fact is that flare-ups do occur—I witness them every year in campgrounds. If you'll just locate your stove far enough away from tent, dining fly, clothing, etc., the occasional flare-up you might get will be unlikely to hurt anything. But it would be even better to learn how to use your gasoline stove precisely so that flare-ups don't occur. This just takes practice, and the common sense to read and follow the manufacturer's directions carefully.

A spark-producing stove starter gets my highest recommendation. Keep it always close at hand.

By my observation, the most common cause of flare-ups is the operator pumping the unit vigorously when the flame is flickering, as opposed to burning steadily. This causes liquid fuel to accumulate in the basin beneath the burning port, which in turn can cause a flare-up when the flame finally catches.

Don't overpump the appliance when it is not burning correctly, for example if it's a little bit cold. If you do get a bad flare-up, turn off the stove, let it cool down, detach the gas tank, then—away from the table and food—turn the appliance upside down. You may well see a fair amount of liquid fuel come pouring off. Alternatively, after the stove has cooled you could try to use a paper towel to sop up the bulk of the accumulated fuel; what little you don't get should evaporate quickly.

CHEESE OMELET

2 eggs	2 T. grated American or
2 T. water or milk	Swiss cheese
Salt and pepper	1 tsp. butter

Beat eggs well in a bowl. Add water or milk and seasonings, then cheese. Heat the butter in a medium skillet. A nonstick pan is ideal for omelets. The pan, in any case, should be quite hot. Pour in the egg mixture and immediately force the edges back toward the center using a spatula. The soft part will run out to the edges. Again force it in toward the center. You may have to do this three times. Pull the whole omelet to the side closest to you, then fold it in half as you slide it to the far side of the pan. Slide out onto a suitable plate for serving. ✦Most any hard or semihard cheese will do. SERVES 1.

As obvious as it may sound, one of the most important things is to avoid running out of fuel in the middle of the meal. A typical tank of two pints will burn for at least two hours at medium-high flame, so you should never have a problem if you'll just make it a point to fill the tank before each meal no matter how close to full it may be. If you do run out while cooking, you have to let the stove cool down, refill the tank, and get it going again. If darkness is approaching, or it's raining, this can be especially troublesome.

It seems to me that a camp stove burns somewhat hotter in the center than does a home stove. This may be because a gasoline camp stove puts out somewhat more BTUs than a typical home-range burner. At a high setting, a camp-stove burner can burn your food quickly, so it's important to adjust the flame as necessary and stir that food around more than you normally would.

A butane stove has a place in a general camp setting, providing—as here—an extra burner. A hot dog roll is being warmed on a bread warmer made just for campers.

As the pressure goes down, you'll start opening the valve to get more flame. Also, if you open the valve to the second (or third) burner, the flame on the first burner will naturally go down and this will require another adjustment. Then of course after you periodically pump the gas tank, the flame initially shoots up higher. It's true that if the generator and all gaskets on the stove are in perfect shape, the amount of adjusting will be minimal. But you still must pay close attention to what you're doing. With the thinner than usual cookware many campers use, burned foods become more common. This is why I so highly recommend cast iron: Its heaviness helps to compensate for the vagaries of camp cooking.

ESCAROLE AND BEAN SOUP

1/4 lb. great northern beans	1 T. olive oil
1/2 lb. escarole	2 cloves garlic, minced
4 cubes chicken bouillon	

Soak beans several hours or overnight. Drain off any remaining water. ✦Separate the escarole into leaves and wash well. Add leaves to a pot of boiling water and cook 5 minutes. Drain, cool slightly, then chop coarsely. ✦In a quart of simmering water, dissolve the chicken bouillon cubes or packets. Add oil and garlic, beans and escarole. Simmer, covered, until beans are tender or at least 30 minutes. Serve with garlic bread. ABOUT 4-5 SERVINGS.

As a result of the frequent regulating you will do, a burner will sometimes go out. If the stove has been on for more than a few moments it will be very hot and if you try to gingerly sneak a little match under a pushed-aside pot you will burn your hand. Get one of those starters described in chapter 1. Keep it in your kitchen box, and it will provide thousands of lights without the burned fingers and the resulting fiery epithets.

To change a generator on a camp stove, you will probably need both a box or open-end wrench of the correct size and a pair of ordinary adjustable pliers. Be sure to have the tools you need, along with a spare generator, since a stove will not operate properly if at all with a clogged or damaged generator. Since this can be a slightly tricky task, I suggest that you change your generator at home. I've found that a generator can last a few seasons with normal use. In that span of time you might forget how you changed it the previous time.

Whatever stove you use, you'll find that pots with folding handles make the best camp cookware, since they're more compact.

Camp stoves will get dirty and messy from spilled food. Don't let this build up—get right after it each day or at least after each camping trip. I like soap pads for cleaning my camp stove. They're usually abrasive enough to clean, but not hard enough to scratch the paint to any degree.

Stoves will get scratched, though, and then they'll start to rust quickly since they are made of ordinary steel. As necessary, touch up your camp stoves or lanterns with red primer; add the paint later, in a matching color.

ITALIAN PORK CHOPS OR CHICKEN

Olive oil
3 cloves garlic, coarsely chopped
2 medium-thick pork chops
1/2 of a large bell pepper, chopped
1 16-oz. can Del Monte stewed
  tomatoes with juice

2 small onions, chopped
1 8-oz. can tomato sauce
1 potato, sliced
Dried oregano and basil to taste
Salt and pepper to taste

Sauté garlic in oil. Add chops and brown. Add all other ingredients except potato and seasonings. Cover tightly and cook 20 minutes. Add potato and season to taste. Cover, cook about another 30 minutes. Adjust seasonings as necessary. Serve with Italian bread. ✦I've found that this recipe works equally well with chicken pieces, with no other changes. SERVES 2.

If you buy a new stove, it will come in a nice, sturdy cardboard box. It makes a good storage case, so unless you have a better container save the box.

Gasoline should not be left in lanterns or stoves over the winter. If it happens, by all means dump it and replace it with fresh fuel in the spring. Also, manufacturers advise that if a can of fuel has been opened for a year, it's best to dump it and start the season with a fresh can. I admit, I don't do this. Be conscientious about where you dump the fuel, if you do. Your friend at the local gas station may have a large tank into which you can drain the old fuel.

Butane stoves are very much a part of the camping scene, mainly in backpacking, but they're far less popular than the other two types. Illustrative of this popularity gap is a camper's supply catalog I have in front of me. It lists seven gasoline models, six propane models, but only one butane model. The butane stove shown is a one-burner job. There is more on butane in part 2 of this book. Suffice it to say here that butane is rarely used in general campground settings. Note, too, that propane and butane are not interchangeable, so if you purchased any kind of butane appliance you couldn't use a propane canister in a pinch, and you couldn't include your butane appliance in a bulk propane hookup.

The good old simple Sterno can has warmed many a dish, and it will continue to do so. They even make little stoves that house the Sterno can. Comprised of jellied alcohol, a seven-ounce Sterno can will burn for approximately two hours. While it is more than adequate for heating up a can of beans, it should certainly not be considered a primary cooking implement. Recently, I saw a folding "stove" for the seven-ounce Sterno can and its cost was a modest $7.50.

RED CABBAGE GRETA BRANDIN
GRETA BRANDIN

1 large head red cabbage	2 T. light corn syrup
4 large sour apples	1/2 cup red wine
1/2 stick butter or margarine	

Chop cabbage. Peel, core, and chop apples. Meanwhile, be melting the butter in a 12-inch cast-iron skillet. Add the syrup, stir well, then add the cabbage and apples. Stir well, turn heat to low, cover, and cook about 30 minutes. Add wine, stir, cook 15 minutes more, still over low flame. SERVES 8-10.

The wood-burning shepherd stove is still a functional, important part of the camp cooking scene, especially in pack-in camps in the Rocky Mountains. This semicollapsible sheet-metal stove lets you avoid altogether the need to bring fuel into the hinterland with you; you burn the wood you find on location. A typical shepherd stove will weigh about 30 pounds so it's rarely used for backpacking (though with a group of people one person could easily pack the stove). But it is used often on pack-horse trips, where outdoor lovers bivouac in ridgepole tents. The pipe of the shepherd stove runs right up through the roof of the tent, the tent section around the pipe being insulated with special material. The stove not only heats—its primary function—but, with some models, does a fine job as a supplementary cooking stove. Some shepherd stoves can even be used for baking.

There are a great many ways to create your own "stove" out of what's at hand. Cinder blocks, coffee cans, truck wheels, and many more objects can be used as cooking stoves through the use of a little ingenuity. Some of these tricks are touched upon in other parts of the book.

Safety and Other Tips for Using Gasoline Camp Stoves

1. Read and follow the instructions that come with the appliance.
2. Use appropriate fuels.
3. Refuel outdoors and away from any ignition source.
4. Avoid spillage of fuel (the leading cause of accidents). Use funnel to fill tank.
5. Never refuel tank when stove or lantern is lit or even hot.
6. Check fuel carefully—be certain about contents of fuel can before using. Kerosene cannot be substituted.
7. Use in ventilated area away from flammable objects. Allow one foot of clearance all around and three feet above appliances.
8. Don't use as a heat source; use as intended.
9. Inspect for extreme corrosion and leaks. If appliance has been sitting around for long periods of time, a few drops of oil on the pump shaft or pump gasket may be necessary to ensure a tight seal.

Safety and Other Tips for Using Propane Camp Stoves

1. Read and follow instructions that come with stove and propane cylinder.
2. All stoves consume oxygen. Do not use in unventilated areas.
3. Use a stove as a cooking appliance only. Never alter a stove in any way. Never use stove as a space heater. Never leave stove unattended while it is burning.
4. Never allow tents, sleeping bags, clothing, or any flammable material to come close to a stove that is operating.
5. Never install or remove propane cylinder while stove is lit, near flame, pilot lights, other ignition source or while stove is hot to touch.
   6.Never store propane near flame, other ignition sources, or where temperatures exceed 120°F.
7. Keep all connections and fittings clean.
8. Propane is heavier than air and will accumulate in low places.
9. If you smell gas, leave the enclosure immediately and ventilate thoroughly.
10. If using refillable propane cylinders, check all hoses and fittings for leaks using soapy water. Never use a flame. Always keep refillable cylinders outdoors, never inside house, camper, tent.

Chapter 5
COOKING OVER WOOD FIRES

There are very clear and identifiable reasons why outdoor cookery is more difficult and thus more challenging: a limited number of utensils and ingredients, lack of running water, the intrusion of natural phenomena such as rain or bugs or darkness, limited preparation space, and the list goes on. Well, along with all these dilemmas, the outdoor cook faces another very significant one, and that is a variable heat source. With gasoline-fueled stoves it is a very real problem. Over charcoal in a hibachi or grill it's a bigger factor. Yet it is when cooking over a wood fire that the dilemma is the greatest. With wood, the heat is both variable and unpredictable, creating chaos where there was once an orderly ritual of recipes with exact cooking times and other neat formulas. First you have to be good at making wood fires, then good at keeping them going, then good at cooking over them. The last phase, the actual cooking, is one where instinct usually must prevail. Luckily there are great rewards for all this, for cooking with wood is economical, effective, and satisfying.

This past summer I was at a campground located on the banks of a well-known trout stream. It was 8:30 P.M., just before dark, and I hadn't a fire going as I'd eaten only a light snack that evening. But I had prepared my fire pit, and I had split the rather large hunks of wood sold to me by the campground. In only a few minutes I had going a cheery blaze, and I gratefully plopped down in my chair in front of it—it had been a long day. As I was with a group of some 20 people, the clean-burning fire soon attracted a number of others who pulled up chairs or just a piece of grass. Meanwhile, on the site right next to mine, a friend was trying to get his own campfire going. *That* turned out to be quite a project.

In the hour or more that he fooled with it, he apparently tried every technique but the correct one. At one point, I looked over and shuddered as I saw white gas being poured onto the wood. White gas is extremely flammable, and a bounce-back to the can would not be out of the question, but luckily there was no live heat in the fire pit. In any case, when the match did get tossed on, the gas popped and immediately there was a small grass fire burning all around the fireplace. Of course the thick logs still didn't start, and by this time most of the man's dinner guests had wandered over to my fire anyway.

To make the story short, I later heard someone say that our friend had tried to start the logs directly with some commercial fire-starting cubes purchased at a camp supply store. This might have gotten some kindling going, but not a log measuring five inches in diameter. The man kept trying, but while he was clearly making a scene of himself I didn't feel it was my place to meddle unless he asked for help. Finally, someone with a hatchet did go over and cut enough slivers off a log to get the fire started, but it must have taken an hour and a half total time. Half the people in camp had already gone to bed.

This story is worth relating because it makes a number of points. First and foremost, a good fire is not automatic, even in a civilized setting and even in bone-dry weather. Coleman Fuel, fire-starting jelly or cubes, and other store-bought giz-

Have all your firewood gathered and stacked before you even start the fire. You'll need a gradation of sizes, as shown here.

mos won't do a thing at all unless you learn some basics of fire building.

Of all those basics, the most important is this: You must start a fire with small pieces of wood or other material and gradually build up. This usually means tinder, stages of kindling, and then logs.

A good fire is important. At a campground where cooking with wood is the exception rather than the rule, not being able to get one going will seldom mean that you'll go hungry. But what about the evening social fire? Without a nice fire it can often be a long, drab evening. Then, too, you may be a campground goer who also backpacks. Now, woodsmanship and specifically fire making takes on more importance. In the backcountry or even at an off-the-road campground, it can mean everything if the little backpack stove won't start. And quite obviously, if you really get into the outback, a fire very well could save your life one day. So learn how to make a fire, no matter how great or meek your outdoor ambitions.

The Flame Source

Romantic fire-starting tricks that helped you to get Boy Scout or Girl Scout merit badges certainly do have their place in the outdoors, and they have saved lives. I'm talking about magnifying glasses, bow and string, or flint and steel. As far as I'm concerned, anyone who strikes off more than a mile into the woods without waterproof matches is a grossly unprepared individual. The techniques just mentioned are so terribly difficult versus the dependable match that the only real reason to turn to them would be to practice your survival skills. I recommend that all serious woodsmen study survival techniques, but that's not what this book is about. For the practical camper near home or on the trail, matches are how you will start your fire.

Interestingly, certain backwoods guides I've tripped with rely almost exclusively on disposable butane lighters. These lighters will be adversely affected if they're immersed in water, but they are essentially very dependable and permit one-hand fire-making. Just remember not to dispose of one in the fireplace or it may go "pop" like a .22 shell.

For a deep-woods excursion, I'd also carry waterproof matches, and I'm sure the guides I mentioned do too. But near the road or off it, please don't even consider regular paper matches. Wooden kitchen matches carried inside a waterproof metal or plastic case are what you want. Now you'll notice that just above I referred to waterproof matches. Regular wooden matches are not at all waterproof, so the case you carry them in should be. Such matches, by the way, can be struck and lit on any rock if they are the white-tipped variety; the blue-tipped type must be struck on the special striker plate on the side of the box. I just cut out that striker plate and slip it inside the match case.

CAMPFIRE CHILI WITH RICE
LIBBY'S FOODS

1 13½-oz. bag Success-brand brown rice
1/4 cup chopped scallions
1 15-oz. can Libby's chili with beans

1 14½ oz.-can Mexican-style stewed tomatoes
1/2 cup grated Monterey Jack or Cheddar cheese

Submerge rice bag in two quarts boiling water. Boil, uncovered, for 10 minutes. Combine chili and tomatoes ("chili-style" stewed tomatoes are an acceptable substitute) in a saucepan and heat. Serve over rice. Sprinkle with cheese and scallions. SERVES 3.

True waterproof matches can be purchased. These will start even when wet, although I'm sure there's a limit to that. Even these are best carried in a waterproof can. Last year, I used one called a "Hurricane Match," which is supposed to light under any condition and be windproof. It burns extremely hot and fast but then it burns way down more quickly than you would want it to. Remember that all such specialized matches will be much more expensive than regular wooden kitchen matches.

Tinder

Next we come to tinder. Again, it's far better to be prepared than to make do with some difficult trick. Let me list some things you can lay your match to with the hopes of getting some kindling going. It will be obvious which ones apply to campgrounds and which to the backcountry. Some of this crosses over into what I would call light kindling.

> Newspaper
> Paper bags, cardboard
> The dry, dead, scraggly twigs or branches on the bottoms
>   and tops of some conifers
> Corn cobs (can be soaked in parafin first)
> Knots from resinous trees like pine
> Seeds from certain plants, for example cattails
> Birch bark from standing dead trees
> Paper dinner plates
> Small chips from any dry, dead wood
> Small sticks from leaning or standing dead wood
> Fuzz sticks (described in this chapter)
> Napkins or paper towels (soak in bacon grease)
> Commercially made tinder
> Certain types of dry moss
> Dead, dry weeds
> Very dry grass
> Pine cones
> Dried and opened seed pods from many weeds
>   (especially late fall through winter)

If I'm heading to a campground, I'll toss a big pile of newspapers into the back of the truck. The more the better. Newspaper is not only free and easy to start, but it can help rejuvenate a dying fire as well as start a new one. Newspaper rolled up into a kind of log will burn slowly and will eventually ignite some fair-sized wood.

No cardboard or paper should ever be trash-canned on a camping trip. Recycle it by saving it for the fire pit. When you buy your groceries at the country store, try to get the clerk to put your brown bags inside cardboard boxes. Then you have both tinder and kindling at your fingertips.

Whether you're in a civilized place or on the trail, you should know about natural sources of tinder, some of which are listed above. Truthfully, it is not a bad idea to bring a little bit of tinder when you go into the woods, and again those little 35-mm film cans are tough to beat. The tinder I carry is an extraordinary fire starter and I happened upon it by accident.

A friend of mine makes hand-planed bamboo fly rods. When I was at his shop a few years ago I saw this big pile of long, thin shavings on the floor and the wheels started to turn. Not only do the shavings compress incredibly well, but they burn instantly and fiercely upon the application of flame. I can cram enough into one film canister to start at least 10 fires under normal conditions. Bamboo-rod making is a reborn art in this country, and it would be worth asking around to see who in your region is practicing this fine craft. You might want to check with better sport shops in your area. If you can't track such a craftsperson down, just use a little imagination and keep your eyes open for other types of tinder.

A few years ago while backpacking for trout, I had a fire-making lesson really hammered home to me. We were camping on the floodplain of the river we were planning to fish. It was late May, and although conditions were nice and dry there was everywhere evidence of the earlier floods we knew had occurred. All around us were tons of white, sun-bleached driftwood, sticks of varying sizes, and clumps of very dry-looking grass, all of which looked as if it would burn like the blazes. This brought a smile to my face, but when I tried to start a fire I was amazed at how this good-looking stuff smoldered and smoked. It didn't take me long to get the picture. Even though it hadn't recently rained, the wood (from tinder to logs) was still sitting on or very near to the ground and dampness had settled in. What appeared to be a fire-making panacea turned out to be literally a washout.

The always popular key-hole fireplace. A fire is made within the large area of the fireplace; the resulting coals are raked into the narrow end, over which two lightweight grills have been propped in this photo.

A fuzz stick is really kindling turned into tinder. Place four or five of these teepee fashion and light from underneath.

It wasn't until I looked above waist-level that I was able to find what I needed.

Peeling bark from a standing dead birch tree is always a good choice. Paper birch is the species of bark most accommodating, but yellow birch and river birch are also worth watching for. The bark should be crumbled into small chards to make tinder. Don't peel a live tree, though, since you would be promoting its demise. Bark from other types of standing dead trees will also work at times.

The very fine, scraggly little branches that grow on some conifers below the level of the greenery and often within arm's length are even better. It remains dry and usable even after a decent rain since it's canopied by the thick, evergreen foliage above it. It will eventually get wet, though, if the rain is an especially hard or lengthy one.

The small twigs of any standing dead tree are the next place to turn. Very often, such wood will be leaning as opposed to standing but it matters not. As long as it's not actually on the ground it will burn. Of course if it's in the open, its effectiveness will be diminished by rainy weather.

On this subject, it would be useful to define tinder. Tinder is very small or very fine material. You might well use two grades of tinder, one a little bigger than the other. But the very first stuff you put a match to should be the finest material you can find. Anything thicker than a pencil is probably too thick. Inexperienced fire builders make one mistake more than any other: They go too large at any stage in the fire-making process.

A fuzz stick is one of those old-time tricks that really does work, and it is something to know if the clouds have opened up. Just take any stick of about one-half to three-fourths inch in diameter and partially trim off shavings all up and down and around it. Arrange several of these sticks teepee fashion, and place your match underneath them.

Kindling

Kindling is the next step up, and the time to gather it is before and not after you've torched your little pile of tinder. Have it all ready, broken or split, and add it on slowly so as not to smother your incipient blaze. There is no hard and fast rule as to what size your kindling should be, and indeed, it won't be all one size but rather a gradation of sizes. Generally, once you have some small twigs burning you lay on some pieces less than an inch thick, then a little bigger. It is at this stage that you must decide the purpose of your fire.

A hinged, metal grilling basket being used to barbecue some spare ribs. Cooking over flames is acceptable, but you have to pay close attention.

There are two primary ways to cook over wood: over flames or over coals. In about eight instances out of ten, you will fare best by using coals. Tenderfoot woodsmen see those nice, orange flames licking up and they just can't wait to put on the pot or the pan or whatever. They're forgetting what all experienced campers know, and that is the basic physics of fires. First, flames rise and fall as wood must constantly be added, so the heat is very inconsistent. Licking flames cook too hot one minute—scorching your food, your pan, and often your hand—and then too cold the next. In addition, as you're adding wood to keep those flames going you're likely to somehow upset whatever cooking implement you're using. Coals, on the other hand, are much hotter and also much more consistent. And, since the fire-building process is over, you can set a pot or pan over coals and tend to other chores while your dish cooks.

Here we get back to the question raised a few paragraphs ago: Just what are you going to do with that nice little fire you've gotten going? Will it be to simply heat tea or coffee? Will it be used to prepare a more elaborate breakfast or dinner? Or will it just serve as a morning or evening social fire? If it is intended for cooking then you should keep in mind the wrist test. That test, and it is a good one, states that any wood thicker than your wrist will take too long to burn down to coals and should not be used. To cook an egg or to boil a cup of water does not take much, so don't waste your wood and your time if that's the extent of your menu. On the other hand, if you need to bake some potatoes or cook a steak or even a pot roast, along with, perhaps, a round of cornbread, you'll need a deeper bed of coals. Even still, there's no call to go to bigger wood. You'll just need more of the wrist-sized stuff. For skillet frying or for boiling water for drinks, spaghetti, vegetables, or freeze-dried trail meals, a two-inch-deep bed of red-hot coals should suffice. For dutch-oven cookery or for very elaborate meals you may well need four inches of coals and a wider diameter of them.

Large or small cooking chore, you just can't start your fire preparations too early. It will take time to gather and cut or split the wood, and it will also take time to arrange your fireplace in many instances. Add this to the typical hour it takes to get to a nice bed of coals. If you're doing all the work, it can easily take two hours from the time you start wood gathering to the time you actually put the food over the coals. This is the biggest reason that most camp meals these days are prepared over portable stoves.

SHORE-LUNCH FILLETS

4 fish fillets, about 1/2 lb. each	1 1/2 T. butter
Mrs. Dash "Lemon Pepper" spice blend	1 medium onion, sliced
	1 4-oz. jar sliced mushrooms
Juice of 1 lemon	1/2 cup dry white wine

Place fillets in your largest plate, platter or pan. Sprinkle liberally with the spice blend then pour over the lemon juice. Marinate fillets in this mixture 10-15 minutes, turning a few times. In a heavy skillet, melt the butter. Break onion into rings and sauté about 10 minutes. Add mushrooms and sauté 5 minutes longer. Slip this mixture out onto a plate. Now add the fillets to that same skillet, then place the onion-mushroom mixture over the fillets. Add the wine, cover, and cook until fish flakes easily, about 10-15 minutes depending on thickness of fish. SERVES 4.

Having carried on about coals, I guess I should acknowledge that like all outdoor chefs I have at times cooked over flames from a wood fire. It can be faster, and it is feasible if you can handle the mechanics of it. First, think in terms of controlled flames, not raging flames. In some campground fireplaces the grill is quite far above the bottom of the fire pit, and while this can preclude cooking over coals it might actually abet your efforts at cooking with flames. Just grease the grill and slap on your steaks, chops, or sausage. Ten minutes of nice high flames and you'll have your charcoal-broiled meat, but you must be very, very careful of not burning your food. By the same token, if you have a pot of liquid on the flames, you must constantly watch that it doesn't bubble over from the close-contact heat. Of course, you must use strictly all-metal utensils—no Bakelite handles, enamel, plastic, or anything that will get burned or disfigured by the flames.

Generally, I restrict my use of flame cooking to backpack situations. Where wood is very limited, or where six miles of tough trail loom ahead, a few cheery flames can boil my morning coffee and then I'm done with it. If the pot gets scorched, a little soap and elbow grease will bring it right back. Other than that, I cook over coals, as do all experienced camp cooks.

Scarcely an outdoor handbook has ever been published that hasn't listed all the different woods and their relative burning qualities. When I see such a chart I always get a good chuckle, because I can hardly remember a camping trip where I wasn't forced to simply use whatever wood was at hand.

"Ash wet or ash dry, a king shall warm his slippers by," goes an old woodsman's

A folding saw is exceptionally useful in camp. Such saws vary considerably in design, but some weigh as little as five ounces.

poem. Yet if nothing but crummy old elm is in the neighborhood, that's what you'll use (even if, as the poem continues, "Elmwood burns like churchyard mold, e'en the very flames are cold").

I have a good friend who is a cabinetmaker. In his old shop he heats strictly with wood. He helps me with my amateur wood projects and I scrounge up burning wood for him every winter. Not only does this man work with wood professionally, but he has burned wood for God only knows how many years. Yet often when I bring him firewood we are both puzzled as to what type it is. I've seen poplars growing in the shade that had trunks which looked like spruces. I've also seen poplars that were so light you had to look twice to be sure they weren't white birches. Numerous trees I can think of have bark that changes radically in color and texture as the tree ages. Often, the bottom 30 feet of a tree can look like any of dozens of other trees, although the upper trunk and branches may retain the characteristic color and texture of the species. Usually, my carpenter friend can tell what he's got when he splits the wood, for the inside of the wood is sometimes a truer gauge of what it is than the bark. But even after splitting, there are times he's still not sure what he has.

In the backcountry, you burn dead wood, and often the leaves will be gone. The bark may also be rotted away or partially so; bark does not last long on dead wood. If there is any point to all this, it's that identifying wood is not as easy as the handbooks make it out to be. You'll have to cut, split, and burn a lot of wood to really pick up this knack. Then, after you've gotten it you'll still have little choice in what wood you cook with a majority of the time. At campgrounds, you will burn the wood they sell you or you will burn what you can quickly gather in the little bit of woods around your particular site. While backpacking, you will use mostly standing or semifallen dead wood, some of it quite far gone with the bark missing. When you do have a choice, and can identify the options at hand, choose softwoods for fast, short fires and hardwoods for long, slow fires. Some softwoods (which generally means conifers or evergreens) are very unpleasant, as they pop, spark, or smoke, but all will do in a pinch. In a similar vein, by no means are all hardwoods (deciduous trees) wonderful for either burning or cooking.

Notes On Fireplaces

Your campground fireplace is 18 inches wide and your logs are two feet long—what do you do? Even at a commercial campground it's great to have a saw. But it's also great to have an axe, because nothing burns like split wood and very wet wood will only burn adequately when it's split.

Last year I stayed at an off-the-road campground where you have to walk a few hundred yards from the car to the campsite. From the standpoint of camp cookery it was an interesting experience because the situation allowed for more gear than backpacking but less than regular car camping. In spite of the slight constraints, we brought an axe and a folding backpack saw and were glad we did. It was very chilly that weekend, and since the woods were full of standing dead birch we kept a nice social fire going mornings and evenings. Using your feet and

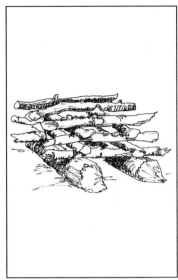

The teepee lay, far left, and the log cabin lay, left. Pictured directly above is the star lay.

some leverage you can break wood that's up to two inches or a little more thick, but with larger wood you really have to cut it. The folding saw weighs only ounces and is worth taking even backpacking.

Cutting wood is often necessary but splitting wood is more of a luxury. On that trip, we did a lot of baking, so fast-burning split wood was essential. On most backpacking excursions, a full-size axe at about three pounds will be just too heavy to bring along. Some people bring a hatchet or small "splitting axe." Either makes a poor substitute for an axe, and so its weight may not be justifiable. When I can't have an axe and a folding saw on a camping trip because of weight or bulk, I'll almost always bring the saw. As mentioned, there are backpacking models that weigh very little and these saws really make the culinary chores easier when you're cooking over wood.

CHUTNEY-LENTIL BURGERS

1/2 cup mango chutney
1 T. mustard
1/4 cup finely chopped scallions
1/4 tsp. salt
2 cups cooked lentils,
  partially mashed

1/4 cup wheat germ or whole wheat
  bread crumbs
1 egg, beaten
Alfalfa or clover sprouts
Sour cream (opt.)

Combine chutney and mustard. Take 1/4 of this mixture and combine with scallions and salt. Add lentils, wheat germ and egg, and form into 4 patties. If possible, chill well. Cook on grill over coals, about 4 minutes per side (a hinged grilling basket would be very useful). Serve on buns and top each with some of remainder of chutney mixture, sprouts, and, if you wish, a dollop of sour cream. ✦Recently, these were very fine served on stone-ground whole wheat hamburger buns. SERVES 4.

Two logs or a few sturdy sticks can be used as bases for a small grill. Here, two pork chops are being grilled.

There are two types of fireplaces: fixed and makeshift. At campgrounds you will encounter a wide array of types, but essentially you will have to work with what you find. Tips for using and modifying these fixed fireplaces are included in other chapters in this book. What we'll talk about here are the kinds of temporary fireplaces you can devise.

Always consider safety first. Don't, for example, make the fireplace so close to the tent that a burning ember is likely to waft over and land on your shelter. It's a small point, but I always try to pitch my tent so the tent opening faces the fire. I like to keep my eye on it, both for esthetic reasons and safety reasons. Who knows, a big wind might come along and juice up a not-quite-dead fire, and if I haven't yet drifted off to dreamland I can get up and do what's necessary. I suppose I should tell you that you should douse your fire before you retire, but I think I'm not alone in liking to drift off to sleep to the pleasant crackle of a fading campfire.

If possible, avoid making your fireplace under or around low-growing vegetation. If the woods are dry, this would be critically important, though if the woods are really tinder-dry don't make a fire at all. Be sure that you clear the ground area down to dirt. If you make your fire on a carpet of ground duff—tangled roots, leaves, moss—a spark could embed itself in this excellent fire medium and smolder without your knowing about it. Days or even weeks later this lethal hot spot could emerge at that point or even travel many yards underground, only to erupt and begin a disastrous forest fire.

The simplest arrangement is a ring of rocks. Don't use porous rocks like sandstone and especially don't use rocks that are wet (for example, from the river). Once heated, the water inside the rocks will turn to steam and this could make the whole rock explode. Use hard-looking, firm, dry rocks. As you assemble these, keep in mind the size of your grill (if you have one along). Also, try to include a couple of big flat rocks in your ring so you can set pots and other things down on them as necessary. Try to keep each rock far enough from licking flames to prevent it from becoming permanently blackened.

If you plan to do some baking with the reflector oven, you'll have some special considerations. See chapter 9. For normal cooking over coals, a keyhole fireplace is an excellent choice.

STEAK WITH MUSHROOMS
Burn a good hardwood fire down to coals. Bring 2 strip or club steaks (or one good-sized sirloin steak) to near room temperature. In a skillet, melt 2 T. butter and sauté 2 cups sliced fresh mushrooms or 2/3 cup canned mushrooms. Add 4 slices chopped, cooked bacon and a dash of Worcestershire sauce. Serve over grilled steaks. ✦Optional: Sprinkle a little crumbled blue cheese over the mushroom sauce while it's still piping hot. SERVES 2.

A keyhole (p. 43) is a way of arranging a fireplace so that it is shaped like an old skeleton key. At the large round end you can keep a fire going, while simultaneously you can use coals from the fire for cooking at the narrower, rectangular end. As the coals burn down, just use a stick to rake in more coals under your grill. It takes a bit of effort and quite a few rocks to make a keyhole, but it's always my first choice when I'm not using the reflector oven.

It is not strictly necessary to contain a fire with rocks. In pristine backwoods places, use only a couple of rocks, to minimize your impact on the area. Keep your fire small and you might be able to skip the rocks completely. In any case, try to avoid blackening rocks by keeping them a bit away from the hottest part of the fire.

For cooking purposes, I'll almost always use the teepee lay to actually start the fire. This arrangement of wood creates a kind of upward funnel effect, and I'm convinced it's the quickest way to start a wood fire. The popular log-cabin lay is OK too, but I think this one is better for social fires. The real beauty of the log-cabin lay is that you can prepare a social fire ahead of time, right from tinder up to logs, because you can just keep adding more layers. In Boy Scout camp, they used to make a big one that had to be eight feet cubed. It was put together during the day by some scouts, so after dinner all we had to do was sit around and wait for the scoutmaster to come along and put the torch to the bottom of the pile. It would then burn for hours with no additional tending. Were you ever initiated with the "O-Wah-Tu-Na-Siam" routine?

However you arrange the small wood to start your fire, once it gets going it really doesn't matter how you add wood. Just be careful not to choke off the blaze.

SAUSAGE WITH SAUERKRAUT
Fill a bowl with cold water and add one 16-oz. can or bag of sauerkraut. Swish sauerkraut around with a fork. After 10 minutes, drain and transfer sauerkraut to a pot. Add 2 cups water, 1/8 cup packed brown sugar, 2 T. minced dried onion, and half of an apple. Simmer 20 minutes. ✦Grill 6 sausages or a ring of kielbasa. When nicely grilled, add these to the sauerkraut with some of the pan drippings. Simmer 10 more minutes or just allow to sit off flame for several hours. ✦If you like your 'kraut quite tart, omit the initial rinsing. SERVES 3.

If you lack a grill, you'll face a much greater challenge in most situations. As discussed in chapter 1, I bring my own full-sized grill to the campground. When I'm backpacking, I bring a simple, lightweight, tubular aluminum grill made just for backpacking (weight, 4½ oz.). A grill makes it infinitely easier to cook over wood, but if you lack one then your best bet may be a two-log fireplace. Just make your fire in the normal fashion, using rocks or omitting them as just discussed. When you have the amount of coals desirable, rake them all together and place a thick log on either side (about three to four inches apart). Now you can (hopefully) straddle the space between the logs with pot or frypan.

Naturally, you could always use rocks in place of the green logs, and if there are a couple of nice, long, basically squarish rocks in the vicinity, go to it.

Another way to arrange your fire is the star lay. When you have mostly large wood for burning, and no implements for cutting or splitting that wood, the star lay comes in handy. After you've begun a fire, just put the ends of what logs you have in the fire. As the ends burn down, push the logs in farther. It's just basic common sense, but it's a method of wood burning that is used more for social fires than for cooking fires.

Personally, as I've stated before, I like to disturb the fire pit as little as possible once the pots and pans have been put on.

An excellent spur-of-the-moment stove can be made from an empty can, preferably one the size and shape of a two-pound coffee can. Completely cut out both the top and bottom and puncture some holes in the side of the can. Place it in the middle of your fireplace or even right on dirt or on a flat rock. Fill it halfway with some already lit charcoal or wood coals. (You could even actually begin the fire in the can. Just put some wadded paper in the upright can and then put your coals on top. Light the paper from underneath.) Then place your small frypan or pot right on top. This makeshift stove will also make some decent toast. To make toast, leave the top on the can, and puncture some holes in that end. Then place the can over some hot, live coals or even over the burner of a camp stove. Place your bread on the top with the punctured holes.

When you cook over wood in the outdoors, you assume a triple responsibility. First, you must not abuse the resource (the wood). Second, you must exercise safety measures so as to avoid forest fires. Third, you must return your cooking area to a natural-looking condition. It goes without saying that you will leave not a trace of any litter on your campsite. But true woodsmen and women go beyond that. Here is the procedure for breaking camp:

1. Douse all flames and coals extremely well with water. If water is unavailable, use dirt or sand. If possible, then go about your other camp-breaking chores. Go back to your fire pit and stir the ashes and remaining bits of coals into the dirt or mud. Ideally, your fire pit should be dead cold before you leave.

2. Take whatever rocks you might have used and scatter them randomly about the area. Do the same with any half-burned logs. If you're in a moderately or heavily used area with established campsites, each having its own

Beechwood fires are bright and clear,
If the logs are kept a year,
Chestnut only good they say,
If for long 'tis laid away,
But ash new or ash old,
Is fit for queen with crown of gold.

Birch and fir logs burn too fast,
Blaze up bright and do not last,
It is by the Irish said,
Hawthorne bakes the sweetest bread,
Elmwood burns like churchyard mold,
E'en the very flames are cold,
But ash green or ash brown
Is fit for queen with golden crown.

Poplar gives a bitter smoke,
Fills your eyes and makes you choke,
Applewood will scent your room,
With an incense like perfume,
Oaken logs, if dry and old,
Keep away the winter's cold,
But ash wet or ash dry,
A king shall warm his slippers by.

Anon.

ad-hoc fireplace, I see no point whatever in disassembling those fireplaces. If anything, these familiar established sites are positive in that they "restrict" campers to just those sites.

3. Cover the dead ashes that you've now doused and stirred into the dirt with some additional dirt. Tamp down with your foot. Make sure there are no burnables under the ashes, just in case a live coal remains.

4. Now do what you can esthetically to restore the area to a natural condition. Police the area and pick up any little tiny bits of foil, cellophane, or paper left by you or the preceding party. Scatter a little ground duff or grass over the area where the fireplace sat. Do the same around the area where your tent sat.

The overwhelming majority of camp meals these days are prepared over stoves. Stoves are easy, fast, efficient, and they leave no scars. Yet in so many instances, a wood fire can be an excellent auxiliary cooking source, and for backpackers it can save the day when the backpack stove fails or the fuel runs out. If you really want to call yourself a woodsman—or woodswoman—practice with cooking fires until you've gotten good at it. It will provide great satisfaction, and will make you one with the woods as will few other skills.

Chapter 6
COOKING ON GRILLS AND HIBACHIS

O f all the types of cooking equipment discussed in this book, grills and hibachis are the ones that people will be most familiar with. Although both are patio fixtures from the big city to the most rural areas, they are also used widely by campers.

Because of their weight and bulk, these implements are pretty much restricted to road campgrounds and similar situations. Some seasonal campers may well use an elaborate grill and, indeed, that grill may even be hooked up to a bulk propane system. But there are many good home-barbecue books that cover such sophisticated equipment. Here, we will talk only about the simpler charcoal grills and hibachis.

If you really go for the taste of barbecued food, bringing one of these to a campground is a smart move. That is because the fireplace at the campground may be unsuited for cooking or your site may not even have a fireplace. Campgrounds provide dozens of different types of fireplaces, many of them makeshift, and woefully too many of them poor for cooking.

If the fireplace doesn't allow for at least some adjustability of the grill, it's going to cause you problems. Another typical dilemma is that the grill (grate) will not sit solidly without wobbling. Then, too, a grill may not even be present, though you'll prepare for this eventuality by bringing your own grill (see checklists, chapter 1).

Hibachi cooking is immensely popular in this country, and the number of shapes and sizes has grown. That is probably because hibachis are very small and very portable compared to standard circular grills, yet they cook as well or better. A standard, single grate hibachi will cook for one or two. A double hibachi will adequately feed three to four people. Beyond that and you're better off going to a larger, circular grill. (To avoid confusion, we'll call the entire appliance the

A heavy-gauge round hibachi. The closely-spaced, flat-topped grill is a good design.

grill unit or just unit and the grate that sits on top simply the grill. Only units that utilize charcoal will be considered here.)

It is just amazing the number of different portable grill unit designs that have appeared in the past 10 years. Fortunately, there are some basic attributes to watch for.

The single most important consideration with a charcoal grill unit is the adjustability of the grill. Ideally, the grill should go as close to the fire as 1½ inches and as far as 5 inches. And there should be at least one step in between. It's extra nice if the grill can be raised to 6 or 8 inches above the fire, which will abet your efforts to keep cooked foods or breadstuffs warm. With the small units you'll rarely enjoy this much adjustability.

On a hibachi, you merely take the grill by its wooden handle and move it up or down a notch. Usually there are three or four notches and the increments are about right. With the familiar circular grill unit with legs, there may be a crank that moves the grill up or down. At the garden store, take your time to examine the mechanism to see how smoothly it does or does not work. With the smaller circular grill units, there will not be any crank to raise or lower the grill. But there might be levels or "steps" that allow adjustability above the fire. Some adjustability is essential.

The grill itself should be plated with nickel or chrome, and the rods should be fairly heavy and spaced close together. Flat-topped rods make for the best grill.

The unit itself should be at least rust resistant. Stainless steel, galvanized steel or aluminum all are in this category. If the appliance is made of ordinary steel, it should be enamel-coated.

Another very important thing to look for is how securely the grill sits on the unit. Wobbly grills will make you curse out loud. Next examine the legs. Are they rigid, or do they allow wobbling and shaking of the whole appliance? Here, you strictly get what you pay for and no more. Another feature to examine is the damper. For the fire to burn well, there should be some kind of damper either at the bottom or at the side of the grill unit. Most hibachis have such a damper, usually just a little sliding window that you can open or close to the extent you desire. Oddly, many grill units do not have a damper.

Ideally, you should be able to add charcoal to the grill during the cooking process, if the fire burns down a little bit too quickly.

There are many more refined outdoor cooking appliances, some of these incorporating rotisseries, shelves, and on and on. While you will see these on occasion at campgrounds, such equipment really gets into the realm of home barbecuing. Again, see the many good books on that subject.

Most of the equipment you need for cooking on a grill or hibachi is included on the checklist in chapter 1. A few more optional items, though, might be mentioned.

For certain types of food, a hinged grilling basket is a godsend. This device really shines when it comes to grilling soft foods like fish. A whole fish being grilled should be turned over once, but if you try to do this with a fork or spatula you risk having your prize catch fall apart. Grilled vegetables can be a surprise treat, but like fish they are soft, and if they don't actually fall apart they might fall through the cracks. Grilling baskets also reduce the risk of burns, since when you have a bunch of food to flip over, all you do is turn the whole basket over by its long handles. Your hand need never be exposed to the very intense heat of the coals. A basket is very useful in two other particular situations: when the grill is dirty and cruddy, and when the rods of the grill are widely spaced (since food could fall through). Thick rods widely spaced are an especial nuisance.

Grilling baskets come in a wider range of sizes and shapes than you probably suspect. Some are for burgers and such, some for vegetables, some for roasts, some for fish. The most commonly seen is the rectangular, flat-folding one used widely for burgers and hot dogs. You may have to hunt around for the others (try kitchen or gourmet specialty shops, or camper's-supply catalogs). Some have depth built into them and these are good for chicken or other thick cuts of meat. Some are shaped like a fish.

Very useful for the serious barbecuer is a rectangular sheet of metal used as a "topper" over an existing fireplace grate or grill unit grill. It is meshlike, to prevent foods from falling through the wider grill it is intended to cover. Toppers are now used extensively for barbecuing fish.

On my checklists, I list pot holders. If you do a lot of cooking over any type of coals, you might want to add one or two fireproof mitts. I probably will this season.

A long-handled basting brush is nice to have. I don't bring one camping but I would if I were to do any rotisserie cooking.

A stiff-wire brush, obtainable at any hardware store, is useful for cleaning the grill. More on that in a moment.

Getting it Going

Next comes the topic of fire starting. Most people use charcoal briquets, which are all of a uniform size. For the best results, use 100 percent hardwood briquets; you'll likely find that brand names are worth the slight extra price. Start the meal farther ahead of time than you think you should. For a typical barbecue meal, mound together 20 to 30 briquets (my experience is that you're better off with too many than too few). It will take an average of 30 to 40 minutes for this many coals to get to a uniform gray, the right time to start cooking. A larger mound of briquets can take a surprisingly long time to get to the right stage—up to an hour or more, depending on the wind, shape and design of the grill unit, and whether or not the briquets have been exposed to dampness. Needless to say, always store your briquets out of the rain and protected from dampness as much as possible. Keeping the entire briquet bag within a large plastic bag is good procedure. If they do get damp, lay them on a tarp in the sun for a few hours.

It almost never will hurt to start your fire too soon, for more briquets can always be put on. But fires started too late have messed up more than a few camp meals. This can loom especially large in summer in certain places, when you must finish supper before the mosquitoes start buzzing around. They're almost always at their worst just before dark.

Instant-light and quick-light charcoal briquets are preferred by some. To these, you may only have to apply a match. They are more expensive and some experts say the smoke from them can impart a bad taste to food if they are not allowed to burn down far enough. I never use these.

To start regular briquets, flammable liquids or jellies are most often used; liquids are easily the more popular. Sold in pint-size or quart-size cans, the liquid fire starters have been made extremely safe in recent years...so safe that you may actually struggle to get a fire going with them. Still, it's about the best wheel in town unless you have electricity and can use an electric fire starter, always my top choice for backyard cooking. If you lack a liquid or jelly fire starter, tightly crumpled wads of newspaper placed under your coals may work, but the liquid starter is easily the better option.

POLYNESIAN BARBECUED BEEF

1/4 cup soy sauce	1/2 tsp. ground coriander (opt.)
2 T. lemon juice	1/2 tsp. ground ginger
1 T. oil	1/2 tsp. dry mustard
1/2 tsp. ground cumin	1½ lbs. boneless beef
1/2 tsp. garlic powder	sirloin, one inch thick

At home, combine all ingredients except the meat. Blend well, bring to camp in a suitable vessel. ✦In camp, trim away fat from meat, cut into long, one-half-inch-wide strips. Place meat in marinade in plastic or stainless steel vessel. Marinate at least 1 hour at room temperature or several hours in the cooler. ✦Thread strips on skewers, cook on grill over hot coals, about 7 minutes total. Do not overcook meat! It should be pink inside. SERVES 4-6.

Drizzle or squirt a half-cup or more of your liquid starter onto the piled-up coals.

Replace the cap on the starter and move it away from the grill unit. Always make sure no flammable materials are near the grill unit. Quickly after applying the starter, drop on a match. As mentioned, these starters are so safe now that flare-up is very unlikely to occur. If anything, you may have to toss on a couple of matches. Do not apply liquid starter or any combustible liquid to live heat. Do not use gasoline to start charcoal, and do not use any type of homemade concoction. Do use the same common sense that you would use in any situation where potentially dangerous heat and flammable substances are present.

Let's next talk about care and cleaning of your grill unit. Then we'll move on to tips for using the unit, including specific recipes and general formulas for certain types of commonly grilled foods.

Lining the bottom of your grill unit with aluminum foil will make cleanup easier and may somewhat lengthen the life of the unit by buffering its bottom and sides from the heat. Be sure to place the foil shiny side up to reflect heat upward.

Charcoal grills are like cast-iron pans: They're far easier to clean when they're still very warm. Forget the nonsense about the heat sterilizing the grill. Do you really want a thick layer of crud on the grill you'll be placing your food on? Do your guests? Be a conscientious camp chef and clean the grill each time. Of course, a black, hard, carbonized film will accrete on any grill. It's the sticky, gooey crud that I object to.

By all means, wait for it to cool a little if you have to, but try to get to it when it's still very warm. Here's where those fireproof mitts really help. Take the warm grill and if possible, completely immerse it in warm, sudsy water. Remove it later at your leisure and scrub it with a wire brush or a soap pad. If dunking it is not possible—usually it won't be at a campground—just wipe the still-hot grill with a cold, wet rag. The cold water will turn to steam and the steam will help to remove food particles and charred crud. Then use a wire brush, or as a second choice, a wad of crumpled aluminum foil.

By a very wide margin, stainless steel makes the best metal for a charcoal grill. It is the most easily cleaned and is far more durable than regular steel. Do not use shelves from an old refrigerator as cooking grills. Such shelves are said to be coated with undesirable substances.

If you've lined your grill unit with foil, you can, once the coals are down to warm ash, simply fold the foil up and remove the whole thing to a trash bin. The bottom of the grill unit can then be quickly wiped with a damp cloth. Last, put in a new foil liner. If you wish, you can even rub the grill with a little oil and place it in a clean place. Now you're all set for the next meal, and when that meal comes you'll be glad you were so fastidious, since cold, dirty, cooking equipment is miserable to clean.

Using charcoal grill units effectively is really nothing but a lot of little tricks. It is probably best to discuss these tricks concurrently with the specific types of dishes they can be applied to. But first, here are a few general suggestions.

Flare-ups are a frequent problem when cooking fatty foods. Some people use a little spray bottle of water to squelch the flames when they get too high, but this fine spray of water will explode as steam and cause ashes to fly up onto your

Picnic table space is always at a premium in a campground. This enterprising camper brought his own folding table, replete with umbrella!

food. One solution, if the unit permits, is to insert a tray or piece of cardboard between the coals and the food when you spray. Or, remove the food momentarily if it's convenient. If you do the latter, you may not have to spray, since the flames will quickly subside when denied those fatty drippings. Here's another example of why tongs are so useful outdoors. If you're constantly handling your meat, poking it continually with a fork will let escape all the juices. If you have to stab a cut of meat on the grill, try to insert the sharp points into the fatty portion of the meat.

Some barbecue books include detailed tables showing cooking times. The vagaries of outdoor cooking usually make a mockery of any such tables. You just have to develop a feel for when something is done. It does help, though, to know the factors that affect cooking times outdoors.

Believe it or not, the temperature of the food being cooked is extremely significant. A very cold steak just thawed out, for example, could take twice as long as one at room temperature. Avoid grilling frozen, partially frozen, or very cold meats. The cooking times for these will be very hard to judge, and the outside may be blackened before the inside is cooked.

The outdoor temperature is significant, but I find the wind to be much more so. On a windy day, the heat above the coals will be severely dissipated and everything will take longer to cook. The direction of wind is also important. It's best to keep a charcoal grill unit out of the wind as much as possible. (This is not always true with wood fires built on the ground. You may want to build your fire with the opening facing the direction the wind is coming from.)

Fine Points of the Game

Preheat the grill before placing food on it. Then rub it with a little oil or grease. If you're cooking a fatty steak or chop, cut off a hunk of fat and spear it with a fork, then push the fat with the fork across the surface of the grill. Taking these steps will greatly lessen the chance of food sticking. It also helps if the food, especially meat, is not too cold.

If the steaks or chops you're cooking are thin ones, slash the fatty edges at half-inch intervals. This will help prevent the meat from curling. The thicker the cut of meat the less of a problem this will be. Never crowd your steaks and chops on the grill. They'll come out crisper and much more appetizing if the heat is allowed to circulate around them. Remember that once you flip the meat the internal temperature has been greatly raised, so it will not require as much time on the second side.

Place the meat about two inches from the coals, farther if the fire is very hot. Searing the meat with very intense heat does not seal in the juices. In fact, tests show that such searing may actually make for drier meat. Medium heat seems to produce the best grilled steaks and chops. If the steak or chop has a lot of fat on the edges, trim some of this before you start cooking. This will help prevent flare-ups before they occur.

Do you like a little smoke flavor to your grilled meat? Just cover the meat with a large pot lid or a tent of aluminum foil for the last few minutes of cooking. These days, even many small grill units come with their own smoke covers. It could be said that the cover is the single most significant development in portable grill units in recent years.

If you wish to add a distinctive smoky flavor to the meat you can toss onto your fire some hardwood chips, the same ones you would use if you were smoking foods in your home smoker. The manufacturer of one such smoker recommends the following hardwood chips for the following foods: hickory chips for ham or bacon, alder chips for game, applewood for poultry, and cherry chips for all dark meats and game. You can purchase these chips through the same outdoor catalogs that offer those small, homemade smoker units, or from specialty retail stores. Some foods, especially fish, can be extremely tasty if first baked (indoors or outdoors) then exposed to 10 minutes or so of controlled smoke from hardwood chips. This works superbly well with whole trout.

It is often said that you can tell how done a piece of meat is by the juices that run from it. If the juice is quite red, the meat is rare; if the juices are pink, it is done; if clear, it is overdone. This is true with red meat. With chicken, the juice will never be as blood red, but pink juice will probably indicate that the chicken is not quite done while clear to yellowish juice will indicate that the bird is done to satisfaction. Remember, today's fatty chicken is harder to overcook than beef, and people will be less picky about how well done it is anyway, as long as it is done. With chicken, if you poke it with a fork or knife to some small degree you won't hurt anything since its high fat content will prevent drying of the meat. So the juice test is a good one with poultry. Another test with poultry is this: Twist the leg and if it moves freely in it's socket it's probably done. As far as performing the juice test on red meat— beefsteak, pork chops, lamb chops—it's not a great idea since loss of the precious juice will dry the meat. With red meat, you have to develop more of an instinct. I know it's time to turn a steak when a fairly thick, frothy bit of reddish juice emanates from it (without my stabbing it). Also, with red meat I do keep an eye on the clock a little more, since cooking times are relatively short and reasonably predictable. I still refuse to list approximate times, but you can bet that almost all steaks and chops will be done in 15 minutes or less over hot coals.

I just mentioned the "instinct" of knowing when red meat on the grill is done. It's actually a little more tangible than that. Raw meat, as you know, is quite mushy. The more tender the cut the more true this will be. Press the meat as it's cooking with the side of a fork or with a spoon. It becomes more firm as it cooks and this, combined with the look of the meat, will clue you in as to its doneness. This knack, which all good sauté chefs possess, can be cultivated.

Matching Meat and Method

A nice, juicy ham steak, one actually cut from the hind quarter or ham of the pig, is delicious when grilled. You can put it directly on the grill or you can place it in a hinged basket. Compared to a top-quality sirloin or a trio of loin-cut lamb chops, a ham steak is inexpensive and almost foolproof from a cooking standpoint. Such ham steaks will invariably be cured so all you really have to do is heat the meat through. I like my grilled or broiled venison or beefsteak best with just a little sea salt and perhaps a little good mustard on the side. I like my lamb chops very lightly seasoned and with mint jelly on the side. However, a ham steak seems to cry out for a nice tangy basting sauce. Following are two of my favorites. The particular basting sauce will partially determine accompaniments, for example: plain boiled potatoes if you use a very spicy baste, grilled pineapple chunks if you use a sweet sauce, spiced chinese vegetables if you use a sweet-sour baste.

MUSTARD-HONEY SAUCE

1/2 cup honey	1/4 cup mustard
3/4 cup ginger ale	1/2 tsp. horseradish
1 T. cornstarch	1/4 tsp. powdered ginger

Cook all over low heat until slightly thickened, about 10-12 minutes. Use a little to baste the ham or ham slices as they're warming on the grill, then serve the rest as a warm sauce. ABOUT 1¼ CUPS.

ORANGE SAUCE

Soften one cup of butter or margarine to room temperature. Add 2/3 cup orange marmalade and 1/8 cup orange liquer. Beat together using a fork or whisk. Baste ham generously with this mixture as you're grilling it. A dollop can also be placed on each warm ham slice as it's served. ABOUT 1¾ CUPS.

As discussed already, grilling poultry these days is almost foolproof due to the extremely high fat content of most domestic birds. This is a sad testament to America's attitude towards its food. If the public demanded leaner poultry, it would get it. But we see the commercials that sell "tender" for all it's worth and never quite get it that "more tender" is only "more fatty." I admit, I eat less and less domestically raised meat these days, preferring wild game when I have it. In the realm of domestic meat, I dislike chicken especially because I believe its extreme fattiness to be unhealthy. When possible, I recommend that you buy chicken from a specialty farm or outlet that allows its birds to range freely and does not give them hormones, antibiotics, heavily chemicalized feed, or other questionable substances.

Whatever my feelings, campers and all outdoor chefs will continue to grill chicken by the millions of pounds. First, we'll talk about the grilling of chicken parts as opposed to whole birds. If you fancy parts from turkey, duck, capon, or squab, methods would not be very much different.

While it's difficult to overcook today's store-bought chicken, it is quite possible to overcook its skin, a problem only if you like to eat the skin, as most do. Many people can tolerate a slightly underdone steak, but to me underdone poultry is most unappetizing. Thus I usually do one of two things: I parboil the chicken parts for 20 minutes or so, or I prebake them on the grill in aluminum foil (also about 20 minutes). Then I take the partially cooked chicken parts and put them directly on the hot grill. If my guests are in the mood for a barbecue taste, which is almost always the case, I dip the entire chicken part in a bowl of sauce, give the meat a little shake, and then place it on the grill. The rationale is, the less time my hand has to be over the hot coals the better.

Without the parboiling, grilling time can extend to as much as an hour. I try to avoid having to grill anything that I have to watch closely for that long, since I usually have other things to do in camp. Additionally, grilling for that long consumes too much charcoal, which wastes money. Even with the parboiling, the chicken still may need another 20-30 minutes on the grill. From all this you can deduce correctly that you need a bigger fire with chicken than you do for steaks and chops. This is where many camp chefs go astray.

Making a red barbecue sauce from scratch at a campground is work. Best to make a big batch at home and bring some to camp. Here is my own formula for homemade barbecue sauce. Use it on grilled chicken, or incorporate it into barbecued beef. For a lighter touch, use the tangy basting sauce that follows.

TUMBLEWEED BARBECUE SAUCE

1 cup catsup	2 T. molasses
1/3 cup water	1 small onion, chopped fine
1/4 cup vinegar	Dash Worcestershire sauce
2 T. oil	Big dash each garlic powder and
2 T. brown sugar	paprika

Combine all in a pot. Simmer slowly about 25 minutes. ✦ You can strain the sauce to remove the onion, and I recommend this for storage past one day. ABOUT 2 CUPS.

CHINESE CHICKEN BASTING SAUCE

Combine 1/3 cup each of teriyaki sauce, vegetable oil (half sesame oil would be excellent) and pineapple juice. Add 3 T. light brown sugar and 3/4 tsp. powdered ginger. Mix well. Baste chicken frequently as it's grilling. MAKES 1 CUP.

So much is said about hamburgers and hot dogs in other books and articles that I won't go into great detail here. Nonetheless, there is a right way and a wrong way.

First of all, don't forget to bring a spatula! You'll burn your hand and botch up your burgers without one. Make your burgers bigger than usual, since grilling will dry them out to some extent. If someone at your dinner table usually eats two normal-sized hamburgers, try making one very big one for that person instead. It will be juicier and tastier. If you're cooking for a group of five or more, a hinged grilling basket will make your job far, far easier. Place burgers that won't be eaten for a little while towards the back of the grill, but do this well before the burger is completely cooked. The low heat just off the coals will finish cooking the meat through without overcooking it.

JAZZED-UP BURGERS I

2 lbs. ground beef	Few dashes Worcestershire sauce
1/4-1/3 cup finely chopped onion	Salt and pepper to taste
1 egg	

Combine all in a bowl and mix well. Form into large burgers and grill over coals. Baste with melted butter or margarine, or a red barbecue sauce. MAKES ABOUT 6.

JAZZED-UP BURGERS II

2 lbs. ground beef	4 drops hot pepper sauce
1 small onion, finely chopped	Salt and pepper to taste
2 T. sweet red pepper, chopped	Butter
(opt.)	Blue cheese
1/8 tsp. garlic salt	

Combine all but last two ingredients. Form into burgers. Grill on first side. Turn, and top with a mixture of butter and blue cheese, each pre-softened. Grill a few more minutes. **MAKES ABOUT 6.**

A London broil is something of a cross between a steak and a roast, but it is essentially treated like the former. My mother does London broil perfectly, and her recipe goes like this (the simple, quick, tasty gravy she makes would go just fine with any other good cut of steak).

BARBECUED LONDON BROIL WITH EASY GRAVY

2-inch thick London broil	2 T. butter
Natural meat tenderizer	Kitchen Bouquet
1 large onion, sliced and broken into rings	1/2 lb. mushrooms, sliced
	Flour, about 2 T.

Moisten steak on both sides with cold water. Sprinkle on meat tenderizer, piercing meat deeply with a fork every 1/4 inch. Rub with Kitchen Bouquet. Set aside. ✦Sauté onion in butter. When soft, add mushrooms. Sauté 5 more minutes. Sprinkle with about 6 oz. water and 2 T. flour (more or less) to thicken. Add 1 tsp. Kitchen Bouquet. Add the meat drippings if there are any. Optionally, add a splash of red wine or 1 beef bouillon packet. Stir well and cover off flame. ✦Barbecue meat on a grill over coals. Slice on an angle and serve with heated gravy.

Kebab Magic

What would a camp cookout be without shish kebab? Skewer cooking is fun and it has its practical advantages in camp. For one thing, it saves the need for lots of pots, pans, and the washing of these. For another, it makes for quick cooking time for meat, since that meat will be cut into fairly small cubes. A further benefit is that the fast cooking can make for just the right combination of crusty outside and super-tender inside. Skewer cookery centralizes a whole meal—just plop the finished kebab down on your guest's plate. And if you really like that smoky, barbecue flavor, kebabs provide a lot of it since so much surface area of the food is exposed to the heat and smoke.

Some outdoor chefs are of the mind that you have to cook the meat and vegetables on separate skewers, the theory being that the vegetables will require less cooking time. I fly in the face of this seemingly sound advice and mix and match everything on one skewer. This looks nicer and is much more practical since each diner gets his or her own skewer. If you cut the meat fairly small as I do, and use tender cuts of meat in the first place, you shouldn't have a problem with the vegetables or fruit pieces becoming overdone. If you do try a tougher cut, like chuck steak, it should be marinated for two to three hours and, additionally, you should sprinkle on some commercial instant tenderizer 10 minutes before cooking. Use the 100-percent natural meat tenderizers that contain no artificial ingredients.

To me, the quintessential shish kebab is lamb. Unfortunately, unless you can find lamb cubes prepackaged specifically for shish kebab—some tender cut, not stew meat—you'll probably have to buy half a leg of lamb, which is expensive. Cut it into one-inch cubes yourself. Don't ask the butcher to needlessly perform this task for you. He may well charge you more money.

A tender cut of lamb need not be tenderized, but a good marinade can add flavor and make the meat even more tender and succulent. My favorite lamb marinade is presented here.

LAMB SHISH KEBAB MARINADE

Juice of 1 lemon	3/4 tsp. salt
1/4 cup vegetable oil	1/4 tsp. pepper
1/8 cup cider vinegar	1/4 tsp. garlic powder
2 T. each chopped onion and parsley	

Combine all ingredients and allow marinade to sit several hours to develop. Then pour over cubed lamb. Marinate a few hours. Use a little bit to baste your shish kebab while it's cooking. ABOUT 2/3 CUP.

Lamb may be the ultimate kebab meat but it isn't the only one. Beef and pork can also be used. With beef, be sure to use a tender cut like sirloin, tenderloin, rib eye, or round. Tougher cuts should be sprinkled with tenderizer a little beforehand. Any kind of sausage cut into pieces is perfect for kebabs. With pork, an ideal cut for kebabing is a boneless smoked shoulder, which only needs to be heated through. Then there are the tempting seafood kebabs. Either sea scallops or shrimp are superb because their texture is such that they are unlikely to fall off the skewer. One fish that has a scalloplike texture and is excellent for kebabs is monkfish.

Although double-tined skewers exist, I have not seen them around lately. A more available design that also will help keep foods from spinning is the spiral or twisted skewer. A long skewer is better than a shorter one, since you can turn it by its looped end without exposing your hand to the heat. Other than that, there isn't a lot of technique involved. There is some skill, though, in cutting the vegetables and fruit pieces (if used) to the right size and shape. This just takes practice.

By the way, while your guests may well shrink from many cooking chores, most will love to help you put kebabs together. They seem to be fascinated with the resulting artistic effects, so just put the cut-up ingredients on the picnic table and let them go to it. You can suggest that each diner assemble just the ingredients he or she fancies. Then, you can even promote the idea of each diner cooking the kebab himself.

KEBAB KOMBOS
(Thread in order listed and repeat as necessary)

FISHERMAN'S DELIGHT
- Boneless monkfish
- Cherry tomato
- Green pepper
- Large shrimp

Baste with a combination of oil and lemon juice. Sprinkle lightly with dried oregano or thyme.

VEGETARIAN ENTICER
- Red pepper
- Firm tofu
- Whole mushroom
- Yellow squash

Dilute some honey with water and warm. Add a few dashes each of soy sauce and salt and pepper. Baste your kebab with this mixture. Sprinkle on dried and well crushed rosemary.

THE "MEAT 'N' POTATOES" KEBAB
- Potato
- Italian sausage
- Cherry tomato
- Pitted prune
- Onion

Parboil the potatoes and sausage (also onion if you wish) so they're nearly cooked. A very light baste of oil/lemon juice is indicated here, or omit.

SOUTH PACIFIC BROCHETTE
- Canned water chestnut
- Pineapple
- Smoked ham chunk
- Firm banana or plantain

A sweet baste, perhaps with orange juice as a base, would be a good one for this kebab.

BEEF LOVER'S KEBAB
- Canned whole small onion
- Tender beef (marinate if possible)
- Bacon-wrapped whole mushroom
- Tomato wedge

Baste with softened butter seasoned with herbs.

CHICKEN KEBAB SUPREME
- Chicken chunk, from breast
- Orange wedge
- Papaya (firm)
- Carrot

A sweet-sour baste would be appropriate with this combination. Lacking that, baste with sesame oil cut with a little orange juice.

Earlier, I mentioned grilling baskets. Such baskets can be used very effectively with kebabs. Just place four or five of your already composed kebabs into the basket and place the whole basket on the grill. This is a trick to turn to when the items on the skewer are very soft and likely to fall off.

Chapter 7

ORGANIZATIONAL TIPS WHEN COOKING FOR GROUPS

Problem: You're at the seashore leading a group of 25 campers from a club you belong to. Part of what you promised them when you made your pitch at a club meeting was a complete seafood dinner on Saturday night. It is now Saturday morning, and in only nine hours they will expect a fabulous spread of lobster, fresh chowder, grilled corn, baked potatoes, and watermelon—all prepared under campground conditions.

Will you personally have to sacrifice a precious day out of the weekend and miss all the fun at the beach? Will you have to slave over a camp stove all day long? Will the meal inevitably not be ready till 11 P.M.? Will one thing at a time be served rather than the whole meal being ready at once?

The answer to all these questions should be no. And in the process of explaining why, I should be able to illustrate some of the principles of cooking successfully for a large group (more than 12).

The first thing you did was anticipate, weeks earlier, the special equipment you would need in addition to your usual assortment of campground utensils. You decided upon: extra three-burner stove, two very large pots, and a large cooler. A lot of people might have forgotten the cooler, but you knew it would be the best way to keep the cooked lobsters hot as the others were boiling.

The next thing you did, at least two weeks in advance, was order the lobsters: 30 in all, which included five extras in case a few died or in case a few extra people showed up. You then followed up with a phone call to the seafood place three days before arrival to make sure the lobsters would be waiting for you.

You figured there would be no problem with baked potatoes, but you did want to have a crate of the freshest, sweet local corn you could buy. So you lined up a

local farm stand and reserved a crate of 48 ears—two per person though you knew you'd have at least eight or ten left over (which you also knew would mix in just fine with some fresh corn cakes on Sunday morning). From that same farm stand you also ordered a nice, big, juicy watermelon.

You pulled all the strings at work you could to get to the campground Friday midday before the others arrived. You checked in with both the farm stand and the seafood place, and you also checked on where in town to buy a few things like nice plastic plates, napkins, and some candles for a birthday surprise you had in mind. Then you picked up some fresh fish, the potatoes, and a few other things you needed to make the chowder. You figured you would have that soup basically done on Friday night—on Saturday evening all you would have to add would be the milk.

The Friday dinner hour rolls around and people start arriving in loose groups. As the good host you're trying to be, you have a big pot of chili simmering for late arrivals who simply get to the campground too late to want to cook.

At 10 P.M., a head count shows that everyone has made it, so you relax in front of the now cheery fire with a cup of coffee and assess where you are with tomorrow's dinner. You really won't need too much help, but you still assign a few informal committees. Two girls will buy the plates, napkins, throwaway tablecloths, plastic utensils, and some little decorations; these same people will also set up the three picnic tables. Two guys will pick up the charcoal, wrap the potatoes and bake them in the campground "fireplaces" (large truck wheels, really). Another person will soak the corn, wrap it in foil, and steam it on grills (which you remembered to bring) over the same coals the potatoes will be cooking in. Two other cooperative individuals have volunteered to clean up. You figure with the work broken down this way, no one, including yourself, will have to leave the beach before 4 P.M.

DUTCH-OVEN BAKED BEANS

4 qts. dried beans, such as navy or great northern
1/2 cup brown sugar
6 T. salt
1 cup molasses

1 T. dry mustard
2 tsp. paprika
1 lb. salt pork, chopped
2 cups ketchup

Soak beans in cold water to cover for 10 hours. Drain. Cover beans with fresh water and simmer until almost tender. Drain. Mix 1½ qts. very hot water with the other ingredients. Add to the beans. Mix well. Cook in dutch ovens about 2 hours, checking at the halfway point (water can be added or, conversely, the lid can be left off to reduce the liquid). The ketchup is heretical, but I find it adds body, color, and flavor. ✦Three 12-inch ovens will be required. ABOUT 36 SIDE DISHES.

The next day breaks clear, making for a perfect morning of bike riding on the boardwalk, followed by various activities such as shopping, arcade hopping, and of course splashing in the waves. You tell everyone who's not helping out to be at the campground by 6:30. You tell your committee members in no uncertain terms that they must do what little shopping they have to do and be at the campground by 5:00. No one objects. Because you have things so well planned you're really not enslaving anyone or intruding on anyone's day.

Nonetheless, you're the first to sneak off the beach at just before 4:00. It takes you only 15 minutes to pick up the lobsters and produce, and another 15 to pick up some butter, lemons, parsley, and just a few other little things. The meal you're preparing is a simple one, and you planned it that way so there wouldn't be 20 or 30 different things to buy.

The first thing you do back at the campground is put the unhusked corn into water in the big lobster pots. No harm in soaking them a little early. From past experience, you know it's almost impossible to start a cooking fire too soon, so you immediately light up the charcoal. Mealtime is 7:30 P.M. sharp. You're allowing 40 minutes to get a good fire going and another 70 minutes to bake the potatoes. Luckily, your help appears and the vegetables are put on the heat at the correct time.

It's now 6:30 and both big pots are at a rolling boil (the corn having been removed earlier). It will take one hour to cook all those lobsters. You give the job to someone else, instructing that person to quickly put each cooked lobster into the big cooler (which you preheated with some boiling water). The longest any lobster will have to sit will be about 40 minutes and you know the preheated cooler will keep them hot for that long.

It's 7 P.M. You look around and see the situation perfectly in hand. People are relaxing, having a drink, and enjoying the blended smells of the different foods being prepared.

You could have brought too little charcoal—a common calamity—but you

When group size exceeds 10, a second camp stove (above) is strongly indicated. French toast is cooking on one, bacon on the other. Bringing an extra tent (right) for storing food and supplies is also a good idea.

didn't. You could have brought too little butter—you'll need a good five pounds for this meal—but you didn't. You could have made any of a dozen key mistakes that would've confounded you—but for now, at least, you don't foresee any problems.

You add the milk to the chowder and put it aside to be heated at the last minute. Then you remember: Bob's birthday surprise! You sneak the watermelon into the tent and, along with an accomplice, carefully cut off the top in a

Our fireplace was too small so, using rocks, we extended it out several feet. Baked potatoes for 36 people are baking in foil directly in the coals. The tent of foil speeds the process.

jagged, decorative way. Then you slowly pour in a bottle of Sangria and finally stick in a dozen or so candles. All set, the "cake" is propped up in a corner of the tent until the big moment arrives.

Both the potatoes and the corn are almost done, as are the lobsters. You heat the chowder and serve it as a first course, and everyone loves it. Meanwhile, you haven't forgotten to start melting the butter, to be passed around in little paper serving cups. No sooner are your guests finished with the soup than the lobsters, corn and potatoes—along with a green salad someone conjured up—are all put out, piping hot except for the salad.

But wait—someone moans. No claw crackers! You reach calmly into your kitchen box. You picked up a dozen on the way from the beach, and without them or with only one or two there would have been real problems.

Although you had your chowder while standing, now you can sit down and relax with the rest of the crew. No last minute hassles, and everything is done to perfection. In spite of the brief thundershower during cocktail hour, everyone is thrilled with the meal and you are justifiably proud that it came off without a hitch.

But the pièce de résistance is yet to come. Drawing as little attention to yourself as possible you sneak into the tent and light the candles on the watermelon then carry it over to the spontaneous singing of "Happy Birthday." Now, not only have you prepared a feast that 25 people will remember, but you have created a special birthday memory for a dear friend.

Later that evening with the entire group gathered around the campfire, you plan out the activities for Sunday, while everyone tells you how much work that great meal must have been. You just smile to yourself because you know it wasn't a lot of work. It was fun. It only would've been work (or worse) if you hadn't been prepared.

GALA WINE SPRITZER
In a large punch bowl or large kettle, combine 2 bottles (22 oz. each) of pink
Chablis wine and 12 ozs. of pineapple-orange juice (from concentrate OK).
Chill well. Just before serving, add 40 ozs. ginger ale and thin orange slices
and/or mint sprigs. **ABOUT 20 SMALL DRINKS.**

For thousands of years, people have been gathering to banquet together. And no
doubt, for just as many years the responsibility of pulling it all together has fallen
to someone. Is it worth the effort? Well, in modern times, our hearkening back to
the outdoors is mostly ritual, but it does uniquely serve to bring people together in
what is usually a healthy and natural setting. What better way to complete that ritual and cement the bonds of friendship than by drawing the whole group to the table
for a meal worth eating? Whether it's a Texas-style barbecue, a southern fish fry, a
Cape Cod clambake, or perhaps a vegetarian feast somewhere in the great Northwest,
a family-style meal can be the centerpiece for a great camping weekend.

Most people plan, but not many people really plan far enough ahead. You just
can't plan too far ahead. A recent wilderness canoe trip I ran for 12 people was
talked about two years in advance and booked one year in advance. A combined
fishing-hunting trip to Canada that I'm working on is being bandied about three
years ahead.

You don't have to plan that far ahead for a group dinner, but a few months prior
wouldn't be too soon, either.

Estimating Food Quantities

Assuming the campground has already been chosen—and that may very well be
something to do a year ahead—the next thing to assess is how many people are
coming. Choosing the right amount of food for a large group is a real art, and while
it does take some firsthand experience, it is possible to set down some guidelines.

What follows is based not on a buffet-type meal with many different dishes, but
a more normal meal of three or four courses. Obviously, as you add more courses you allot less of each dish to each person:

Bacon	1 lb. per 6 people
Baked potato	1 medium per person
Bone-in chicken	1 lb. or more per person
Boneless brisket	½ lb. per person
Butter	1 lb. per 8-12 people, depending on the meal
Chops, lamb	2 large or 4 small per person
Chops, pork	1 large or 2 medium per person
Coffee (A.M.)	2 cups per person
Coffee (P.M.)	1 cup per person (some will have none)
Corn	1½ ears per person if good corn
Fish (fillet)	⅓–½ lb. per person
Fish (steaks)	½–⅔ lb. per person

Fish (whole)	1 12–16 oz. fish per person
Hamburger	¼ –⅓ lb. per person
Hot dogs	2 per person with rolls
Italian sausage	2 or ⅓ lb. per person
Lettuce, in salad	1 head per 10 people
Live mussels or clams	1½ lbs. per person
Live oysters	2½–3 lbs. per person
Lobster	1½–1¾ lb. lobster per person
Meat, in stew	¼–⅓ lb. per person
Orange juice	1 half-gallon per 10 people
Pancakes	2–3 large or 5-7 medium per person
Pork spareribs	1 lb. or more per person
Shish kebab	¼ lb. meat per person with several vegetables
Shrimp	½ lb. per person (headless, tail and shell on)
Shrimp (head on)	¾ lb. per person
Soup	1 cup (8 oz.) per serving as a first course
Spaghetti	1 lb. per 4 persons
Spaghetti sauce	1 gallon per 25–32 people
Steak (boneless)	⅓–½ lb. per person
Tomatoes, sliced	1 small per person

Buying the food and the right amount of it certainly is the first and foremost hurdle when cooking for a group. But how can you be sure how many people are really going to show? Ah, now there's something that really should be discussed. Because while you'll be doing most of the work, there are things that your guests clearly must contribute. I'm talking about commitments.

CORN CHOWDER
EATON BARTLETT

2 large onions, diced fairly small	One stick of butter
4 large stalks celery, diced fairly small	4 large potatoes, diced
	1 16-oz. can whole kernel corn
Salt	1 16-oz. can cream-style corn
Pepper, sage, and garlic powder	1 12-oz. can evaporated milk

In a large pot, cover onions and celery with 1½ qts. lightly salted water. Add 3 dashes each of pepper, sage, and garlic powder. Add a stick of butter. Cook until vegetables are tender. Do not drain. In a separate pot, cook the diced potatoes in salted water until tender. Drain, add to first mixture. Add both cans of corn. In a saucepan, bring 1/2 cup water to simmer and add the milk. Bring back to simmer and add to chowder. SERVES ABOUT 16.

It's just amazing to me how few no-shows there are when all the money has been collected ahead of time. As an example, I recently hired out a good French

BOTH PHOTOS BY BETTY LOU FEGELY

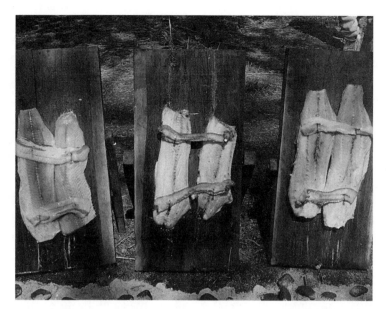

Fish baked on planks in front of the coals takes on an incomparably delicious flavor. Planked shad is traditional at the numerous early spring "shad festivals" in my own Hudson Valley; other types of fish can also be used. Oak is the best wood for fish planking. The optional bacon strips help baste the fish as they cook.

restaurant (owned by a friend) to prepare a venison dinner for my father, myself, and 10 fishing-hunting buddies. The cost was $20.50 per person and to save hassles on the night of the dinner I added in the tax and tip and charged everybody $26. First we called the people we wanted to come to see if they were all free. They all were—or so they said. But when we sent our little informal invitations, we asked everyone to send in a check for the full $26 not later than 10 days before the dinner. Now the tendency might be in a case like this, when you're dealing with friends who you essentially trust, to think that you're being rude asking for money ahead. Yet it seems that no one ever objects when it's an event they really want to attend. And if they don't really want to attend, do you want them on your list? You are responsible to the restaurant (campground, etc.) and at best if guests cancel you have to scurry at the last minute to find replacements. Get the money ahead—no one will mind. Also, simplify the money when possible. Don't collect half then half if you can get the whole tote at once. At the venison dinner I just described, I included the wine in the price but not the drinks, and any predinner, postdinner drinks had to be paid in cash. Thus, I had to get but one check from everyone and there was no bill to split up at the restaurant. The same kind of thinking applies to group cooking out of doors, on camping trips or just picnics.

Miscellaneous

Now that you have the money in hand, or at least lined up, here are a few tips that should help to make your job easier.

When you're cooking for a large camping group, try to avoid darkness if the situation allows. When darkness sets in, try to be down to dessert and coffee, or better yet, cleanup and campfires.

BISCUIT'S AMBROSIA
Eaton Bartlett

4 one-pound cans fruit cocktail, drained
2 8-oz. cans mandarin orange slices, drained
1 10-oz. pkg. miniature marshmallows
1 cup crushed walnuts
1 16-oz. pkg. shredded coconut
4 large bananas
1 pt. light cream whipped with 2/3 cup sugar and 1 T. vanilla

Combine all ingredients except the cream. Whip the cream with sugar and vanilla until somewhat thickened. Fold into the first mixture and stir. Chill if possible. ✦In his lumberjack camp, Biscuit used canned light cream. Nestle is one company that makes this. ABOUT 20 SERVINGS.

When you're running the show and it rains, guess who automatically gets blamed for it? You can't stop the rain but you can bring a dining canopy and/or a tarp. Especially with a large group, a temporary roof can make all the difference in the world. Conversely, having no protection against a cloudburst will not only ruin the morale for that meal but possibly for the rest of the trip.

VEGETABLE SOUP

3 quarts stewed tomatoes
Salt to taste (add a little at a time)
1 T. pepper
2 bay leaves
1 stick butter
6 medium onions, chopped
6 cups chopped celery
12 cups chopped potato
4 cups chopped carrots
2 cups yellow turnip, chopped
2 cups yellow squash, chopped
2 cups uncooked brown rice

In a 24-qt. or larger pot, place the tomatoes along with 5 gallons of liquid. Ideally, the liquid should consist of at least half vegetable stock made earlier, but water alone can be used. Add salt, pepper, bay leaves, and butter. Bring pot to a simmer. Meanwhile, prepare the vegetables in the quantities indicated. The potatoes should be added to the simmering pot immediately after being peeled and chopped, due to the risk of oxidation. Add all other vegetables plus the rice and simmer about 2 hours. Taste and adjust salt if necessary. Other seasonings may be added to taste. SERVES 50.

Don't be afraid to assign committees. If you try to do it all yourself, you'll be run ragged. Dole out the simpler tasks and do the more complicated procedures yourself.

Well before the meal, pull together as many picnic tables as you'll need so the group can eat together. You may well have to do this before you set up your dining canopy.

With certain key items, buy a little more than you think you need. There are certain things, varying from meal to meal, the lack of which will make people extremely contentious. The butter, the paper plates, the salt—whatever you have too much of will get used another time.

With a really large group, 50 or more, set up some kind of serving line so confusion doesn't reign. To make this sort of thing work you have to cleverly place and arrange what tables you have to funnel people in the right direction. You also will need more help, so don't be afraid to ask for it.

Chapter 8

ALL YOU CAN DO WITH CAST IRON

Cast iron has been used for cookery for at least 900 years. It probably was, in fact, the first metal humans ever used for cooking. In the days of the old West, before stainless steel or aluminum even existed, it was a primary material for cooking pots and skillets. In those frontier days of America, all the wagon trains heading west toted their battery of cast-iron cookware. The things that people liked about it way back then haven't changed. And to be honest, the things that people didn't like about it also haven't changed.

Its two great advantages are its weight and its porosity. Because it's so heavy, it heats slowly and evenly and thus thwarts the burning of food. It's weight (actually its heaviness) also permits types of cookery and overall versatility that is not possible with lighter implements. Because of its porosity, cast iron absorbs oil, and when it is properly seasoned, foods stick minimally.

Ironically, cast iron's two great disadvantages are also its weight and porosity, and you might throw in its dirtiness. Not only is it about out of the question for backpacking, but it may even be undesirable for certain types of trips by boat, canoe, or horseback. As for the porosity, if it's not seasoned and then properly taken care of, it will get crudded up from foods sticking to it and it will rust. It's like a good old-fashioned carbon-steel knife: You have to watch out for it, but if you do it's the best way to go. The notorious dirtiness of cast iron also has to do with its porosity. That porosity encourages the buildup of a black crust on the outside, and this will dirty everything it touches. That's why you so often see cast-iron pans hanging from hooks in camp (even though they also look nice).

Cast iron is still used in millions of homes and restaurants. Yet for some combination of reasons, part romantic and part practical, cast iron is, as it has long been, most closely associated with outdoor cookery. As testament to this, one large manufacturer of cast-iron cookware runs as a headline in a promotional brochure: "Great American cast iron camp cookware for America's great outdoors."

Does cast iron deserve this regard, and does it really belong in camp today? I wouldn't be without it.

PINEAPPLE UPSIDE-DOWN CAKE

1 18-oz. pkg. yellow cake mix	1/2 cup brown sugar, preferably light brown
Eggs	1 16-oz. can sliced
3 T. melted butter	pineapple

Empty the contents of the mix into a large bowl and add the required ingredients—usually eggs and water. Mix as directed. ✦Preheat the reflector oven. ✦Into a 10-inch round cake pan, pour the melted butter, then sprinkle on the sugar. Briefly place the pan in the oven to melt the sugar and create the glaze. Remove pan and place 7 pineapple slices over the glaze. A cherry can be placed in the middle of each slice. Now pour the cake batter over this and set the pan into the oven. Bake until an inserted toothpick comes out clean. Cool for 15 minutes then invert onto a plate. Sprinkle with powdered sugar if available. One box will probably make too much batter. You could bake two thinner cakes then use one as a second layer underneath the one with the pineapple. SERVES 8-10.

To my mind, one of the biggest reasons is cast iron's forgiving qualities when it comes to heat. We spoke earlier in this book about a variable heat source being among the camp cook's largest headaches. Cast iron is so heavy and dense that it distributes heat extremely well. Thus if the fire flares up when your back is turned—and distractions are the hallmark of camp cookery—chances are that the calamity that might well occur in an aluminum skillet won't happen. Conversely, if the heat source (say coals) is dying down, the cast iron will absorb heat and continue cooking beyond when the fire is really adequate.

Just as important, cast iron is versatile. For example, in standard frying pans of stainless steel, aluminum, or enamel-coated steel, you can fry and that's pretty much it. But in my 10½-inch cast-iron skillet I can and have fried, deep-fried, braised, stewed, poached, boiled, and baked. Of course with cast iron you can fry eggs or bacon or burgers, and it will work better than the lighter implements. But that wonderful heaviness cooks slowly enough that you can make a stove-top pot roast that needs to cook for an hour and a half (without having to continually add more liquid), a chili or a stew that may have to cook for two hours, or a sextet of biscuits that would burn before they'd rise in a lightweight skillet.

There are almost certainly more types of cast-iron cookware than you're aware of. We'll discuss some of the more popular ones, then add some important tips on the proper care of cast iron. Finally, we'll discuss baking in cast iron.

The Primary Implements

SKILLETS. These range in size from a tiny, three-inch "Miniature Skillet" right on up to what one manufacturer calls a "Paul Bunyan Skillet" measuring 20 inches and weighing 21 pounds! If you consistently cook for just one or two people, a pan of about nine inches (measured across the top) may suffice. But the most commonly used sizes are 8 inch, 10½ inch, and 12 inch. For a large group a 12-inch cast-iron frying pan is not too big, but it will weigh about 7.3 pounds. This is in contrast to a 10½-inch model that will weigh in at just over five pounds. Before you purchase a cast-iron skillet larger than 12 inches, consider going to a legless dutch oven (see below). By the way, the number on a cast-iron pan does not necessarily indicate its size in inches. Rather, the number may be part of an old marking system that had to do with the size of grates atop wood cooking stoves.

I never cease to be amazed at how my 10½-inch cast-iron skillet always seems to be just the right size for what I have to do. In camp, I probably do more than half of my cooking in this pan, and with a capacity of two quarts, it takes the place of a pot for many chores. In the small sizes, seven or eight inches, you might not miss a cover too much. But for nine inches on up, be sure to procure a lid. Only with a moisture-trapping cover will you be able to prepare those long-cooked dishes like stews or pot roasts. Too, with a cover, you'll be better able to boil or steam vegetables. Finally, you just can't bake without a cover. I admit, the cover is expensive, and the store may not even have it—you may have to send for it. I still recommend it.

GRIDDLE. In chapter 10, there is considerable discussion about pancakes. As I mention there, the heat has to be kept at just the right level if your pancakes are to turn out correctly.

Suspending iron cookware on a tripod or (as here) just an iron rod, is an accepted way to cook over coals. This display was set up by several Native Americans at an outdoor exposition.

You can see that when a skillet's lid is removed, moisture as steam is lost quickly. It's worth the considerable extra expense of purchasing a cover for a good iron skillet (the one I'm using here was salvaged from an old cast-aluminum skillet, and fit perfectly). In lower photo, an iron skillet has been lined with foil and will serve to warm up these cinnamon rolls. Here, again, a cover is helpful.

The surface of a heavy, cast-iron griddle will fluctuate less in temperature and thus cook your batches of pancakes very evenly. Two common sizes (in inches) are 19 by 9 and 21 by 10½. Both should fit over most two-burner camp stoves. Most of these griddles have little loop handles at each end, and some even have a long handle like a regular fry pan. Suit yourself. If the griddle you're shopping for does have only small handles at each end, make sure they are raised up to facilitate easy removal from the fire.

There are also round griddles offered through the camper's mail-order catalogs. Perhaps this design will suit your fancy.

I'm willing to bet that pancakes account for three-fourths of all the use a camper's griddle gets. Still, I feel a griddle is worth having along, although mine happens to be cast aluminum with a nonstick finish.

SQUARE SKILLET. This one, spotted in a recent catalog, is square, 9½ inches on all sides and it weighs 5.2 pounds. Its sides are about as high as those on a standard skillet, and they slope out away from the bottom. Although I bake skillet breads like corn bread in my 10½-inch round cast-iron pan, this square one would be even better for this purpose. That's because, with all edges being straight, you could work a spatula in there to lift the bread out without breaking it.

COMPARTMENT SKILLET. This one is sometimes advertised as a "Bacon and Eggs Skillet," but it would also be good for heating up leftovers. It is just like a stainless steel one I have in my kitchen which I use for that purpose once in a blue moon.

OVERSIZE SKILLETS. For large groups there are a couple of oversize iron skillets available, like the Paul Bunyan skillet mentioned a bit earlier. These are too heavy to lift with one hand, so the traditional handle is missing. Rather, there are little loop handles on each end as with an oblong griddle. Really, this type of implement is for use on wood fires, since it's much too big for any camp stove. Burn down to a nice big pit of hot coals, throw on a grill (or omit the grill), and let this brute go to town. The 20-inch size should easily whip up a chili dinner for 12-15 or more. Such huge pans, and they come even bigger than 20 inches, can also be suspended on a metal tripod over the firepit.

DEEP FRYERS. In one outdoor catalog, a "Camp Fryer" is listed and measures 17½ by 9 by 4 inches. It weighs 16 pounds. This is for the bottom part. The "Griddle Top," which can be purchased separately, weighs 10 pounds. You get the picture—this is an awful lot of weight to add to your arsenal of camp cooking implements. If you can abide the weight, iron is superbly well suited to deep-frying, because holding the correct temperature is the hinge pin for success with this cooking method. Since this particular model has a capacity of two gallons, it will serve a large group. You can use the top to this implement as a griddle. Also, the main or bottom part can be used for roasting or other chores.

STOVE-TOP BROILER. This is just like a regular skillet but it has ridges in the bottom to keep the meat out of the grease. If you cook a lot of steaks and chops in camp, this pan will help to give you a real crispy broiled effect.

SPECIAL BAKING PANS. One catalog I have lists several different ones: cornbread skillet (makes eight individual wedge-shaped slices, a nice idea), popover pan, corn-stick pan, muffin pan, French bread pan (makes two loaves), fluted cake pan, Danish cake pan, and breadstick pan. If you're serious about baking, some of these might serve very well in a camp setting, depending on how you do your baking.

There are actually quite a few others available, including a wok, a round French fryer with basket, various kettles, and a slope-sided chef's skillet (a design I especially like).

DUTCH OVENS. Dutch oven cookery is a world unto itself, so I have moved it to later in this chapter.

Care and Seasoning

Some people speak of "seasoning" a brand-new cast-iron implement to prepare it for duty. This has always struck me as a self-contradiction, like Los Angeles Laker or easy diet. True seasoning may take a whole season. Or maybe more than a season. That's why they call it seasoning. Get it?

A dutch oven does it all. Here, water is being heated for dishwashing. A legless dutch oven or even an iron deep fryer could also serve in this capacity.

When you buy a new cast-iron implement, the correct way to prepare it for service is as follows. First, heat it in a slow oven to soften the protective waxy coating used in shipping. Now use some paper towels and wipe it thoroughly. Repeat this until the paper towels remain clean. Next, wash the implement in some sudsy water. This is the first and last time your iron implement should be washed in soap. Dry it well, then take some bacon fat (congealed drippings would be good) and wipe all inside surfaces. Heat your home oven to 250°F. Place the greased implement in the oven and leave it there for one hour. Let it cool naturally at room temperature. Repeat this procedure if you wish. The first few times you use it, try to cook somewhat oily foods as opposed to watery foods. Deep frying would be ideal in these early stages.

Many experts, cast-iron manufacturers included, recommend vegetable oil for the initial treatment. Trust me—use the bacon fat.

A clever camp trick (above) is to start some coals on top of an old grill, to create a flat surface on which to place the dutch oven. Below, the lid has been removed to check progress on a venison shoulder roast. This particular pot roast took 80 minutes, and liquid had to be added once.

It will take a long time before that beautiful, lustrous patina develops. During that time, try to scour it as little as possible. If at all possible, get to the pan while it's still warm. If you can, use a nonmetallic scouring pad such as one made of nylon mesh or some combination of sponge and nylon.

Even after the pan is fully seasoned and shiny, you will sometimes cook things that will stick and burn and a light touch won't do it. In this instance, pour near-boiling water into the pan or place it back on your stove and heat water to a simmer. The pores of the iron will open back up and release the burned-on food. Now you can gently scour it as just described and set it in a warm place to dry. Finally, take a paper towel and swab a little oil on the inside surface. (With a seasoned pan, oil is fine—bacon grease is not needed but would still be good.) Sometimes I'll rub a little on the outside too, if the environment is damp.

The goal in cleaning the pan is to de-season it as little as possible, although in truth, your implement will go through peaks and valleys when it is somewhat more or somewhat less seasoned. Avoid metal scouring devices, which will quickly de-season your pan. Also avoid the use of soap.

If a cast-iron pan has been neglected, abused, or just scoured to the point that its interior carbonized coating is badly scratched, you'll have to reseason it. Just swab it with bacon fat and heat it. Repeat this several times if possible. If you're in camp, you can simply place the greased implement on a grill over a warm fire, or even in your reflector oven in front of some flames. And, as with the initial treatment, avoid watery foods in favor of oily foods the first few times you use the pan again. One coating of oil may close the pores of the metal, but don't think your pan will really be seasoned (or reseasoned) at this point. I've found that it takes many, many meals to truly season a cast-iron pan. In short, the best way to keep an iron pan seasoned is to use it—the more the better.

Some people, by the way, like to use Pam, which is convenient because it lets you spray on your coating of oil, either before or after you cook.

There is something to be careful of with cast iron, even as rugged as it is. Don't put a very cold pan right on the heat, and don't plunge a hot pan into cold water. Try to let the temperature of the pan change more slowly, otherwise it could crack or warp.

MEDALLIONS OF PORK WITH GINGER

1 large clove garlic, minced
1/2 T. oil
4 boneless pork chops, one inch thick each, cut in half
1/8 cup teriyaki sauce

1/8 cup water
1/2 cup chopped scallions
1 tsp. fresh grated ginger (or 1/2 tsp. dried)

In a cast-iron skillet or wok, sauté garlic in oil. Add pork medallions and cook over medium flame about 4 minutes on a side until lightly browned. Add rest of ingredients and continue cooking uncovered about another 8 minutes until pan liquid is reduced to a thick sauce. SERVES 2-3.

When a heavy, black crust develops on the outside of your pan, the remedy is easy. Place it in some hot coals, and when good and hot, knock the crust off by gently tapping it against something hard, such as the edge of the fireplace. Or scrape it off with the edge of some kind of implement. Alternatively, at home, run the crusted implement through a regular cycle in a self-cleaning oven.

Cast iron comes in two primary finishes: natural sand-cast finish, and polished-interior finish. The former is more widely seen while the latter may not even be available in all styles of cast-iron cookware. This is puzzling to me, since I have found that the polished finish will eventually develop a smoother and more beautiful surface. I believe it's worth the extra effort to find the specific cast-iron implement you want in a polished-interior finish.

Dutch-Oven Cookery

Ridgepole tents and wagon trains, horses and heifers, a porcelain coffee pot, wide-open spaces: It's the very stuff of the old West, not to mention nearly every beer commercial on the television. But of all these heady frontier images, none is likely to evoke a tear of nostalgia in the eye of an old wizened camp cook as fast as a real dutch oven. You can almost smell the chili cooking, almost see the cavalry charging and the tumbleweed blowing across the desert.

CHICKEN A L'ORANGE
DON AND SALLY CARRIER

4 boneless chicken half-breasts, skinned
1 orange
1/2 cup flour
1½ tsp. salt
1/2 tsp. paprika
1/4 cup salad oil
1 cup chicken broth
3 sprigs fresh mint (opt.)

Rinse and pat dry the 4 chicken breasts (4 leg-thigh pieces, skinned, may be substituted). Place in a bowl. Grate the rind of the orange over the chicken. Cut the orange into quarters and squeeze juice over the chicken. Marinate 1 hour, turning. ◆Mix the flour, salt, and paprika. Roll the chicken pieces in this. Heat oil in a 12-inch dutch oven and brown chicken lightly on both sides. Cant off most of the oil in the oven. ◆Add the broth, plus the juice and rind that you marinated the chicken in. Cook about another 35 minutes with 13 coals on top and 13 on bottom. Garnish with mint and/or a few thin slices of orange. SERVES 2-4.

It *is* a marvelously adaptable implement. In fact, it is the most versatile cooking implement I know of. Unfortunately, it is so at odds with the instant-gratification mentality of modern campers that I fear my chances of winning the average camper over to it are very slim.

In the Northeast, where I do most of my camping, you'll rarely see a dutch oven in camp. Yet in other areas of the country, especially the Southwest and Rocky Mountains, there exists a whole dutch-oven culture. There are dutch-oven "World Cook-offs," dutch-oven clubs, at least one dutch-oven association, and even dutch-oven newsletters. This is not to mention the ever-growing number of books just on dutch-oven cookery. (One authority I know says he has 19 dutch-oven cookbooks!) I think all this speaks well to the fascination and sheer effectiveness of "cooking dutch."

SEEDED DUTCH-OVEN BREAD

2 cups flour
1 cup whole wheat flour
4 tsp. baking powder
3 T. sugar
1/4 tsp. salt
1 tsp. dill seed
1 tsp. caraway seed
1 can beer

Mix all ingredients but beer at home. In camp, place this mixture in a bowl and add beer slowly until dough cleans sides of bowl. You'll probably use a little less than a can of beer. Knead on a floured surface. Form the dough into a ball. ◆Swab inside of dutch oven with cooking oil. Do not preheat oven. Lay dough directly in oven. Place 1/3 of lit coals beneath the oven, 2/3 on top of lid. Bake about 50 minutes. Can also be baked in a camp-stove oven.

If you live where the "black pots" are already popular—for example Salt Lake City, the apparent spiritual center of this subculture—you will wonder why I didn't devote at least half of the bloody book to dutch ovens.

There are two types. The first is really nothing more than a big, heavy kettle, the legless dutch oven. Old sourdoughs will sneer and itch at this implement even being called a dutch oven, but I like it since it can be used on top of a camp stove as well as in a city kitchen, both in the oven and atop the range. The legless dutch oven will usually have a roundish "dome top" that is termed self-basting since the cooking steam will condense in the center of the dome and drip down on whatever's being cooked. This implement is superb for pot roast, soups, and certain other dishes. I use the one I have mostly at home.

The traditional dutch oven is the only dutch oven for many. It has three legs on the bottom and the lid is flanged. These features allow you to put hot coals underneath as well as on top of the implement. It is for use in wood fires, though most people fire it with charcoal these days. A legless dutch oven really won't substitute because it can't contain hot coals in any way.

There is no doubt, versatility is what has made the dutch oven a chapter itself in the book of outdoor cookery. You can bake in a cast-iron skillet, as we'll discuss. But you can do it four times as well in a dutch oven. Perhaps the second biggest attribute of this storied implement is its slow-cook feature; it really is the original slow cooker (although I'm sure the chefs of long ago did slow-cook in clay pots). Because the dutch oven is so heavy, and distributes heat so slowly and evenly, you can throw in a pot roast, go off fishing, and when you come back in three hours—or five hours—your dish should be perfectly done and waiting for you. This scenario will work sometimes, but the truth is that you must pay some attention to what you are doing.

PARADISE POTATOES
Gerald and Chauna Duffin

6-8 medium potatoes	1 clove garlic, minced fine
1 pint sour cream	1 tsp. salt
10 ounces Cheddar cheese, shredded	1/8 tsp. pepper
1 bunch scallions, chopped	4 T. melted butter
3 T. milk	1 cup Saltine crackers, crumbled

Cook potatoes to two-thirds done. Cool, then peel and grate. Add sour cream, cheese, and scallions. Stir well. Combine milk, garlic, and salt and pepper. Stir into potato mixture. Press into a baking tin or directly into a 12-inch dutch oven. Smooth the surface. Combine butter and cracker crumbs. Spread this over potato mixture. Bake approximately 30 minutes with 10 coals on bottom and 12-14 on top. SERVES 8.

SAUSAGE 'N' BEANS

For each diner, brown 2 to 3 large-size pork link sausages (sometimes called dinner sausages) in a dutch oven set over coals. When meat is nicely browned, cant the oven to eliminate most of the grease. For every 3 sausages, add one 16-oz. can pork 'n' beans or barbecue beans. Stir, cook uncovered 5 minutes. Optionally, add 1/4 cup cubed cheese per can of beans, stir 2 minutes and serve. ✦Can also be done in a skillet, over coals or on a camp stove.

The traditional dutch oven is fired by coals, period. Sure, you can dangle it on a tripod over flames, but such a setup is impractical in most camps. Burning down to a bed of wood coals can take time, sometimes a long time, and here is where the fast-paced modern camper is going to balk. Happily, you can use charcoal briquets, which is not only easier but will also provide more uniform heat. Just start the coals wherever and however it is convenient and transfer them to above and below your dutch oven. For this procedure, it's best to have a small, metal shovel so add that to your checklist.

QUICK BROWN BREAD
HODGSON MILL

1 cup flour	3 T. melted butter
2 tsp. baking soda	1/4 cup molasses
1 tsp. salt	1½ cups buttermilk
1 cup brown sugar	1 egg, beaten
2 cups whole wheat flour	

Stir first 3 ingredients together in a mixing bowl. Blend in the brown sugar and whole wheat flour. Add the melted butter, molasses, buttermilk, and egg. Beat vigorously until batter is smooth. Pour into a 9 x 5 x 3 loaf pan. Bake in a camp-stove oven at 350° for about 45 minutes. ✦This recipe can be used as is for muffins. Pour into greased muffin tins filling 2/3 full. Bake for 20-25 minutes. ✦This sweet bread is more a dessert bread than anything else. It is magnificent when spread with softened cream cheese.

Pre-use preparation and care of a dutch oven is no different from what you do with other cast-iron implements. See earlier in this chapter.

You'll need to use more coals on a cold day. You'll need to use fewer coals on a hot day or a windy day. How many? That will vary, depending on the just-named factors, on what's being cooked, and on when you'd like that dish to be done. In general, I think the tendency is to use too many coals. This can not only burn your food, but if you're cooking with a relatively small amount of liquid, you can set that liquid to a rolling boil and steam it all out of the oven. The oven's lid is tight, but not steam-proof.

An exceptional treat: real baked beans, cooked in a dutch oven set in the coals. See page 71 for recipe.

For baking, try about six or seven beneath the oven and 16 to 18 on top. Arrange them in a checkerboard pattern and not necessarily touching. For stewing, braising, and browning, reverse this: Put two-thirds beneath the oven and one-third on top. Anytime you want to brown what you're cooking, leave the lid off. Also leave the lid off when you're deep-frying.

Dutch-oven experts are very specific about how many coals to use. Usually, in their recipes, the number of coals to use is stated in exact terms.

The lid of the oven makes a pretty good frying pan. Just invert it and place it on the hot coals. The lid is somewhat concave, but that little depression in the center will not be too hard to deal with. If you can, prop your inverted lid up on two rocks or bricks and heat from the coals will circulate more effectively around it.

As discussed earlier, never try to cool the oven too quickly.

Clean it and store it as you would any other piece of iron cookware, but keep the lid ajar so condensation cannot take place inside. This is especially critical when the oven undergoes a rapid temperature change or when it's stored in a very moist environment. When I take my oven out to use it again, I always take a slightly oily paper towel and wipe it inside and out to remove any dust that may have accumulated. Some people use an old burlap sack to scour the oven. For that matter, some devotees store the oven in a burlap sack.

The classic, traditional dutch oven is made of cast iron. To the irritation of traditionalists, but to the delight of the more pragmatic, aluminum dutch ovens are now made and may be gaining popularity. Not subject to rusting, the aluminum ovens need far less care and weigh much less—about seven pounds, vs. 18 pounds in the popular 12-inch size. The main disadvantage, in the opinion of some, is that aluminum, being soft, flakes off and minute quantities of it eventually wind up in the body. One other small concern is that aluminum is more reflective, and so more coals may need to be used.

A dutch oven is meant to be set down directly on the ground, but sometimes there are advantages to propping it off the ground a bit. Below, dutch ovens have been "stacked." Coals are placed between the ovens as well as above the top one and beneath the bottom one.

My oven is iron. I no longer use any aluminum cookware, either at home or in camp. I would, though, like to try the relatively new stainless-steel dutch ovens that I see advertised from time to time.

Rectangular dutch ovens do exist. They're harder to clean and not very popular.

What size oven should you buy? It's quite an important consideration.

They range from about 8 inches to 16 inches, measured across the top of the oven. Because of the extravagant weight, you might be tempted, out of sheer fear of that weight, to go with one of the small sizes. A great many camp cooks of my acquaintance use the 12-inch (six-quart) model. That's the one I own. There is also a strong following, especially among the cognescenti, for the 14-inch size (eight-quart). There's no doubt about it, if you purchase a smaller one, say 10-inch (four-quart), you will repeatedly be frustrated that your oven is "just a little bit small." Sixteen- to 22-inch dutch ovens do exist. I saw a 16 today in a hardware-store display, but ones larger than this are hard to find.

COOKS FALLS FLANK STEAK

Start about 25 charcoal briquettes. Into 2 cups bread stuffing (store-bought, or see p. 173) mix 2 sweet Italian sausages—skinned, cooked, and crumbled. Cut a pocket in your beef flank steak and stuff with the stuffing. Heat the dutch oven over 15 coals and heat 2 T. oil till hot. Brown the flank steak very well on both sides. Add 1 small onion chopped and 10 oz. water in which you've dissolved a beef bouillon packet. Cover the oven, put rest of coals on top, and cook about 75 minutes, checking once and adding a little more water if necessary. Thicken the gravy if desired with a flour-water mixture.

As with the reflector oven, you can set things down directly in the dutch oven, or in tins or pans and then down in the oven. This depends completely on the recipe. Certain things will have to go in their own tins, for example muffins and batter breads. Very sugary dishes can glop up the oven and these, too, are often best placed in tins first. The tins I recommend for camp cooking are discussed in chapter 1.

Dutch-oven accessories are available, most typically from the companies that make cast-iron cookware. One good example is the Lodge Manufacturing Company of South Pittsburgh, Tennessee, one of the largest makers of iron cookware. Let's look at what they currently offer.

Dutch ovens do of course get dirty, so Lodge offers cloth covers for most any size dutch oven you might have.

When you remove a dutch oven's lid, to check on the food or perhaps to add liquid or additional ingredients, where will you set the lid down? Because it will likely be damp or wet, it will pick up dirt easily. Thus, a special stand for the oven's lid is available. If you lack this, an old (but clean) board will do.

You'll need some kind of hook to lift the oven's lid so you can both check progress and remove the food for eating. If you fashion one it should be at least 18 inches long to keep your hand away from the heat. This lifter can also serve to move the entire oven by its bailing handle. I should note that some people use a "pot-grabber" clamp for removing and replacing the oven's lid. I prefer the lifter. Some commercially made lid lifters actually steady the lid as it's being raised from the oven. The fork at the end of the lifter is what accomplishes this. Serious black-pot chefs like to have both a long and a short lifter, and both made just for dutch ovens. Part of the rationale for this is that you can use one to lift the pot by its handle and the shorter one to tip the pot, for example to cant grease or other liquid (this need arises fairly often). In the Lodge brochure, both a 15-inch and a 40-inch lifter are listed.

It's nice to have a whisk broom, to sweep off the lid of an oven. This will help to keep ashes from getting into the food.

Dutch-oven tables are available but this item would be out of the sphere of the average camper.

Skillet Baking

Through the years, a lot of famished campers have queued up to my camp stove and watched me bake over an open flame. Once they start chomping, they don't seem to miss the romance of the dutch oven or the reflector oven at all.

We all know that it never rains on camping trips, and I know for certain that it never rains on my camping trips (that's why during the most recent drought summer my friends threatened to take up a collection and ship me out to the Midwest to help the situation). But in those terribly rare instances when the clouds do burst, both reflector-oven and dutch-oven cooking can be difficult. Nestled cozily under my canopy, camp stove humming cheerily, gin and tonic in hand, I unhook my 10½-inch cast-iron skillet, swab the bottom with oil, and pour in the grainy yellow batter that will, anon, be a perfect round of corn bread. I also have made biscuits and small loaves of bread in the skillet. True, the bottom will often be burned, being only $\frac{5}{32}$ of an inch away from the flame. But I don't let it worry me. In fact, I can sometimes avoid this completely by lining the skillet with foil, or by using a small baking tin. With the stove turned fairly low, and the lid on tightly (I'll add a gasket of aluminum foil), I'll have my biscuits in 20 minutes or my corn bread or spoon bread in 35 minutes. When baking in this manner, check halfway through, as the items may get done quite quickly.

SHENANDOAH CORN BREAD

1 cup yellow cornmeal　　　　1/2 tsp. salt
1 cup all-purpose flour　　　　1 cup milk or skim milk
1/4 cup wheat germ　　　　　1 egg
1/3 cup sugar　　　　　　　　1/4 cup oil or melted butter
4 tsp. baking powder

Mix all dry ingredients at home and place in a plastic bag. In camp, combine milk, beaten egg, and oil and mix well. Blend into the dry ingredients. Pour into a baking tin or a 10-inch cast-iron skillet and set into the reflector oven for about 40 minutes. Could also be done right on the camp stove, in the covered skillet. ✦This one is a bit sweeter and moister than most corn breads. ✦Crumbled, this is a particularly good corn bread for stuffing poultry. Saved for this purpose, it freezes very well.

A cast-iron skillet can also be set directly in the coals, for baking. Since you lack the legs of the dutch oven, you should try and use a few 1½- to 2-inch-thick rocks to prop it up. You might even be able to scatter a few coals on top, although the convex shape of the lid will not abet this effort. I'm not saying this is an ideal setup, only a possible one. For cooking with coals, you just can't beat a dutch oven.

The lid of a dutch oven makes a suitable on-the-spot frying pan. Eggs, bacon, flapjacks, hamburgers, and other things may be cooked in this fashion. A whisk broom is useful for sweeping ashes from the oven's lid.

Chapter 9
REFLECTOR OVENS AND OTHER MEANS OF BAKING

"You do more cooking than anybody I've ever met," Debbie stated to me one time, trying to put it somewhat politely.

"What, pheasant under glass *again,* Capossela?" Bob always says when I'm baking something in my reflector oven.

"You mean you *bought* that pie crust?" Greg said sarcastically one time.

Every once in a while you get a sincere remark: "Homemade sourdough cinnamon rolls—that sounds incredible!"

There are other ways of baking at a campsite, but for sheer romance, challenge, and mouth-watering anticipation, there is really nothing like a reflector oven. Dutch-oven fans will protest, but you just can't watch the drama unfold in a dutch oven.

It is a metal contraption, always aluminum as far as I know, that works on the principle of reflected heat. They vary in size and even somewhat in design, but they all feature two angled surfaces that reflect the heat from an open fire up and down respectively, and a level surface towards which that heat is reflected and on which you put the item to be baked.

The reflector oven is usually placed on the ground, its front edge about six to ten inches from the flames of an open fire. Actually, the oven can be moved at any time closer to or farther from the flames and that is the main way you regulate the heat. Unlike most cooking done with wood, coals will do you no good unless you have a gigantic pile of them. You need flames, and you must keep those flames up for however long your dish takes to bake. A fire with plenty of flames is quite hot, so it won't take you much longer than it would to bake the same thing at home in your oven. For example, drop biscuits should be done in 10–15 minutes, rolled biscuits or scones in 15–20 minutes, a fresh cobbler in 45–50 minutes. You can cook main dishes too, like vegetables and casseroles, but with these your cooking time may run past the one-hour mark. Once you go past an hour

There are actually several reflector oven designs, some more compact when folded than others. The principle is the same with all of them, though.

you spend too much time tending the fire and you use too much wood. The reflector oven is really at its best when it comes to simple breadstuffs and various dessert goodies that get done in 30 minutes or less.

ROYAL RAISIN SCONES

1¾ cups all-purpose flour	1/3 cup butter or margarine
3 T. sugar	1 egg, beaten
2½ tsp. baking powder	1/2 cup raisins
1/2 tsp. salt	4 to 6 T. heavy cream

At home, blend flour, sugar, baking powder, and salt. Cut in butter or margarine until mixture resembles fine crumbs. ✦In camp, stir in the egg, raisins, and enough cream so dough is moist. Turn out onto a floured surface and knead lightly for 15 seconds. Roll or press dough till it's a half-inch thick. Cut into circles 2½ inches round (top of a glass will work nicely). Place on your ungreased oven tray. Bake about 15 minutes in your reflector oven, turning pan once, until nicely golden. Remove tray immediately to cool. Serve very warm with presoftened butter or margarine and sweet preserves. Like all biscuits, best served immediately after baking. MAKES ABOUT 8.

WILD-BERRY COBBLER

1/3 cup sugar	4 cups fresh fruit
2 T. cornstarch	Additional sugar
3/4 tsp. cinnamon	Bisquick
1/4 tsp. nutmeg	

At home, mix 1/3 cup sugar, cornstarch, cinnamon, and nutmeg, and place in a plastic bag. Label it "Cobbler" and say "Add 4 cups fruit." When you luckily come across wild strawberries, raspberries, blackberries, blueberries, or other berries, simply mix the rinsed, cleaned fruit with the dry mix, adding more sugar to taste if the fruit isn't too sweet. Fold into a suitable baking tin. Then mix 1½ cups Bisquick with about 1/2 cup cold milk. It should be fairly thick, but thin enough that you can still spread it over the fruit mixture. Bake in a reflector oven till the biscuit dough is golden brown, about 30 to 40 minutes. ✦Any biscuit dough prepared to the right consistency can be used for the topping. **ABOUT 8 SMALL SERVINGS.**

Cooking effectively with the reflector oven (sometimes called the reflector baker) is really nothing more than a series of little tricks. As with all aspects of cooking with wood, a certain instinct must replace the clearly defined formulas of conventional cookery. Nonetheless, a number of concrete tips can be passed along.

With flames, the variability of the heat is far greater than it is with coals. Combine this variable with others like air temperature, wind velocity, and shape and design of the fire pit, and you can easily see how no two dishes will ever bake in the same amount of time. Thus, timing your dish to get done at the correct moment within the framework of the whole meal can be very challenging.

As mentioned elsewhere in this book, most people wait too long to start any kind of cooking fire. If you have an adequate wood supply, start it a little early but don't crank the fire up so high that you waste your wood. Just get it going and that way when the last-minute cooking chores arise just before dinnertime you won't have to fuss with starting a fire. You can just quickly build up the one you already have burning softly.

There is an axiom in the backcountry that you choose a cooking site first and then decide if it's also a good campsite (although you'd probably look for water first of all). This may not be the criteria used by everyone, but I assure you it's the way the camp cook approaches it.

Sourdough cinnamon rolls in a reflector oven (top photo) placed very close to the fire, to promote browning of the tops. Bottom photo shows the rolls, about to be placed into the oven, set down on my specially fashioned baking tray.

Campgrounds are no different. Some sites will have good fireplaces well located while others will have broken-down fireplaces poorly situated. After I've chosen my site, one of the first things I do is set up my reflector oven next to the fireplace. There it stays for the rest of the trip. After tent erection and other primary chores I'll go back to the fire area and see how I can modify it for easier cooking. Some tips and photos along these lines are presented in chapter 5, and some of these tips will have relevance for the reflector oven. Here, I'll restrict myself to tips on actually setting up and using the oven.

In any outdoor setting, fireplaces will vary greatly. Indeed, at some campgrounds the fireplace's design may be such that you can cook with coals but not with flames. Assuming the fireplace you find on your site has at least one open face, you now must make minor adjustments to compensate for ground that slopes or is bumpy.

If the ground directly in front of the fireplace is smooth and at the same level as the bottom of the fire pit, simply place your reflector oven on the ground. If you do need to prop it up, a common situation, then keep something in mind: You may be forced to move the oven closer to or farther from the flames during the cooking process. Thus, if you use five or six odd-size rocks to prop up one or both ends, everything is liable to go out of whack when you try to move the oven. Better to use two big, smooth, flat rocks, one on each side. Then, if the oven need be moved to regulate the heat, it will still sit squarely on those same two rocks without tumbling over.

BASIC PIE CRUST

2½ cups all-purpose flour	1 cup Crisco or butter
1 tsp. salt	Ice water
1 T. sugar	

Combine the flour, salt and sugar in a large mixing bowl. Cut in the shortening using a pastry blender or two knives. When dough is pea-sized, make six little wells in it. Put 1 T. ice water into each well. Mix each little section with a fork, pushing each one off to the side on a lightly floured surface. Gather up any dry flour as you do this. Do not overmix. Form all sections into a ball. Cut in half. Roll out on waxed paper. Makes a top and bottom for an 8-inch pie.

RUN-THE-RAPIDS PEACH PIE

1/2 cup sugar (more if peaches aren't sweet)	3 fresh peaches, peeled and mashed
2½ to 3 T. cornstarch	3 more fresh peaches, sliced (peeling opt.)
Dash salt	1 prebaked 9-inch pie shell
1/4-1/2 cup water	Whipped cream (opt.)

Combine sugar, cornstarch, and salt, and bring in a plastic bag. In camp, place this mixture in a pot and stir in water and mashed peaches. Bring to an easy boil, then cook over medium heat, stirring constantly (about 5 minutes) until mixture is smooth and thickened. Cool. Place sliced peaches in pastry shell. Pour well-cooled cooked mixture over these. Chill about 2 hours. Serve with whipped cream if you have it. ✦A pie shell can be easily prebaked in a reflector oven, about 10 minutes. Or, skip this step by using a store-bought graham cracker crust.

Because of their collapsible design, some reflector ovens are a bit flimsy. Avoid knocking into it while baking, and warn others in the group of this. Nothing's worse than having the contraption fall apart to dump your would-be feast into the ashes. This can happen even if you don't knock into it, by the way. If you are clumsy when opening the back to rotate the baking pan and you jostle the oven too much, the baking shelf (with some models) can slip off its rather precarious

The Formica-laminated camp kitchen door is perfect for kneading bread, and most other food-preparation tasks.

edge. To thwart this, bend the lip that cups the back edge of the baking shelf. Then it won't slip out so easily. If your oven is of a slightly different design than this, you'll have to evaluate it to see both where the pitfalls lie and how you can modify it to make it more stable.

You should have two thick potholders or fireproof gloves to work with your oven. You'll need both hands protected to move the oven in or out, and you'll also need both hands covered when you remove the finished product; usually, one hand opens the back flap while the other lifts out the baking tray. You'll also be opening the back flap from time to time to check progress and to rotate the baking tin.

To get back to the actual fire for a moment, there are a couple of things to keep in mind. First, as you build up the flames immediately before baking you must lay the wood in a way that's propitious to what you'll be doing. For one thing, you may want to keep the wood towards the front rather than the rear of the fire pit. You may find, too, that a teepee lay (see chapter 5) will be the best wood arrangement for baking. You have to be a little bit of an engineer in creating a perfect fire for this type of cooking. Then, unless you're baking quickly done biscuits, you'll probably have to add wood or otherwise tend the fire during the baking. Be certain that the whole mass of burning wood doesn't come tumbling towards the oven, thereby upsetting it. Also be careful that a hot, burning stick doesn't slip underneath the baking shelf. This will serve to burn the bottom of whatever's baking.

The highest heat will be towards the front edge of the oven. Thus it is usually necessary to rotate the baking tin. If you've laid two neat rows of biscuits directly on your baking tray (not to be confused with a baking tin) you can simply turn the tray 180 degrees. You'll know the time is right when the biscuits in the front row are golden brown. If I'm using my square tin, I'll turn it three times. A round baking tin, as for a pie, can be rotated a quarter turn every so often. If you have trouble with some of the baked goods not browning to your satisfaction, but eventually getting done, you may have the oven too far from the flames.

Either that, or the flames aren't strong enough. To improve the chances of achieving a nicely browned top spread on a little melted margarine, or better yet, a thin wash of beaten egg.

WORLD'S FASTEST BISCUITS

Add 2/3 cup milk to 2¼ cups Bisquick prepared baking mix. Stir, and as a dough begins to form, beat well and continue to beat 30-45 seconds until the dough is smooth. Drop by large spoonfuls onto your baking tray, sprinkling cinnamon over some of the biscuits if you like. Place tray into reflector oven, bake about 15-20 minutes. MAKES ABOUT 8-10.

CINNAMON SUGAR TREATS
ORONOQUE PIE CRUSTS

Thaw a store-bought 9-inch pie crust until it is soft but still cold. Prick the bottom and sides all around with a fork. Rub the bottom and sides of the crust with 1 T. softened butter. Sprinkle with a mixture of 2 T. sugar and 1/2 tsp. cinnamon. Bake in your reflector oven until golden brown. When cool enough to handle, break into pieces and serve.

CAPPY'S MIXED-FRUIT MUFFINS

1 cup all-purpose flour	1/4 cup sugar
1/2 cup rolled oats	1/2 cup mixed dried fruit, chopped
1 tsp. baking powder	1 egg, beaten
1 tsp. baking soda	1/2-3/4 cup milk
1/2 tsp. salt	

At home, mix together the flour, oats, baking powder and soda, salt, and sugar. In camp, add the fruit, egg and milk. Beat only about 20 times until the dry ingredients are moistened. Fill muffin cups to 3/4 full. Bake in a reflector oven about 20-25 minutes. MAKES ABOUT 8.

In chapter 1, I have a baking tray on my camp kitchen checklist. This essential item was once a flat, one-half-inch-deep cookie tray that I cut down to exactly fit the length and width of the baking shelf in the reflector oven. I learned the hard way why this item is needed.

The first year I bought my oven I just placed the biscuit dough directly down on the baking shelf. Starting out with a cold oven this was not a problem, but when the biscuits were done and I wanted to quickly remove them, how was I to do it? You can move the entire oven away from the heat, but as mentioned, these ovens are flimsy and you risk having the whole thing fall apart with the goodies still in it. If you open the back flap and remove the biscuits one at a time with a spatula, the last ones removed may become overdone. You also must repeatedly subject your hands to high heat.

I made another unhappy discovery that first summer. I made from scratch a blueberry pie, one that even had a homemade crust. As my guests and I dined on venison stroganoff, we watched in great anticipation as the pie browned deliciously. All went well until the last 15 minutes of cooking. At that point, the pie started bubbling over, spewing its sticky, red juices onto the oven's baking shelf. This is a real faux pas for two reasons. First, no one in camp wants extra cleanup chores. And second, a reflector oven should be scrubbed as little as possible so as not to dull that reflective shininess.

Coincidentally, early the next year I took a backcountry trip, and the guide on that trip happened to have the very same reflector oven I had. But he was better prepared: He had a baking tray that I copied just as soon as I got home.

Since you can't buy one, you'll have to make one. It's best to pick a pan that has low sides, as opposed to a true cookie sheet that may lack sides altogether. Measure the baking shelf in your reflector oven and then carefully cut the tray just a bit smaller than the dimensions of the oven's shelf. You will wind up with a sharp edge probably on two sides where you cut. But these types of baking trays are very soft metal and can be bent easily. Rather than trying to sand the sharp edges down, take a pair of pliers and methodically bend up about one-sixteenth of an inch all the way around the cut edge. Then take a hammer and crush the now folded metal down. No more sharp edges to cut the cook.

Don't bake without the tray in place. Biscuits or scones go directly down on the tray. Pies, cobblers, most breads, and muffins go in their respective tins and then down on the tray. This way, anything that bubbles over will do so on the tray, not on the oven. When the item is done, open the back flap of the oven and remove the entire tray, to be set aside in a convenient spot for cooling. Since your baked dish may well get done at a critical point in the preparation of the meal, this is better than having to remove hot biscuits one at a time when other things have to be tended.

The softwoods often shunned for general wood-fire cookery are not a taboo in reflector-oven cookery. Yes, they will pop and maybe even spit a few cinders into your goodies, but they burn hot and fast and that's what you want for reflector-oven baking. To better guarantee hot, bright flames that will stay that way, use split wood whenever possible. A hard-to-burn wood that is unsplit will be even tougher to burn, and since you often won't know what type of wood you have in your hand it's always best to split it. If you do use softwoods for the quick flames they afford, don't worry about bad flavors getting into your food. You're cooking in front of the flames not on top of them, and it's doubtful (unless there is a lot of smoke) that any ill flavors will work their way into the food in the oven.

If you've earlier split wood for both cooking and the evening social fire, carefully squirrel away your baking wood and even hide it if you have to so late afternoon kibitzers won't wander over to your fire pit and burn it up on you. Use relatively small wood for baking. Wood that's split roughly two inches wide by one inch thick would be good. Whole sticks should be no more than about one to two inches in diameter. If the fire starts to burn down with your baked dish only half done, you must get that fire going quickly again and big, thick wood won't do it.

Also, have plenty of baking wood ready. It's never fun to run out of wood when you need it, but running out in the middle of a baking procedure really messes things up in a big way. On a recent backpacking trip I was on, our hired guide had an assistant who sometimes looked to get out of doing chores. One time after splitting a small amount of wood for supper the assistant turned to the guide and said, "How much wood do you want me to cut?" The guide turned to him and said, "Enough so I don't run out." I think the assistant got the message.

Reflector ovens are fairly inexpensive at, currently, about $25.

Sourdough Cookery

As with dutch ovens, entire books have been written about sourdough cooking. I keep learning new facets of this venerable art form, and will pass along a few tips here.

The puffy texture of breadstuffs is caused by some leavening or rising agent added to the dough before baking. The most common leavenings used today are dried yeast, baking powder, and baking soda. Cream of tartar is used, too, often in combination with baking soda. Without getting too heavily into the chemistry of it, gas is released by reactions involving the leavening and that gas causes the baked good to rise.

Baking powder, baking soda, and cream of tartar are inert chemicals, but yeast is a living organism. It is a single-celled fungi that converts starch to sugar for its food. When conditions are right—namely, heat, moisture, and a starchy medium—yeast multiplies rapidly and releases alcohol and carbon dioxide. It is this gas that "stretches" the glutinous structure of flour, and thus makes whatever's baking rise properly. With sourdough baking, yeast is the method of leavening relied upon.

Long ago, before dry yeast or artificial leavenings existed, backwoods roamers and explorers needed to have some means to leaven their breads, biscuits, and hotcakes. It was thus found that an active if sometimes dormant yeast culture could be kept going a long time. The milieu was a simple mixture of a starchy food product and water, the "sponge" or "starter" with which all sourdough baking begins. Not only did sourdough leaven the breadstuffs of prerefrigeration campers, but it imparted a wonderful fragrance and taste as well—something the chemical leavenings cannot do. The slightly "sour" taste of sourdough comes, of course, from the alcohol expelled by the yeast as it grows.

It is all too true that the gas-producing fungus in yeast will die at too high a temperature or too low a temperature (although starter can be frozen and later reactivated in water). Thus, it's something of a myth that this country's early explorers were able to keep their starters going indefinitely. Starters died back then, as they sometimes do now even with the availability of modern refrigeration. How did the pioneers prepare a new starter?

The best way, they found, was with potatoes. Hardy, easy to store, and loaded with starch, potatoes were widely used by camp bakers for centuries, especially in the northern United States and Canada.

My three favorite camp baking tins, dimensions given in chapter 1. Quite often, I'll also bring a 6-cup muffin tray.

But the potato-water method is not the only method of starting a starter. A simple mixture of dry yeast, flour, and water will do it. Since the dry yeast method is the faster of the two, that is the one I will describe. The hopelessly traditional should poke their noses into one or more sourdough cookbooks, where more than ample dissertation on the potato-water method will be found.

That does lead to an interesting question: Does the particular starter you use influence the baked good you're preparing? Indubitably, yes. Starters can be made with potatoes (a method that often does incorporate some flour), white flour, whole wheat flour, and still other flours. The character of the baked good will be very much dependent on the character of the starter. Moreover, many authorities claim that a starter improves and deepens in complexity with age. One day I visited a friend of mine, a master chef, at his restaurant. He was distraught because his special starter had died and he could no longer make his highly regarded Danish dark bread.

"Why don't you just make a new starter?" I asked.

"It just wouldn't be the same," he answered somewhat morosely.

A simple starter for the modern camper goes like this. In a plastic, glass, or ceramic bowl, mix two ¼-ounce dry-yeast packets with two cups of water (its temperature should be 105°-115°F). Then add two cups of flour. Stir well with a wooden spoon, to create a thick batter. Cover the bowl loosely with a towel and keep in a warm spot overnight. At home, I use the oven with the pilot light on. By the next morning, the mixture should be bubbly and have a light, pleasant, alcoholic smell to it. In camp, if it's cool out, it could be a couple of days before the starter is ready. Once it is ready, keep it in the cooler since the gas-producing fungus will die under too high a temperature. The night before you plan to bake, remove the starter from the cooler and add two cups of water and two cups of flour to increase its volume. Keep the whole batch in a warm spot and by morning it should be bubbly and ready again. I've found while tent camping that if the night-time temperatures are anywhere from about 50°F upward, the starter will properly come back to life. If it's not quite bubbly the way I like it by breakfast, I'll try to set the bowl in the sun or next to the camp stove or the fireplace to wake it up.

In reality, there are airborne yeasts all around us, and a simple mixture of flour, water, and sugar placed in the open will attract them. But the starter will take longer to form by this method, and most campers will not want to wait a few days to actually have a starter to work with. Once you do have your starter, take one or two cups to incorporate into your recipe and return the rest to refrigeration. This "mother sponge" will then be there for you when next you plan to bake.

SOURDOUGH BUTTERMILK BISCUITS

2 cups flour	1/2 cup butter or margarine
1 tsp. salt	1 cup sourdough starter
1 1/2 tsp. baking powder	1/2 cup buttermilk

At home, sift together flour, salt, and baking powder. Cut in the butter or margarine. Bring this mixture to camp. ✦In camp, mix starter with buttermilk. Stir this into flour mixture and continue stirring until a soft dough forms and cleans the side of the bowl. Turn onto floured surface and knead gently for 30 seconds. Roll or press down dough to form a circle 5/8 inch thick. Cut into two-inch biscuits. Place on your lightly greased baking tray and brush with melted butter. Cover and allow to rest for about a half hour. Bake in your covered iron skillet over the stove about 15 to 20 minutes or until a toothpick inserted in the middle comes out clean. **MAKES ABOUT 10.**

SOURDOUGH BREAD

2 tsp. dry yeast	3 T. powdered milk
3 T. warm water (about 115°F)	2 T. melted butter
3 T. plus 1 tsp. sugar	3 cups all-purpose flour
2 cups sourdough starter	Up to 3/4 cup whole wheat flour
1½ tsp. salt	Lukewarm water, about 1/2 cup

In a small bowl, dissolve the yeast in 3 T. warm water and add 1 tsp. sugar. Set aside to proof. ✦Mix starter with rest of sugar, salt, powdered milk, and butter. Add flour and enough water to make a moist dough. When dough cleans the sides of the bowl, turn out onto a floured surface and knead until smooth and elastic but not too dry. Shape and place in a well-greased 9-inch loaf pan. Cover with a cloth and set in a warm spot until doubled. Bake in your camp-stove oven set at 350° or in your dutch oven, about 50 minutes. ✦Using all white flour will produce a lighter if somewhat less interesting loaf. **MAKES 1 LOAF.**

At home and at my Catskill Mountain cabin I keep my starter in a one- or two-quart plastic pitcher, stored in the refrigerator. Wisdom has it that the cap on whatever vessel you use should be left slightly ajar, to let gas escape. When I go camping, I transfer about 1½ cups of the starter to a crockery container in which soft cheese is sold. It has a rubber gasket and a snap-closing lid. I keep the lid tight in transport, but loosen it up upon arriving in camp.

The acids in sourdough will attack and even pit metal. You can both damage your cookware and impart ill tastes to your food by storing sourdough in metal. Use plastic, glass or—my favorite—earthenware. A wooden spoon should be used for stirring, although in reality, short-term contact with metal implements will harm neither the sourdough nor the implements.

The real secret of keeping a sponge going a long time is to use it frequently. Each time you take it out of refrigeration and add new flour and water, it seems to rejuvenate the starter. If you don't bake at least once a week, take the starter out anyway. Add the ingredients, let it sit out overnight, then just discard the excess if the vessel has become too full.

Sponge that's not being used often should be stirred occasionally. Under refrigeration the yeast is semidormant, and the sponge will be flat looking. A slightly yellowish to amber liquid will rise to the top. Stir this into the sponge from time to time. If the color of the surface liquid changes to an unappealing gray, your starter may have died on you, although experts tell me that a starter is actually quite hardy and may still be viable beyond when we think it is.

Backpackers need not forego the pleasures and inimitable camp fragrance of sourdough goodies. Just take some starter and pour globs of it onto wax paper. As soon as it sets up a bit, turn the mounds from time to time with a spatula, which will quicken the drying. Take these little dried cakes with you and reactivate them by soaking them in warm water. When the mixture starts to "work," add a little flour and additional water and you'll have your backcountry sponge.

SOURDOUGH CINNAMON ROLLS

1½ cups sourdough starter	2¼ to 3 cups all-purpose flour
3/4 cup milk	1½ tsp. cinnamon
1 tsp. vanilla	1/3 cup sugar
2 T. sugar	2/3 cup chopped nuts
3 T. butter or margarine, melted	Glaze (see below)
1 tsp. salt	

These are incredibly light, and you have to stop yourself from eating the whole batch. They will not last long on the picnic table. Tops will brown better in a dutch oven but instructions given are for reflector oven. To your starter add milk, vanilla, 2 T. sugar, and 1 T. melted butter or margarine. Add salt and enough flour to make the dough clean the sides of the bowl. Turn out onto a floured surface and knead until smooth and elastic, incorporating more flour if necessary. Dough should be soft. Place in a greased bowl, turning

A standard-size, two-burner camp stove (right) working overtime. Inside the camp-stove oven, a nice loaf of Irish soda bread is baking. Coffee, made earlier, is warming on the left, as is a pitcher of pancake batter prior to cooking (the left side burner is off here). On top, a chunk of foil-wrapped venison sausage bread is being warmed for the upcoming brunch. Above, the inside of the camp-stove oven is shown. Note that the level of the grate is adjustable.

over once. Cover, set in a warm place free of drafts and let rise for about 1½ to 2 hours. A tent heated by the midday sun can be excellent. ✦Punch dough down, and roll it into a rectangle about 15 inches long by 8 inches wide by 1/2 inch thick. Brush dough with rest of butter, melted, and sprinkle with (premixed) cinnamon, 1/4 cup sugar and nuts. Roll up jelly roll fashion beginning on a long side. Cut into one-inch-thick slices. Place on your baking tray, pregreased, with the cut side of the roll facing upwards and with sides barely touching. Cover and let rise again, about 1 hour or until doubled in bulk. Preheat reflector oven to hot. Slip in the baking tray with rolls and cook until done. If desired, drizzle onto the still-warm rolls a mixture of powdered sugar, milk, and a few drops of vanilla. This glaze will really help the finished product. ✦Best, by far, when eaten immediately after 5 minutes of cooling. MAKES ABOUT 16.

Dried sourdough—either the sponge or drippings from a recipe—is brutal to clean. It dries into a kind of tenacious glue, so wipe it up immediately if you spill any.

Besides the recipes presented in this section, a recipe for sourdough pancakes may be found in chapter 10.

The Camp-Stove Oven

A camp-stove oven is specifically designed for use atop gasoline or propane-fueled camp stoves. The only model I'm aware of at present is made by Coleman and measures 11⅝ by 11¾ by 12¼ inches. This is the open size, with length, width, and height listed in order. Since this implement folds flat for storage and transport, its height is only two inches when folded. It sets up easily, and sits squarely atop a standard two-burner camp stove. It is made of heavy-gauge steel and is fairly rugged. Its weight is about five pounds.

The camp-stove oven is certainly easier and more reliable than a reflector oven, even if it is less romantic. That is not to say that it should completely replace the reflector oven. For one thing, the camp-stove oven must be preheated, and it can take 15-20 minutes or more to get to the baking temperature you desire. With quickly cooked things like biscuits the reflector method is thus easier, since there is really no setup time—this assuming you have a fire going anyway. The camp-stove oven really shines when it comes to loaf breads and cakes which would take a fairly long time in a reflector oven. It's distracting watching over a fire for 45 minutes or more, but with the camp-stove oven you don't have to pay as close attention. You do have to pay some attention, however, since the device has no thermostat. It has only a visible thermometer. When it gets too high, you turn the stove's flame down. When it gets too low, you turn the stove up.

HEALTHY BANANA BREAD

1 cup regular or vanilla soy milk	1 tsp. pure vanilla
1/4 cup apple sauce	1/2 tsp. salt
1/4 cup honey	2½ tsp. baking powder
1 cup mashed bananas (about 3 small ripe ones)	2½ cups whole wheat flour
	1/2 cup chopped nuts

Set reflector oven in front of the fire to preheat. Mix soy milk, applesauce, honey, bananas, and vanilla in a bowl. Add this to combined dry ingredients. Mix well. Pour into a loaf tin. Cook until a toothpick inserted comes out clean. ✦I use aluminum-free baking powder, obtainable in health-food stores. MAKES 1 LOAF.

As with any other implement, you'll pick up a few tips after using it a few times. For example, you may find that you'll do best setting the moveable grid a few notches above the lowest setting, especially with cakes. I think you'll also find that baked goods will get done more quickly than you expect in this appliance. Although it can take a good 15 minutes or more to get to 350°F, once you do get there the oven holds the temperature well. Unfortunately, opening the door to check progress can make the temperature quickly plunge back down, a problem in cool weather.

An important tip with the camp-stove oven is to not use such a large baking tin that you block off circulation of air. Use a smaller one. Another tip is to keep the oven out of the wind as much as possible. When preheating the oven, turn the stove's burner up to the highest setting, but when you set the item in to bake, turn back the flame to medium or you may burn the bottom of the food even though it is in a baking tin.

The camp-stove oven has at least one obvious and substantial drawback: It ties up your stove. Although it's best to place it directly over one burner (as opposed to attempting to straddle both burners), it really takes up about two-thirds of a standard size two-burner stove, as the photo on page 106 clearly shows. Few campers are so well prepared that they venture forth with two camp stoves, and with the oven tying up the works, how do you cook? One solution is to do your baking ahead of time. A two-layer cake for a birthday surprise or a nice loaf of sourdough bread can be baked in the afternoon before the evening meal commences. The baked goods will then keep perfectly well until evening or even for a day or two if they're wrapped properly, even if that piping-hot goodness will be gone. On one wilderness trip I took, I noticed that our outfitter would bake two loaves of white bread every afternoon in his camp-stove oven. Or, if the day was busy, he'd do it in the evening. In either case, he would not serve it right away. Rather, he would wrap the loaves well and store them in his food pack to be used with lunch the next day. Lunch on that particular excursion was a light one of cheese, peanut butter, jelly, dried beef, and the bread. The outfitter later explained to me that he used to serve crackers with the lunchtime snacks, but the crackers for 12 people for 10 days got to be very bulky. The camp-stove oven solved the problem, because while he did bake certain things in his reflector oven, baking full-sized loaves of bread in it would have been just too time consuming and too much trouble.

The camp-stove oven opens up a tremendous new dimension to the camp cook. As long as you have a tarp or fly you can bake delectable dishes even in the pouring rain. Not only that, but the oven can be used to reheat leftovers, baked goods or otherwise.

Foil Baking

You can do some wonderful baking in various types of cast-iron implements. By all means, if you like to bake in camp turn to chapter 8 and see what a versatile material cast iron really is. Here, we'll turn to some miscellaneous ways of baking foods in camp.

The first several of these involve the use of aluminum foil. While I generally shun aluminum cookware, because it is such a soft metal, I don't fear the use of aluminum foil since it is not scraped as a pot often is.

Use the heavy-duty kind when possible, as it is less likely to puncture. It is perfect for baking potatoes directly in the coals or on top of a grill over the coals. The trick to making nice baked potatoes that are still moist is to cook them quickly with high heat. I demonstrated this to a group of about 25 campers on a recent trip to an island we camp on in New York's pretty Lake George.

On this annual trip, sponsored by a club I belong to, all campers share in the cooking. For each meal, about three or four people are appointed, and they do everything from cooking to cleanup. The next meal, a different crew takes over. Sometimes the crew does a good job, and sometimes they just get through it. But of all the mistakes I've seen made, the most common one is this: They wait too long to start the charcoal for the evening barbecue.

Last year, myself and three others were assigned to do chicken, corn, baked potato, and salad. Fortunately the meal came out well, but it did take a few little tricks.

I rolled the potatoes in a double thickness of aluminum foil, meaning that there were actually at least three layers of foil between the potato and the fire. I started the coals early, and when they had burned down to the right stage I put the potatoes on. I purposely used a lot of coals to get a very hot fire going. Now, we did have grills over the large charcoal fire we'd made, but we needed those grills to cook the chicken on. The potatoes had to go right into the coals. The extra layers of foil prevented the skins from burning (many people like to eat the potato skin, but if it's become very black it's unappealing). Then, to cook the potatoes as quickly as possible, I made a "tent" of aluminum foil over them. I pushed the edges of this tent down to really keep the heat in. The result was that the potatoes cooked in only about 40 minutes, and they were nice and moist the way most people like them.

The crew at supper the next evening was assigned to make London broil, corn, and baked potatoes. They waited too long to start their fire, though, and got behind on the meal. With everything else done, including the meat, they were still poking away at the potatoes which were not going to get done until they were good and ready. First, they had the wrapped spuds on top of the grills rather than in the coals. They also did not cover them with a foil tent as I had the night before. The total cooking time must have been 90 minutes for those potatoes, and then they had been poked with a long fork so many times that they had really dried out. No one knew why Friday's potatoes turned out better than Saturday's potatoes, but I knew.

Foil, then, is most useful in camp, for baking as well as a host of other things. For foods that take a long time to cook it can, for example, prevent excessive drying out. Poultry comes first to mind here. Chicken and other domestic poultry is very fatty, and takes a long time to get done. A good solution is to wrap the bird parts in foil. Add a little butter, some paprika or other seasonings you like, and perhaps a little white wine. Seal them up in foil and bake for about 20 to 30 minutes. Then, for the last 15 to 20 minutes (more or less) put the pieces directly on the grill and brush on barbecue sauce if you so desire. You'll have the charcoal-barbecue taste but your birds won't be dried out and blackened beyond recognition.

You can do this with a steak, too, especially a frozen steak. Frozen meat put on a grill over even very hot coals will take a surprisingly long time to cook. By the time the inside is done, the outside may well be overdone. I like to slap on a dab or two of butter, wrap the steak tightly in foil, and prebake it on the grill with the grill fairly close to the coals. There is no way to suggest cooking times here, you can only go by experience and instinct. Frozen meat is diabolical: It seems to take forever to get past the raw stage, but once it does it quickly goes to the well-done stage. In any event, prebaking it in foil will prevent dry-out, and after all, it only takes a few minutes directly over the hot coals to impart a smoky charcoal taste.

I pulled another trick on that Lake George trip I mentioned. The chicken was cooking nicely on the grill—we had parboiled it but we could have also prebaked it as just described—but the coals started to burn down to the extent that we weren't getting any flare-up. I knew most people would want at least a little bit of charcoal flavor and blackness on their chicken, so I took a bottle of vegetable oil and drizzled it slowly over the hot coals. This gave us five minutes of controlled flare-up that resulted in some perfectly barbecued chicken parts. Note that you must have an extremely hot fire for this to work. If you get only smoke, stop immediately or you'll impart a bad taste to your food.

When you slow-bake meats (especially roasts) in aluminum foil, it's best to wrap the foil tightly with relatively little air space. This will reduce steaming and give the meat a better chance of browning. You'll probably want to start your roast on the grill but you can put it directly on the coals (still wrapped of course) for the last 20 minutes or so to promote browning. Again, you can unwrap the roast and place it directly on the grill near to the coals to give it some flavor during the final stages of cooking.

With vegetables you want the opposite effect. Fold the foil so there is an air space and the natural juices of the vegetables will create steam that will ensure a succulent end product. I believe you will like vegetables cooked this way. They come out juicy and a little bit snappy if not overcooked, and little flavor is lost. Try different kinds of vegetables singly and in combination, and don't be timid about experimenting with different seasonings. I like to add a little butter to these foil-wrapped vegetables, and the melted butter combined with the juice from the vegetables creates a thin sauce that is heavenly. Always reserve this sauce and dole out a tablespoonful to each diner. With all vegetables baked in foil, resist the urge to poke the pouch to see if the food inside is done. You'll lose those wonderful and healthful juices.

Fruits, too, can be baked within foil. Baked apples properly dressed up are delicious and even more so when served with some good, vanilla ice cream. This is a pure, earthy dessert that fits the outdoors and goes particularly well with a fish or game dinner. The baked apple recipe in chapter 21 is not a foil recipe, but it will give you some ideas. Bananas, also, can be baked in foil. One of my favorite baked fruits is peach halves stuffed with whatever moves me at the moment (canned peach halves are best). Mincemeat, pan-toasted pecans, maple syrup, a little brown sugar—it's easy to turn peach halves into a simple but delicious sweet-tooth tamer. Both bananas and peaches are delicate, though, so wrap them well in foil and bake on the grill, not directly in the coals.

One of my favorite camp dishes is baked, stuffed fish. I own a special hinged fish basket that does a super job of cooking a fish in the two to four pound range over open coals. This special basket has legs on both sides so it can simply be turned over halfway through. It's a fine implement, and you may be able to locate one in a gourmet cook shop or a sportsman's mail-order catalog. If you lack such a basket you can use a double thickness of foil to cook your prize catch. A fish as you know is very fragile and often falls apart when turned over on a grill. A smart trick is to put the fish on a well-greased grill over very hot coals first, before it has gotten soft. After a few minutes you will have imparted some charcoal flavor to it and you can then wrap and bake the fish stuffed or unstuffed. If you don't care to stuff it, just sprinkle the inside and outside with salt and pepper and a little onion salt; alternatively, you can insert some very thin onion slices into the cavity.

Much more on fish cookery outdoors is to be found in chapter 13. Also, some "lightweight tips" involving the use of aluminum foil are presented in chapter 19.

BAKED STUFFED FISH A LA JACQUES

Gut, gill, and scale a 2- to 3-lb. fish, but leave on head and tail. (Trout need not be scaled.) Lightly salt and pepper cavity. Stuff fish with bread stuffing, page 173. Place fish in a hinged grilling basket, pre-greased, and cook over the coals. Keep about 2 to 3 inches from coals. Turn once during the baking. Serve with pan-heated French fries and a green vegetable. ✦If you lack the grilling basket, wrap fish in a double thickness of foil and bake right in the coals or cook on a suitable grill over the coals. SERVES 2-3.

CAMP PEACHES EXTRAORDINAIRE

Take a one-pound can of halved peaches and place them in a baking tin, casserole, or fireproof skillet, hole side up. There should be about 5. In a separate skillet, sauté 1/2 cup crushed pecans in 1½ T. butter until golden. Spoon nuts into the peaches, then sprinkle dark brown sugar over all (filling can overflow into bottom of baking dish). Bake about 20 minutes in your reflector oven. ✦Variation: Substitute walnuts for the pecans, and mix in some raisins (walnuts can also be sautéed for extra flavor).

Chapter 10
WHEN THE ROOSTER CROWS

The smell of coffee brewing, the feel of a down bag that you've just warmed up after climbing into it for the night, the compelling sight of a campfire beneath starry skies: These are some of the classic images etched into the senses of most campers. At least one more has to be added for me, and that is the smell of bacon wafting across the campsite and perhaps into the very tent where I'm lying listening to the woods wake up. I believe if I ever gave up bacon completely, I'd still have to cook it in camp a few times a year for whatever part of my soul that is renewed by its aroma and all the images it conjures.

Unfortunately, what bacon is to camp cooking, cholesterol is to bacon, and the days when most people can accept all that saturated fat are about over, or should be. Nonetheless, once every camping trip I thumb my nose at the C word and take my fix of bacon. The other three days—or eight or twelve—I try to eat more healthfully. To me that means first and foremost lots of fresh fruit and vegetables, a high percentage of it eaten raw, whole grains in all their variety, and sometimes some nice vanilla yogurt with raisins. I love eggs, home fries, French toast and pancakes, but I make them the distinct exception and not the rule. I also have this thing for panfried trout first thing in the morning, but meat is something I usually skip at breakfast.

The breakfast meal can be two radically different things to the two main types of camper: the campground goer and the backwoods traveler. Campground breakfasts often drag on leisurely and quite robustly until nearly noon, with everyone sharing and sharing alike. The backpacker, though, often is anxious to get on the trail and so breakfast is typically the simplest and fastest meal of the day. In this section of the book the recipes are geared largely to the well-stocked base camp or campground, but a great many of them should also prove valuable to the deep-in hiker.

CAMP COFFEE

Put 8 cups cold water and 9 slightly rounded tablespoons ground coffee in a pot along with 2 halves of an eggshell. Bring this to a boil and remove from heat to steep. After 10 minutes, add 1/4 cup cold water to settle the grounds. Works best in an enamel coffee pot.

STRAWBERRY YOGURT SWIRL
CELESTIAL SEASONINGS, INC.

4 Strawberry Fields® herb tea bags
1 cup boiling water
2 T. honey

2 cups ice cubes
16 oz. strawberry yogurt

Pour boiling water over tea bags and steep for 5 minutes. Remove tea bags. Add honey to tea. Allow to cool slightly. Pour over ice. Swirl in yogurt. Stir vigorously and serve. SERVES 4.

SOY MILKSHAKE

1 ripe banana, cut in pieces
1½ cups vanilla soy milk

1 cup (sliced) strawberries
or blueberries

Mash banana and other fruit by whatever means you can. A potato masher is excellent. Add soy milk and stir well. Serve cold. SERVES 1 OR 2.

The Exciting World of Grains

It's my belief that grains are not used more in our culture because there isn't enough understanding of them. People are confused about what they are, where they come from, the different forms in which they are sold, and how to cook or prepare them. Grains are an ideal food for campers. They're nutritious, not prone to spoil, clean and easy to transport, inexpensive, and easy to prepare.

At the back of the book is an appendix titled, "A Grain Primer." It provides more than a good initiation to grains. Here, now, are the cooking formulas for some of the more popular processed grain cereals.

WHEATENA®. This is a true whole-grain cereal, with all parts of the wheat kernel present. For 2 people, combine in a saucepan 1½ cups water, ¼ tsp. salt, and ½ cup Wheatena. Heat to a rapid boil, stirring occasionally. Cook 4 or 5 minutes over moderate heat to desired consistency, still stirring. Remove from heat; cover until ready to serve. Taste before adding more salt. Top with milk, fruit, sugar, butter, etc. as desired.

CREAM OF WHEAT®. For 2 people, heat 1¾ cups water or 2 cups milk, plus

¼ tsp. salt, to almost boiling. Slowly stir in ⅓ cup Cream of Wheat, stirring vigorously to thwart lumping. Return to boiling over medium heat. Reduce heat, cook 2½ minutes or until thickened, stirring constantly. (These directions are for "Quick" Cream of Wheat.) Serve with milk and any desired toppings.

CREAM OF RICE®. For 3 people, heat 2 cups water with ½ tsp. salt. Pour in slowly ½ cup Cream of Rice, stirring constantly; boiling should not stop. Cook and stir over moderate heat for 30 seconds. Remove from heat, cover and let stand 3 minutes. Serve with milk and any desired toppings.

FARINA. Milled from sweet, hard wheat. Both farina and cream of farina are available and there doesn't appear to be much of a difference. This recipe is for farina. For 2 servings, heat 1½ cups water and ¼ tsp. salt to boiling. Slowly pour in ¼ cup farina, stirring constantly. Return to the boil. Reduce heat; simmer 2 or 3 minutes or until thickened, stirring frequently. Milk can be substituted for the water. Serve with milk and fruit or other desired toppings.

One busy morning in camp I set a half-quart of milk on a grill over some coals. My aim was simply to heat the milk for use with some hot cereal, but I forgot the pot and a good 45 minutes went by. Although a heavy skin had formed at the top I didn't think the milk had ever actually boiled. It was clear that I had a lot less milk than I'd started with, but I didn't give it too much thought. I finally made a big pot of Cream of Rice (in a separate pot) and used the heated milk as a topping.

We just about flipped at how good that cereal tasted. I'd made my own condensed milk! Since that morning, I've tried my "sweet milk" in all types of hot cereal, always with delicious results. Reduce the quart of milk to about half then try this formula.

SUNRISE SWEET-MILK CEREAL

Pour a quart of milk into a pot and set on lowest flame for about one to two hours. It should not boil, but you should see steam rising from it. The skin can occasionally be removed. When reduced to about half, pour in 1/3 cup Cream of Wheat cereal in a slow, steady stream. Stir, following directions on package. Add salt to taste. ✦Alternatively, you could cook your favorite hot cereal with water and just use your sweet milk as a topping. Other toppings can include maple syrup, sugar, salt, fruit, raisins. My personal favorite is a pat of butter along with a tablespoon of maple syrup. If your sweet milk takes too long to condense, and breakfast is already complete, put it in the cooler and use it the following day.

Fruit for Breakfast

The value of raw fruits and vegetables in the diet can no longer be doubted. Quite simply, for all our joy of cooking, it's hard to believe that we can really improve on what the good earth has provided. Ripe fruits are tempting, sweet, succulent, beautiful, varied. It just seems such a shame to cook them, and I do it rarely. Since as the camp cook I assert my right to push my opinions on others, I have found clever little ways of making my camping guests eat their fruit, like good little boys and girls.

People are lazy. Put five whole oranges on the table in the morning and four will be there when breakfast is through. Now cut those oranges into 10 wedges each and only half an orange will be left over. Next day, take four fresh apples and leave them on the table through the morning meal. Three may remain, but nothing will remain if you'll cut and core the apples, and sprinkle them with cinnamon and sugar. Get the picture?

How to make fruit more interesting? Let's list some ways:

1. Core, cut, and reduce to easy size as just discussed.
2. Take citrus fruit and scoop it out of its skin, place in a large bowl with all the juice. Remove pits. Add a bit of water. Drizzle on a small amount honey or sugar. Stir. Make sure small bowls are available. Mixed citrus fruits are especially pleasant.
3. Put out coreless, seedless pieces of fruit along with bowls of granola, chopped nuts, raisins, toasted seeds, and yogurt. Again, make sure bowls are available so guests can mix and match as they please. Most days, skip the fatty main dish completely, and just serve the fruit with various toppings.
4. Whether you have canned fruit or fresh, make sure some is always available for topping on a cereal.
5. Learn which spices marry especially well with what fruits. Sprinkle banana strips with a little nutmeg, sprinkle apples and pears with cinnamon, liven up avocado with a dash of lemon juice, try a sprinkle of ground allspice on melon slivers.
6. Soak some pitted or pitless prunes the night before and you won't have to cook them at all. Serve with the juice in the A.M. and they should all go.
7. When fresh fruit is scarce, set out some of the less typical dried fruits. Dried figs, mixed dry fruits, dried apricots—all these will go because they're set to eat as is.
8. Finally, a little milk goes well on most noncitrus fruits. Try soymilk. I like vanilla.

FIVE-MINUTE FRUIT SALAD

2 bananas, sliced	1/2 cup chopped nuts (almonds,
2 apples, cored and sliced thin	hazelnuts, wild nuts, etc.)
6 ozs. dried figs or dates	Lemon juice

Mix fruits and nuts then sprinkle lemon juice on top. Serve immediately. Since apples and bananas are available year-round, this satisfying salad can be made at any time. SERVES 2 TO 3.

If you have to cook your fruit, at least make sure that what results is sheer delight. In your dutch oven you can make the sensational baked apples described in chapter 21.

Eggs & Other Things

In spite of still growing concerns about cholesterol in the diet, eggs continue to be immensely popular in camping breakfasts. Just below, I show a utensil-less way of cooking eggs. Here are a few of a more conventional nature.

EASTERN SKY DELIGHT

6 slices toast	6 hot poached eggs
Butter	1 cup white sauce
1/2 cup canned deviled ham	Watercress

Butter the toast generously, then spread with the ham and arrange all slices on a platter. Place a freshly poached egg on each slice. Top with the sauce, garnish with some fresh watercress and serve. SERVES 3-6.

HASH 'N' EGG ON ENGLISH
LIBBY'S FOODS

2 split, buttered English muffins   4 eggs
1 15-oz. can corned beef hash

Fry muffins lightly on buttered side. Wrap in foil to keep warm. Heat hash in same skillet, stirring occasionally. Make 4 indentations in hash. Carefully break 1 egg into each indentation. Cover skillet and cook until eggs are set. Break apart carefully with spatula and serve over muffins. SERVES 4.

Here's how to make perfect scrambled eggs. If possible, use a slope-sided chef's skillet. This is one of the few instances where I like nonstick finishes. Melt two tablespoons of butter in it and twirl the pan so the bottom and sides are both coated. Meanwhile, break your eggs into a bowl and add one tablespoon of cold milk per egg. Beat well with a whisk or fork. Pour half of the now-melted butter into the eggs, and stir. Turn the heat under the skillet to a rather high medium. After one minute, pour the eggs in and let them set for about five seconds. Then beat with a fork till fluffy and light. The key is really the skillet temperature. Too hot a skillet will make eggs stick, and will kill any chance of the eggs coming out fluffy and a little moist on the inside.

Still-warm ashes that may include some embers from the previous night's camp-fire can be used to cook eggs. You should have "soft-boiled" eggs in five to ten minutes, hard-cooked eggs in a bit more than that.

A satiny-smooth iron skillet and some floured trout—all that's needed now is some bubbling hot butter and a few wedges of lemon.

Almost everyone likes French toast. Here's a French toast recipe with a twist, followed by a time-honored cornmeal recipe.

SUNUP ORANGE FRENCH TOAST

French bread loaf	1 tsp. grated orange rind
2 eggs	1 tsp. vanilla extract (opt.)
1/2 cup orange juice	2 T. sugar

Cut French bread crosswise into slices about 1½ inches thick. Beat eggs, mix with rest of ingredients. Dip bread into mixture, fry in butter or margarine until golden on both sides. Serve with butter and maple syrup.

FRIED CORNMEAL MUSH

Bring 2 quarts water to a boil and add 1½ tsp. salt. Slowly add 2⅔ cups cornmeal in a steady stream, stirring constantly with your wooden spoon. Turn heat to low. Stir frequently. After about a half hour, when mush is thick, smoothe the top. Let set in the pot placed in the cooler or just outside if it's cool out. Next morning, serve fried in slices, and top with a bit of salt and/or butter and/or maple syrup. ✦ While still warm, the mush makes an excellent substitute for potatoes. Great with stews and innumerable other dishes.

Meat and Potatoes

The best way to make sure your bacon comes out crispy is to separate the slices, cook them slowly, and keep draining off the grease. Because bacon seems to often get done before the rest of breakfast, try to keep it warm. The best idea is to serve bacon within 5 to 10 minutes of cooking, or right after it has crisped up.

A somewhat less fatty breakfast meat is a smoked pork butt, cut into slices. You can brown it but I prefer to just heat the thickly cut slices in water. This is excellent with eggs, pancakes and French toast, and much easier and faster than making bacon or even sausages. Generally, these pork butts are cured and so only have to be heated through.

The key to making good home fries is to boil the potatoes the night before. Then try this recipe, my own creation.

MOUNTAINTOP HOME FRIES

3 medium potatoes	Oil and butter
1 medium sweet potato	Few dashes each garlic powder,
2-3 T. chives (fresh, frozen, or	paprika and cayenne
dried)	Salt to taste

Bring a pot of water to the boil. Wash the skins of the potatoes but do not peel. Boil potatoes including the sweet potato for 6 minutes. Remove potatoes and cool. Wrap spuds tightly and store overnight some place the critters can't get at. ✦In the morning, heat your 10-inch cast-iron skillet. Add oil and butter. Scrape the skins from the potatoes, chop, and add to pan. Add a little more oil if too dry. Add seasonings. Cook approximately 15-20 minutes on low-medium flame. Potatoes should have just a bit of crispness left, and should be golden, not brown. SERVES 3-4 AS A SIDE DISH.

Roschti is a sensational Swiss potato dish that I first sampled when traveling through the Alps many years ago. My good Swiss friend Teresa later gave me the recipe, which emigrated here with her. Again, it's critical that the potatoes be boiled the night before.

ROSCHTI
TERESA MACCABEE

3 medium potatoes	Cooking oil, about 2-3 T.
Boiling salted water	Salt, pepper, and paprika to taste

Wash the potatoes but do not peel. Drop into boiling salted water to cover. While still slightly hard, remove from heat and drain. Run cold water over to stop the cooking process. Wrap and set aside overnight. ✦In the morning, add oil to your cast-iron skillet and heat. Peel potatoes and grate coarsely directly into the skillet. Sprinkle on a little each salt, pepper, and paprika. Turn potatoes a few times until light brown. Cook a little longer till slightly browner. Serve hot. SERVES 3.

Pancakes and a Little More

The key word in making pancakes is "cakes." That's what you're doing, baking a bunch of separate little cakes. It's a good thing to keep in mind, because like any

cake, hotcakes can be botched in any one of a number of different ways.

Pancakes are almost always made with some combination of flour, milk, egg, shortening, and leavening (leavening is omitted with crepes). Sometimes a dash of salt is added. I always add a little sugar. When you buy "instant" or "easy" pre-packaged pancake mix, these ingredients are usually in there in one form or another. Needless to say, all different types of fruit and occasionally nuts are added to hotcakes.

With the easiest types of store-bought mixes, all you add is water. This is the "complete" type of pancake mix, but I find the pancakes to be most drab. With some others, a fresh egg or fresh milk might be required. These are often much better, a fine example being Pepperidge Farm Buttermilk Pancake Mix. These mixes are reasonably foolproof, although you still have to maintain a proper griddle temperature while cooking.

Pancake mixes abound. Some taste almost as good as 'cakes made from scratch. Still, no other pancake seems to have the lightness and flavor of sourdough pancakes (below).

Among the premixes you can buy regular or white flour, buttermilk, or buckwheat. These are the most popular although I'm sure there are others. Recently, I came across a premix for "Swedish thin pancakes." These turned out to be quite good.

If you want to make pancakes from scratch, you have two primary options: You can use a yeast-based starter or you can use a simpler form of leavening like baking powder or baking soda. Sometimes both of these latter two are used in the same recipe. In either case, the leavening is necessary to help the cakes rise. Some day you'll forget to put in the leavening and you'll wonder why your hotcakes came out looking like beer coasters.

FARMHOUSE CORNMEAL PANCAKES
CONNETQUOT STATE PARK PRESERVE

1 cup yellow cornmeal	1 egg
2 T. sugar	2 T. melted butter
1 tsp. salt	1/2 cup milk
3/4 cup boiling water	1/2 cup all-purpose flour

Bring the cornmeal, sugar, and salt pre-mixed. In camp, add the boiling water and allow to stand 10 minutes. Beat together the egg, butter and milk. Add this to the first mixture. If possible, sift the flour. Add this to the batter and stir or whisk until smooth. Cook like pancakes on an ungreased hot griddle. ◆These moist cakes are good with butter alone. Or, serve with strawberry preserves, with or without the butter. SERVES 6-8.

BUCKWHEAT CAKES

1 cup white flour	2 cups milk
1 cup buckwheat flour	1 T. honey
1 tsp. salt	1 egg, beaten
4 tsp. baking powder	1/4 cup melted butter or oil
1/3 cup chopped walnuts	

At home, combine the flours, salt, baking powder, and nuts. In camp, combine the other ingredients. Beat the mixed dry ingredients into the liquid mixture. Cook cakes on a lightly greased griddle or skillet. MAKES 8 TO 10 LARGE CAKES.

Some premixes advise that you let the batter "rest" after mixing in the liquid. I feel this is always a good idea, even with scratch pancakes. If you're working with cold batter—leftover or just made earlier and kept cold in the cooler—definitely try to warm it up a bit first. Place it next to the fire or the stove or in the sun or any place where it will pick up a little bit of heat. Cold batter is very flat looking. Batter that's ready to cook with has a lighter and sometimes bubbly or frothy look. This is especially true of yeast-based batter.

BASIC GRIDDLE CAKES

2 cups flour	2 cups milk
1 tsp. salt	1 large egg
2½ T. sugar	2 T. melted butter
2 tsp. baking powder	

If possible, sift together flour, salt, sugar, and baking powder (can be done at home). Add milk, well beaten egg, and butter. Mix well. Cook on well-greased griddle. SERVES ABOUT 6.

I have found that white-flour and buckwheat-flour pancake batter stores extremely well (batter made from whole wheat flour far less well). I've used it two, three, and even four days later and have found the cakes to be every bit as good. Just keep it in the cooler and warm it up a bit before using. Stir all batters well after storage and even between batches while cooking. Do not store in aluminum vessels. Try to store your batter in plastic, stainless-steel, or ceramic containers.

Usually, the inspiration for camp pancakes is a morning gathering of people (pancakes for one is not very rewarding). In consideration of this, use a griddle. With one, you can make six at a time and get on with the project. If you make fewer at a time, as most any skillet will force you to do, the whole thing will go too slowly. The first cakes cooked will get cold while they wait for the others to get done. Or, the people at your picnic table will eat their breakfast one pancake at a time.

JIM'S WHOLE WHEAT PANCAKES

2 cups stone-ground whole wheat
  flour
4 tsp. baking powder
1 tsp. salt
2½ T. sugar

2 eggs, beaten
2½ cups milk
6 T. melted butter
1 T. maple syrup

After much experimentation I finally perfected this recipe, which should make nice, dark, high cakes. If you can't get stone-ground flour, regular whole wheat is OK but might require less liquid. At home, sift the flour, and combine with other dry ingredients in a plastic bag. In camp, beat eggs, add 1½ cups milk. Stir in melted butter and maple syrup. Add this to flour mixture. Add rest of milk carefully; batter shouldn't be too runny. For smoothest batter, use a whisk to stir and mix. Let sit for 10 minutes, preferably in a warm spot. Cook cakes on a lightly greased griddle. SERVES 8.

Unless you're intentionally making crepes, keep your pancake batter just a little on the thick side. I think you'll like the results better. Never add all the liquid at once when you're making the batter! Add a little at a time until you reach the right consistency. You can always add a bit more liquid but if you add too much you're forced to add more dry ingredients and you can wind up chasing your tail.

Assuming you're starting out with a good recipe, the really key thing is griddle temperature. Every batter has a temperature that it likes best but generally the thinner batters should be ladled onto a slightly hotter surface. Correct temperatures will range between about 380°F and 400°F, but of course there's no way to gauge that in camp. You simply have to observe the cakes as you cook them.

WHIPPED MAPLE BUTTER

Soften 1 cup butter or margarine to room temperature. Beat with an electric mixer at high speed until smooth and creamy. Gradually add 1/2 cup maple syrup while beating constantly. Bring to camp in a suitable vessel. Excellent over pancakes or French toast. MAKES 1½ CUPS.

APPLE JUICE SYRUP

3/4 cup apple juice
1/2 cup packed brown sugar
1/2 cup light corn syrup

1/2 tsp. lemon juice
2 T. butter or margarine
Dash each cinnamon and nutmeg

Put all ingredients into a small saucepan and heat just until mixture comes to a boil. Reduce heat and simmer about 15 minutes, uncovered, until sauce thickens slightly. Serve warm over pancakes or, especially, waffles. ◆The butter will quickly separate and rise to the top as the sauce cools. If you wish to keep the butter, there is no choice but to reheat the sauce each time to reincorporate the fat. ABOUT 1½ CUPS.

In a similar vein, every recipe will result in a slightly different looking cake, but there will always be one right look for each batter recipe. Whether you get that right look depends more than anything on griddle temperature. If the temperature is too low, the cake may be uniformly light colored and may be untextured and without appeal. If the temperature is too high, the cake may come out sort of slick looking and shiny, may have dark spots, and will not rise properly.

NANA'S CREPES
ROSE ZAJICEK

3/4 cup all-purpose flour	1/3 cup water
1/4 tsp. salt	2/3 cup milk
2 T. sugar	1 T. melted butter
2 eggs	1/2 tsp. vanilla (opt.)

Mix flour, salt, and sugar with a fork. In a separate bowl, beat eggs with a whisk and add water, milk, butter, and vanilla. Add liquid mix to dry mix, combine with a few quick strokes. Let stand at least 30 minutes. Fry in a lightly buttered skillet (a 6- or 7-inch nonstick skillet would be ideal). SERVES 3.

Since you have to guess at griddle temperature, start with a small test pancake. If it looks good, lay a whole batch down. By the time you get to the second or third batch, you'll probably have to turn down the flame. If you do additional batches, you may well have to turn the flame back up again. And so on. All you can do is try to cook as many pancakes as possible at just the right temperature—you can't make them all perfect. Because of the need for adjusting the heat, a camp stove is a better choice for making pancakes than is the lid of a dutch oven set over coals, or a skillet set over coals.

CRUSTY SOFT SPOON BREAD
DANIELLE BRANDIN

1/4 cup flour	3/4 tsp. salt
3/4 cup cornmeal	1 egg
1 tsp. baking powder	1½ cups milk or skim milk
1 T. sugar	1 T. butter

Bring the premixed dry ingredients in a plastic bag. In camp, blend together the egg, beaten, and 1 cup milk. ✦In an 8 x 8 baking pan, melt the butter. Blend the egg-milk mixture into the dry ingredients. Pour this batter into your pan. Now pour rest of milk evenly over the top and do not stir. Bake in your reflector oven about 45 minutes. Cool 10 minutes then serve promptly. ✦This moist bread is a nice break from regular corn bread, which can be very dry.

Again, every batter recipe will produce a different looking cake, but there are some almost universal signs of success. A nicely done cake usually is fairly light in the center, with golden brown rings towards the edge of the cake. Cakes that look light and inviting usually are. And those that look a little bit funky usually are.

Eight delicious pancake recipes are presented in this book, six within this chapter. I have to admit, I've never had another pancake that compares with sourdough pancakes. They are unique in that they contain no milk—that's the main reason they are so light.

SOURDOUGH PANCAKES

2 cups sourdough starter   3 T. oil
  (see p. 103)   1 T. melted butter
1 egg   1 tsp. baking soda
2 T. sugar   4 T. water

Mix starter, egg, sugar, oil, and butter till well blended. Dissolve soda in water in a separate cup. Fold into batter. Stir gently. Cook on lightly greased griddle on your camp stove. SERVES 3.

Chapter 11

PLEASING LUNCHES, HOT AND COLD

I can recall many a memorable camp breakfast. Once it was a seashore omelet which used up not only my leftovers but everyone else's as well. It had two cut-up lobsters in it, vegetables of every hue, and God only knows how many eggs.

Coming back to me, too, is more than one fabulous camp dinner. I recall baked lake trout, cooked just minutes out of the water, on a fishing trip to Hawk Lake, Quebec. Then there were creamy fish chowders with pink-fleshed Maine brook trout, shish kebabs of museum-quality design in Hampton Bays, hearty dutch-oven pot roasts along Montana rivers, and fresh berry pies in the Florida Keys.

I can scarcely remember a camp lunch though, and maybe it's better that way. If when the wheel of fortune has spun you've been knighted camp cook, this, the midday meal, is where you get a little break.

A high percentage of campers are where they are for some particular reason: fishing, sightseeing, hiking, photography, mountaineering, swimming. Thus, lunch is the meal they will least have on their minds. There are two implications here. One, if you are in fact running the culinary show, you can promote the idea of each person seeing to his or her own light lunch. On the other hand, if you feel like making lunches, don't push them on people who have a lot of other good things to do between 10 A.M. and 5 P.M. Roll with the flow when it comes to lunches.

In the preceding chapter, there are ideas for serving fresh fruit so as to make it disappear from the picnic table. You can do the same exact thing with fresh vegetables.

It's doubtful that people will descend upon your midday offerings if they consist of just cut-up raw vegetables. But place a tangy dip in the middle and watch them fly away. Here are a couple of recipes.

COURTESY COLEMAN, INC.

BLUE CHEESE DIP

4 oz. cream cheese

4 oz. blue cheese

1/2 cup lowfat plain yogurt

2 T. mayonnaise

1½ T. finely grated fresh onion

Salt to taste

Dash of garlic powder

Get both cheeses very soft. Mash together with all other ingredients. Like most dips, it will be better the next day, but bring to near room temperature before serving. ✦A dash of lemon or lime juice could be added. Finely chopped walnuts is a marvelous addition.

GUACAMOLE DIP

Cut 2 small ripe avocados, remove the pit, then remove the pulp. In a bowl, mash the pulp with 1 T. lemon juice, 1/4 tsp. salt, 1/2 T. finely grated onion (or a little more), and 1 small clove garlic, crushed and finely chopped. Taste and add additional salt if desired. A small dash of Tabasco sauce can also be added. Mix and let stand overnight. Bring to camp in a suitable vessel.

A wide range of vegetables can be used raw as crudités, but some of the best are: yellow squash, red (sweet) pepper, green (bell) pepper, cherry tomatoes, cauliflower, broccoli, zucchini, endive, cucumber, carrot, yellow pepper, and snow pea pods.

Simple Soups

On a chilly day there's scarcely a better midday meal than soup. And it can be a meal by itself. I sometimes like to bake biscuits in the morning and put them aside to be served with soup at the lunch hour. Soup, bread of some sort, and a piece of cheese will revive the spirits on a wind-blown spring or autumn day when the weather has been less than kind.

JIM'S STOMACHACHE BROTH

2 qts. spring or well water
1½ packets chicken bouillon
4 cups chopped potato
1 cup loosely packed chopped parsley
1 cup chopped celery

1 cup chopped carrot
1 cup chopped tomato (about 1 medium one)
2 large wooden spoons of honey (about 3 to 4 T. total)

Bring water to a simmer. Add all other ingredients and simmer for about 30 minutes, covered. Turn off heat and allow to steep another 15-20 minutes. Strain, discarding vegetables. Reheat broth to warm before serving. ◆This very alkaline broth is good for an acid stomach.

CAMPER'S MEATLESS PEA SOUP

1 cup dried split peas
1 bay leaf (opt.)
1 medium onion, chopped small

1 8¼-oz. can sliced carrots
2 chicken bouillon cubes or packets
1/2 tsp. garlic powder

Rinse the peas in cold water, stirring vigorously. Drain. Cover the peas with 4 cups cold water and soak several hours or overnight. Do not drain. Add the bay leaf and onion and cook about 45 minutes or until the peas have fully disintegrated. Remove and discard bay leaf. ◆Mash the carrots coarsely and add to the soup pot with the other two ingredients. Stir very well, cook 10 minutes. ◆As with most soups, you can add water to thin or remove the cover during cooking to thicken—but the carrots provide thickening so add them first. SERVES 6.

AUNT JOAN'S EASY CHICKEN SOUP
JOAN CRONIN

3 chicken quarters, skin removed
1½ qts. water
3–4 chicken boullion cubes or packets
1 onion, choppped

2 ribs celery with leaves, chopped
2 carrots, chopped
Parsley
Pepper (opt.)

Any chicken parts totaling about 3 lbs. will be acceptable. Cover them with the water and add all the other ingredients. Bring to a boil, reduce heat, and simmer on low, covered, about 60 minutes. Use a large spoon to force some of the meat off the bone. Uncover and simmer about another 30 minutes or until "it's soup." Cool. Skim fat. ABOUT 5-6 SERVINGS.

HARD-TIMES TURKEY SOUP

Butter
1½–1¾ lbs. turkey necks,
  backs, and thighs
1 10¾-oz can Campbells Golden
  Mushroom soup, undiluted

Seasonings to taste
1 13¾-oz. can chicken broth
1 onion, diced fine

Sauté turkey pieces in butter until golden. Season as you wish (try a little Poultry Seasoning). Add soup plus 2 soup cans of water, broth, and onion. Add fresh or dried parsley if you have it. Simmer 75 minutes. Remove turkey pieces, pick meat off bone and reserve for sandwiches. Or, return now boneless meat to pot and serve in the soup. ✦I made this soup for $2.89! SERVES 4.

Salads

Sometimes, a small bowl of salad and a hunk of good bread is nourishment enough to make it through those long afternoon hours. Any one of these several good salads can be put out between high noon and 2 P.M. First is an original from my sister, who makes the best green salads I've ever had.

CAROLEE'S SALADE NOUVELLE

Break up, into bite size pieces, one small head of red leaf lettuce, one head of endive, and one cup of arugula. Wash, dry very well, and place in the cooler to crisp, preferably 4 hours or more. Serve with your favorite vinaigrette or try this fancy one: 6 T. sesame oil, 1 T. balsamic vinegar, 1 T. raspberry vinegar, 1/2 tsp. salt, 5 turns of fresh pepper, 1 tsp. Dijon mustard, dash dry tarragon. Certainly, this dressing could be made at home and brought to camp. Add slowly to your greens as you toss—don't overdress the salad! ✦My sister Carolee likes to add freshly-shelled green peas to this salad. SERVES 6.

NINETY-SECOND COLE SLAW

In a large bowl or pot, empty a 16-oz. bag of prepackaged cole slaw blend (often just a mixture of shredded cabbage and carrots). Add 1/2 cup each of mayonnaise and lowfat plain yogurt, plus 1/2 tsp. of salt, 1/4 tsp. pepper, add 1½ tsp. each of sugar and celery seed. Stir well. Chill and let set 4 hours or longer. ABOUT 8-9 SIDE DISHES.

MOM'S EASY TOMATO SALAD

2 large ripe garden tomatoes,
  sliced 1/2 inch thick
Chopped onion to taste
Garlic powder

Oregano
Salt and pepper
Oil
Wine or tarragon vinegar

Place sliced tomatoes on a large plate. Sprinkle on finely chopped onion (red onion is ideal) and seasonings to taste. Drizzle on oil (about 1½ to 2 T.) then vinegar. Allow to marinate for a few hours if possible, turning occasionally. Optionally, chopped fresh basil can be sprinkled over all. SERVES 4.

ZITI GARDEN SALAD
RONZONI

1 lb. ziti
1 cup Italian salad dressing
2 cups broccoli florets, cooked
1 large red pepper, in thin strips

1/2 cup pitted black olives, halved
1/2 cup finely chopped parsley
1/4 cup grated parmesan cheese

Cook the ziti according to package directions. Drain the pasta and rinse quickly with warm water. Combine with all other ingredients and toss well. Serve with additional cheese if desired. SERVES 4

JIM'S UNBELIEVABLE POTATO SALAD

3 medium cloves garlic, finely minced
4 liquid ozs. oil
2½ lbs. baby new potatoes (white skin)
2 T. finely minced onion

3 T. fresh parsley, finely chopped
1½ tsp. sugar
1/2 tsp. salt
Freshly ground pepper
1-1½ T. vinegar

Let garlic sit in oil 20-25 minutes, then remove with a slotted spoon and discard. Add all other ingredients to the oil except potatoes. Whisk or stir well. ✦Wash potatoes. Lightly salt 2 qts. of water. Boil potatoes about 5 minutes. Remove from flame. Potatoes will continue to cook in the hot water. Test every minute until most of hardness is gone. Drain immediately and pour cold water over until potatoes are luke warm. Do not peel. Slice potatoes 1/3-inch thick. Small potatoes, which are best, will yield only 3 slices each. Potatoes must be luke warm, not cold. Pour batter over, stir well, and let sit 1 hour. Serve warm or at room temperature. ✦Small red-skin potatoes are an acceptable substitute. ABOUT 6 SIDE DISHES.

More Substantial

Big appetites can occur at midday. Many of the recipes in the next chapter (as well as many other chapters) should stay the thronging pot-lid lifters. Here are a few additional ones.

A spectacular omelet made for Sunday brunch at a New Jersey shore campground. It used up all the leftovers and fed about 12 people.

KASHA-STUFFED TOMATOES
WOLFF'S BUCKWHEAT PRODUCTS

3 large ripe garden tomatoes
1/2 cup chopped onion
1 clove garlic, minced
1/4 cup butter or margarine
1½ cups cooked kasha

1/2 cup packed, soft bread crumbs
1/2 tsp. salt or to taste
1/4 tsp. pepper or to taste
1/8 tsp. rosemary

Cut tomatoes in half crosswise. Scoop out much of pulp but do not pierce bottoms. Drain pulp well, and reserve. ✦Cook onion and garlic in butter until onion is tender. To this, add tomato pulp and rest of ingredients. Fill tomatoes with mixture. ✦Add 1/2-inch water to the bottom of your dutch oven and heat. Bake tomatoes about 20 minutes. MAKES 6 SIDE DISHES.

NORTH COUNTRY STUFFED PEPPERS
GIBBS WILD RICE

1 medium onion, chopped fine
1 large carrot, chopped fine
1/2 cup celery, chopped fine
1/2 lb. ground beef, venison, or
  other game meat

1¼ cups cooked wild rice or
  brown rice
Salt and pepper to taste
6 large green bell peppers
8 oz. Cheddar cheese, shredded

Sauté onion, carrot, and celery in butter or oil until soft. Push aside and sauté meat until lightly browned. Stir all together, simmer on low for 10 minutes. Turn off heat and add rice. Stir well, season to taste. ✦Wash peppers, remove tops, and clean insides. Add stuffing. Top with shredded cheese. Bake in dutch oven for about 35 minutes; or, wrapped in foil in the coals. ✦You can soften your peppers by steaming them in a pot with a little water for about 10 to 12 minutes before stuffing them. This will reduce the baking time. SERVES 3-6.

AMERICAN-STYLE CHILI

1 medium onion, chopped
1 medium green Italian pepper,
  chopped
3/4 lb. chopped beef or venison
1 8-oz. can tomato sauce
1/4 cup water

1 16-oz. can red kidney beans
1 T. chili powder, or to taste
Dash each Worcestershire and
  Tabasco
Salt and pepper to taste

Fry onion and pepper in a little oil or fat. Push aside, then add meat and brown lightly. Add all other ingredients, stir well. Simmer slowly, uncovered, about 30 minutes. Serve over white rice or noodles. Toppings can include chopped scallions, shredded cheese, and sour cream. SERVES 4-5.

Towards Healthier Beverages

Most people drink at least some coffee and carbonated soda, but I doubt there are many who see either as something healthy to introduce to one's body. In coming years, I hope more cookbooks (outdoor and otherwise) will offer many more recipes for healthy beverages than has been the case to date. Here are three contributions to that cause, and a few are found in other chapters.

CAROB MILK

4 cups milk or skim milk
1 T. honey
6 T. carob powder

1/2 tsp. vanilla extract (opt.)
1/4 cup ground peanuts

Combine all ingredients in a pitcher or large bowl and stir or whisk vigorously. Serve as cold as possible. SERVES 4.

DAIRY-FREE CAPPUCINO

In a pot, combine a cup of brewed coffee (half-day old OK) and a cup of plain soy milk. Bring to a full boil. Immediately pour into two mugs and top with cinnamon. Sugar may be added to taste. SERVES 2.

SLEEPYTIME NIGHTCAP
Celestial Seasonings, Inc.

8 Sleepytime® tea bags
4 cups boiling water
1 tablespoon honey

1/4 cup plain or flavored brandy
1/2 tsp. lemon juice

Pour boiling water over tea bags. Steep 4 minutes. Add honey and stir until dissolved. Pour in brandy and lemon juice. Serve warm. SERVES 4.

Chapter 12
DINNERS WORTH TOASTING

Aglass of O.J. at 8 A.M. and gorp at noon might be all there's time for on a camping trip, but rarely is the evening meal skipped. No matter what you cook, query the others to see what time they wish to eat. Depending on the activities planned, it could be any time between about 4 P.M. and 10 P.M.

One-Pot Wonders

Although it's not universal across all cultures, in America the largest meal of the day usually consists of several separate courses or dishes. In camp, this can make for mighty big work for both you and the dishwashers. Salvation is at hand, however. It comes in the form of one-pot meals, the great ally of the camp dinner chef! There is almost always something intrinsically hearty and pleasing about these dishes, and they really cut back on preparation time. How fast can you make a one-pot meal? With a little forethought, just minutes.

You'll have little trouble coming up with combinations for one-pot camp meals if you'll just keep a few principles in mind. First of all, for a one-potter to be truly filling by itself, it will probably have to incorporate some kind of protein. Chili, of course—whether with meat or without—is a great example. If you do choose to forego the meat, you can have both heartiness and nutritive value by adding beans. A few types of beans come frozen, but more kinds come canned. In either case, the beans will have been precooked which means you don't have to soak them and/or precook them in camp.

A good alternative to beans is pasta, in any of its myriad shapes and forms. For example, pasta added to a comparatively thin soup can really add body, and sometimes turn that soup into a one-pot main meal. A good tip here is to stick to the faster-cooking pastas, no matter how you plan to use them.

A final tip before we get to some actual recipes: Poke your nose into some oldtime cookbooks, and look under the "casserole" section. The tuna casseroles of yesteryear may not be so chic today, but they are all one-pot meals that can serve the camper well.

LONG TRAIL DELIGHT

1 lb. lean ground beef or venison	Dried Italian seasonings to taste
1 cup chopped onion	1½ cups thinly-sliced zucchini
2 cloves garlic, minced	4 ozs. dry wide egg noodles,
2/3 of a 28-oz. can crushed	precooked
tomatoes in puree	1 cup shredded Cheddar cheese
Salt and pepper to taste	

In a large skillet, brown meat with onion and garlic (with beef, no oil may be necessary). Add tomatoes and seasonings. Simmer 10 minutes, stirring. Add zucchini, cook 10 more minutes. Blend in noodles. Continue cooking on low flame 5 more minutes. Serve piping hot with a little cheese on top. SERVES 3-5.

PASTA FAZULE (PASTA E FAGIOLI)

Fry 2 large cloves garlic, chopped, in olive oil. Add 1 small onion, chopped. Cook 5 minutes. Add 1/2 of a 6-oz. can tomato paste and two 8-oz. cans tomato sauce. To taste, add salt, pepper, and dried Italian seasonings. Cook about 20 minutes. Add one 32-oz. can tomato puree and up to two 8-oz. cans water. Cook another 10 minutes. ✦Separately, cook about 1⅓ cups dry ditalini. Drain. ✦Add one 16-oz. can cannelinni beans, with its liquid, to the sauce. Add more water if necessary to make a rather thin sauce. Add cooked ditalini to the sauce just before serving. ✦Chopped Italian sausage or kielbasa can be added to the sauce for extra flavor. Any raw sausage used should be sautéed first. With or without meat, sauce will be better the next day. SERVES 6.

APACHE CORN

Cook 1 lb. diced, hickory-smoked bacon until it starts to crisp, decanting grease about three times. Add 1 small green pepper, chopped, and cook about 7 minutes. Add one 8-oz. can whole kernel corn, drained, 4 beaten eggs, and pepper to taste and stir well. Cook, stirring, until eggs are fully set. SERVES 3.

MOROCCAN PORK WITH COUSCOUS

Couscous	2 cups canned pork (fully cooked)
2 T. butter	2 T. red wine
1 medium onion, shredded	4 dates, cut crosswise into about 4
1 carrot, shredded	pieces each

Cook the desired amount of couscous in a pot. (To make this a one-pot meal, you could cook the couscous in a steamer or colander over the pork mixture.) ✦In a heavy skillet, melt the butter and sauté the onion and carrot until soft. Add the pork (leftover fresh ham, shredded or slivered, may be used). Stir, add wine and dates. Cook about 5 minutes on low-medium flame. Serve over the couscous. SERVES 4.

On the Side

Preparation of many types of foods well suited to the evening meal are presented in a number of other chapters, especially 5, 6, 8, 13, and 14. One thing not discussed at great length elsewhere is side dishes. Here, I've carefully selected a handful of well-tested side dishes that are relatively easy to make in a camp setting.

BUTTERY TARRAGON GREEN BEANS
LAND O'LAKES BUTTER

1 lb. fresh green beans, trimmed	3 T. unsalted butter
1 4½-oz. jar small whole	1/2 tsp. dried tarragon
mushrooms, halved	

Bring a pot of water to the boil. Cook beans until they are crisply tender, about 6 minutes. Drain, cut in half or thirds, set aside. In a separate pot, melt butter. Add mushrooms, cook over medium heat 3 minutes. Add tarragon and beans, stir well. Cook another 2 to 3 minutes. MAKES 5 HALF-CUP SERVINGS.

BARBECUE BEANS

4 slices bacon, cut up
1 medium onion, diced
1 15-oz. can baked beans, drained
  well
1 15-oz. can lima beans, drained
  well

1 15-oz. can kidney beans, drained
  well
1/4 lb. cubed American or
  Monterey Jack cheese
1/2 cup packed brown sugar
2 tsp. Worcestershire

Sauté the bacon pieces in your dutch oven, stirring well, about 7 minutes. Decant half the grease, add onion and sauté until slightly colored. Add all other ingredients. Stir. Bake about 30 minutes until bubbly hot. SERVES 6.

BEAVER BROOK SALAD

1 17-oz. can French-cut green
  beans, drained and cut
1 16-oz. can baby peas, drained
3 stalks celery, chopped small

1 medium green bell pepper,
  chopped small
1 large onion, sliced extremely thin
1 4-oz. jar sliced pimentos, drained

Combine the above and drain. Marinate in this mixture:

1/3 cup sugar
1/2 cup oil

3/4 cup tarragon vinegar
1 tsp. salt

Refrigerate 2 hours or more before serving, stirring gently from time to time. Better the next day. ABOUT 8 SIDE DISHES.

SUNSHOWER SALAD

2 medium cucumbers
Salt
Cayenne
Pepper

Tarragon vinegar
Sour cream
Paprika

Peel then slice cucumbers very thin. The crescent blade on a two- or four-sided grater is very useful for this. Salt the slices liberally, and let sit for up to several hours. Wash twice in cold water to remove salt. Squeeze with hands to remove most excess moisture. Place in a bowl. Add a dash of cayenne and a few dashes black pepper. Drizzle on approximately 2 T. vinegar. Add 3 T. sour cream or enough to make as creamy as desired. Taste, adjust seasonings as necessary. Add a little more vinegar if needed. Sprinkle with paprika and serve cold.

LIMA AND TOMATO SCALLOP

1 1-lb. can stewed tomatoes
1 1-lb. can green limas
2 T. butter
2 T. flour

1/2 tsp. salt
Dash pepper
1 cup buttered bread cubes, from 2
  slices toast

Drain liquid from tomatoes and beans into a 2-cup measure. There should be about 1 1/3 cups. In a 10-inch cast-iron skillet melt the butter then add the flour; stir to make a roux. Simmer briefly until mixture bubbles. Stir in combined vegetable juices, bring to the boil, boil 1 minute. Add salt and pepper to taste. Add vegetables and toss lightly. Cook on your camp stove on low for 15 minutes. Sprinkle on the bread cubes and serve hot. ◆Alternate methods: Cooking time is short enough that a reflector oven can be used. In this case, use a suitable vessel, such as a baking tin, and cook about 30 minutes, adding the bread cubes halfway through. You could also bake your scallop in the dutch oven, which will give you the best shot at achieving a nicely browned top. SERVES 5.

Meatless Main Dishes

In the breakfast chapter, cereal grains and their preparation are given full discourse. But what wondrous and appetite-filling main courses you can also make with many of these grains. Yes, you can spoon a delicious, velvety, meat 'n' gravy dish over a mound of rice, and yes, you can serve that nutty kasha on the side with beet soup. But what about composed dishes with grains? It happens to be my favorite way of utilizing them.

Here are two with grains and two without. These, too, are essentially one-pot meals. The first is rather involved (though very filling) so make it at home and bring to camp.

VEGETARIAN CHILI

1½ cups low-salt tomato juice
1/2 cup bulgur wheat
4 cloves garlic, crushed
2 medium onions, chopped
1 cup chopped green pepper
1 cup chopped carrots
1 cup chopped celery
1 28-oz. can crushed tomatoes
2 T. vegetable oil

2 cups kidney beans, canned or
    dried and soaked overnight
1/4 cup dry red wine
1/2 cup water
3 T. tomato paste
1 tsp. Mrs. Dash "Original" spice
    blend
2 tsp. chili powder or to taste

Bring tomato juice to a boil and pour over wheat. Stir, cover and reserve. ◆In a large pot, cook the vegetables in a little water until tender, about 12 minutes. Add all other ingredients including soaked wheat and simmer 20 minutes. Adjust seasonings, simmer 10 more minutes. Garnish as desired with shredded cheese, scallions, corn chips, sour cream, etc. Better several hours later or next day. ◆Unless you like your beans somewhat crunchy as I do, precook them by boiling for 12 minutes. SERVES 6-8.

BROWN RICE AND CARROT CASSEROLE

3 cups cooked brown rice	2 T. olive oil
1/2 cup chopped onions	1 T. finely chopped parsley
2 medium carrots, chopped	1/2 tsp. sea salt
1/4 cup chopped celery	1/3 cup shredded cheese (opt.)

Cook the brown rice in a pot. In a separate pot or skillet, cook onions, carrots, and celery in 1/4 cup of water until almost tender, about 8 minutes. Add more water if necessary. Stir in olive oil, parsley, and sea salt. Turn into a suitable baking dish (1¾ qt. minimum) along with the cooked rice. Stir well. Bake, covered, for 20 minutes. Sprinkle shredded cheese on top and bake, uncovered, a few minutes longer until cheese melts. SERVES 4-6.

SCALLOP SPAGHETTI

1 stick of butter	Salt and pepper to taste
3 garlic cloves, mashed	1 pound spaghetti
1 pound fresh mushrooms, sliced	1 pound scallops

Melt half the butter in a skillet. Sauté the garlic with the mushrooms, about 10 minutes. Reserve this mixture to a bowl. ✦Heat a large pot of water for spaghetti. ✦Melt the other half of the butter in the same skillet and sauté the scallops, stirring gently, until they turn opaque (if sea scallops, cut in half). Add mushroom mixture and salt and pepper to taste. Cook spaghetti, drain, then toss with the scallop sauce, incorporating a generous few tablespoons each of chopped parsley and grated cheese if available. SERVES 5-6.

AUTUMN LEAVES CASSEROLE

1 head garlic	1½ cups milk or buttermilk
1 large sweet potato	Salt and pepper to taste
1/2 medium head cauliflower	Dash nutmeg
4 broccoli spears	2 cups heavy whole wheat or
2½ T. butter	multigrain bread, broken into
2½ T. flour	pieces.

Bake the unpeeled whole garlic head for 1 hour (can be done in foil in the coals). Reserve. ✦Peel the sweet potato and cut into chunks. Cut cauliflower and broccoli into pieces. Steam the three together about 6 minutes, then turn into a suitable baking dish. ✦In a small pot or skillet make a white sauce with the butter, flour, and milk (recipe follows). Take 7 medium cloves from the baked garlic, peel, mash well, and add to the white sauce. Add spices to taste. Stir and cook 2 minutes. Pour sauce over vegetables. Toss. Top with bread cubes. Bake in camp-stove oven at 350°F for 20-25 minutes. Can be done in a dutch oven with or without a baking dish. ✦The remaining garlic cloves can be served as an appetizer, spread on toast squares or crackers. SERVES 6.

BASIC WHITE SAUCE

2 T. unsalted butter   1 cup hot milk
2 T. all-purpose flour   Salt and pepper

Melt butter slowly in a small saucepan (cast iron not best). Gradually stir in flour until smooth. Gradually add hot milk, stirring continuously. Simmer 3 to 4 minutes, till thick. Add salt and pepper (white pepper if you have it) to taste. For a thicker sauce, use 2½ T. of the flour. For a thinner one, use 1½ T. flour.

Salad Dressings

A simple, crisp green salad can often round out a meatless main dish that, by itself, might not quiet the crowd. If you've been weaned on those horrendous bottled salad dressings, your taste buds will glory in a crisp salad dressed only with a light vinaigrette. Here's the basic formula. Two other simple but enticing salad dressings may be found on page 215.

BASIC VINAIGRETTE

In a jar, combine 8 T. olive oil, 2½ T. vinegar, 3/4 tsp. salt and 1/4 tsp. freshly ground black pepper. Cover and shake well. ✦The variations to this are endless. Consult any comprehensive home cookbook.

Soups

The best seafood soup I ever tasted was made by the late Eaton "Biscuit" Bartlett, a great lumberjack camp chef who once owned the Maine hunting camp I stay at. Like many great recipes, it is the picture of simplicity. The one following it is also practical enough for many camps.

BISCUIT'S LOBSTER BISQUE
Eaton Bartlett

3 lobsters, 1 to 1½ lbs. each 1 12-oz. can evaporated milk
1/2 stick butter   Paprika

Boil lobsters. Remove meat and cut it into pieces. Sauté the meat in butter in a saucepan over low flame. In a separate pot, boil one quart lightly salted water. Add the milk. When simmering, add the lobster in butter. Sprinkle on paprika. SERVES 6-8.

MUSHROOM-BARLEY SOUP

2 13¾-oz. cans low-salt beef
  broth
2 cans water
1/2 cup whole barley
1/4 tsp. garlic powder
1/4 tsp. sage (opt.)

1/2 cup green pepper, chopped
1/2 cup onion, chopped
1 4½-oz. jar sliced mushrooms,
  drained
2 T. margarine or butter

In a large deep pot or dutch oven, combine broth, water, barley, garlic powder, and sage. Simmer one hour, covered. In a heavy skillet, sauté pepper, onion, and mushrooms in butter until onion is tender. Add to broth mixture. Simmer, still covered, an additional 20 minutes. ABOUT 6-8 SERVINGS.

Desserts

The Freudian needs of sweet-tooth people like me must be respected. Just remember the words of Gael Greene, food critic for *New York* magazine: "I was so stuffed I thought I was going to die—but only a fool would die before dessert."

SWEET NOODLE PUDDING
MUELLER'S EGG NOODLES

1 lb. medium egg noodles, cooked
  and drained
6 eggs, beaten
1 8-oz. pkg. cream cheese, softened
1½ lbs. cottage cheese

1 16-oz. jar applesauce
1 cup raisins, preferably golden
1 cup sugar
1/2 cup sweet butter, melted
Nutmeg and cinnamon to taste

Drain noodles and cool slightly. Turn into a 12-inch dutch oven and mix with all other ingredients. Stir well. Bake for 1 hour. A camp-stove oven can be used but you'd have to halve the recipe. ✦I tried freezing leftovers of this. It freezes poorly. SERVES 12-15.

Chapter 13

TIPS AND TECHNIQUES FOR THE LUCKY FISHERMAN

There is no list of multisyllabic package ingredients to worry about when you pluck a brook trout from an icy pure headwater stream, sauté it over the campfire, and eat it right there next to the tent. No processed, supermarket food will ever compare with such a meal. Bring a fishing pole camping, and the following few pages should show you that these two activities are a match made in heaven.

You can smoke your catch; you can sauté it or deep-fry it; you can make a sassy fish chowder; you can stuff and bake it, over the coals in foil or in a hinged grilling basket. You can also poach your fish, or boil it and then fashion it into some savory fish cakes. You can steam it gently, cool the flaked meat, and serve it in a cold salad with some freshly picked wild greens. You can cook your fresh-caught fish in any one of dozens of different ways. Just be sure not to take more fish then you need for dinner. There are more people fishing than ever, and the endless bounties of lake and river shown all too vividly in the "stringer photos" of old-time camp cookbooks are no more. If you practice "no-kill" angling, that's fine and a personal choice. If you do like to eat fish, greatly restrict your kill so that it's less than what the law allows.

Although many anglers won't acknowledge it, freshwater fish in general are not as good tasting as saltwater fish. Fish from fresh water are also more variable in flavor. It depends on the species, the particular body of water, the time of year, and other factors. You would be wise to at least consider these things when you choose your cooking method. A plain, unadorned poached fish better be good tasting by itself, since there will be little to hide or enhance that flavor. At the other extreme, a very iffy-tasting fish can be made quite palatable when combined with certain other ingredients into the Parmagiana recipe found later in this chapter. In between these two, the camp chef can introduce other flavors in various ways and to varying degrees.

BETTY LOU FEGELY

Some cookbooks give options when they present a fish recipe. In other words, they tell you all the various species that will work with that recipe. Usually, the criterion they use is the relative fattiness or leanness of the fish.

My approach is different. I do talk about treatments for specific species—for example trout, very popular with campers across the northern United States—but when I talk about options, I mention not so much specific species but mild fish, assertive-tasting fish, and strong-tasting fish. Especially with freshwater fish, just listing the species won't work. Trout vary tremendously in how they taste, and so do freshwater bass and many other species. Personally, I think almost all freshwater fish taste dramatically better in winter, and that's one reason why I'm an ice fisherman. Saltwater fish are, admittedly, somewhat more predictable (for example, bluefish will be strong tasting no matter where they are taken from).

Most of the following fish recipes are relatively simple and doable by the average camp chef in a typical outdoor setting. A few, though, are difficult enough to be best left to the well-stocked base camp.

Let's start with the simplest and most common technique for fish cookery.

Sautéing

Technically, there is a distinction between frying and sautéing. The dictionary states that sauté means "to fry quickly in a little fat." In the definition for fry, the word "quickly" is not included. However, in this book I am using sauté and fry interchangeably. When I use the term deep-fry, it means fried in a pan or pot with a substantial amount of oil so that what's being fried is totally immersed in the oil or nearly so.

PERCH ROE WITH HAM

2 large yellow perch roes	Lemon juice
Thick slice from a smoked	Parsley
pork butt	Worcestershire sauce
Flour	Capers
Butter	

Unlike trout roe, perch roe is delicious, especially in winter. Remove the sacs carefully from two female perch. Boil a small pot of water. Turn off heat. After 2 minutes, drop in the whole roes. Remove after 2 minutes with a slotted spoon. ✦Cut the ham (bacon could also be used) into pieces and sauté. Meanwhile, dredge the cooled roes in flour. When ham is golden, drain off some of the fat, then add a pat of butter. Add roes and sauté gently for five minutes each side. Add about 1 T. each of lemon juice and chopped parsley. Add a few dashes Worcestershire and 2 tsp. capers. Stir pan well. Serve each roe over toast, with some of the sauce. SERVES 2.

A hefty northern pike, soon to be dinner for these successful camping piscators.

Onions and French fries, and coffee from an old enameled pot: good accompaniments for a fish dinner.

BETTY LOU FEGELY

Any mild-tasting fish can be cooked by a simple sauté. You can do a whole small fish, but I always prefer fillets these days. By practicing diligently with my fillet knives, and learning the peculiar bone structure of each species, I have found that I can now fillet almost any fish. Whatever route you go, understand clearly that a high percentage of your dining guests will be turned away by fish with bones in it. I admit I almost always panfry very small trout, but most other fish, including all panfish, undergo the knife.

Take the quickly rinsed fillet and dry it on a paper towel. On a plate or on foil or wax paper, spread out a tablespoon of flour. Sprinkle on a little salt and pepper and onion powder if you wish. Optionally, add a little each of either dried tarragon or dill. Press your fish into the seasoned flour then put it aside five minutes to set the coating.

To your cast-iron skillet, add a pat of butter or a little each of butter and oil. Heat the pan to moderately hot. Sauté the fillet about three to five minutes per side depending on thickness. A thin fillet may only have to be cooked 90 seconds on each side in a hot pan. The goal is to get the coating to a golden color, not a burnt-looking brown color, so don't use too hot a pan. Remove the fish to a plate and cover with foil if possible to keep it hot. Now melt a little more butter in the pan, squeeze in a teaspoon or less of lemon juice, add some chopped parsley or one of the above-mentioned herbs and stir and scrape the pan to form a sauce. Serve at once over the still piping-hot fish. Dole out a lemon wedge to each diner.

TRUITE AUX TROIS HERBES

6 five- to seven-inch wild brook trout	2 T. wild wood sorrel
Buttermilk pancake mix	2 T. each chives and parsley
Butter and oil	Lemon juice

Gut and gill the fish and remove heads if you wish. Rinse, pat dry. Dredge in pancake mix. Sauté 3 minutes on each side in a 10-inch cast-iron skillet in which you have heated some butter and oil. Remove fish from pan, split open, and remove all bones and fins, heads and tails. Keep very warm. ✦Add more butter to same pan. When bubbly hot, add herbs, plus a few squeezes of lemon juice. If necessary to serve fish very hot, reheat it skin side down in same skillet. Serve with sauce, garnish each plate with a few sprigs of sorrel with stems. SERVES 2-3.

At lunch time, I like to make a sandwich out of a sautéed fish fillet, but if it's a leftover that's been stored in the cooler I set it outside for a while. Served cold it's not as good. I like fillet sandwich on camp-made sourdough bread, but second to this I like a good quality grainy white bread (preferably fresh made). If you have a little mayonnaise, that can moisten the sandwich. Lacking mayo, use a little extra butter when you cook or reheat your fish and then press your slice of bread into the pan just before composing your sandwich. For a quick tartar sauce combine a little mayonnaise and chopped sweet pickle or green-pickle relish. A slice of sweet or sour pickle is the perfect accompaniment to a fish-fillet sandwich. A bit of lettuce or watercress on top will also elicit a sigh of contentment.

SALMON GASPÉ
BOB AND NAN ZAJAC

In a heavy cast-iron skillet, melt a stick of butter in 4 T. of oil. Add 6 salmon steaks of 1/2 to 3/4 lb. each and season with salt and pepper to taste. Spread sliced onion rings over steaks. Cover skillet, using aluminum foil first then skillet cover, or just the foil if that's all you have. Cook at medium heat for 10-15 minutes. Do not remove cover during cooking. Serve with baked potatoes and fresh fiddlehead ferns. A good Chardonnay would be a wonderful accompaniment. ✦Can also be done with landlocked salmon or trout, preferably specimens over 5 pounds. SERVES 6.

If your first camp meal tells you that the fish you're catching are just a little on the assertive-tasting side, enhance your sauté as follows. Dip the fish in plain flour, then in beaten egg, then in seasoned bread crumbs. Let sit 10 minutes to set the coating and proceed as above. Seasoned crumbs from the supermarket are quite highly seasoned and some even have cheese in them. The flavors they will introduce will serve to sublimate any off-flavor in the fish.

One day at our seashore summer camp, an aspiring angler picked up the fillet knife and decided the time had come to learn how to fillet flounder. The thin fillets turned out a little scraggly, so without explanation I quietly cut them into strips and made the "fish fingers" in the following recipe. Any small or slightly ragged fillets, or pieces of fillets, can be put to very tasty service in this recipe, an original of mine.

FISH FINGERS WITH CHAMPAGNE CHEESE SAUCE
Pop open a bottle of bubbly and first have a toast to your good fishing luck. With the other hand, dip those small fillets or fish strips in milk, roll in very fine plain bread crumbs, and sauté in butter. In a separate small pot, be melting about 6 ozs. of soft spread-type Cheddar cheese ("crock cheese"). A double boiler is ideal but not strictly necessary. For each 6 ozs. of cheese add 1½ tsp. Dijon mustard, a dash of ground sage (opt.) and 1/3 cup of the bubbly. When the drained fish fingers are cool enough to handle, dip them by hand into the sauce. A superb prelude to a seafood dinner.

If you wish to sauté your fish whole or with only the head removed, the problem is this: If you go through the trouble of coating the fish nicely, the entire coating may wind up in the garbage if the person chooses not to eat the skin of the fish. With certain species, like small trout, the scales are so small that the entire skin can be eaten. With other fish, you must scale the fish and then a crisp skin is sometimes palatable. If past experience tells you that the fish before you has skin not to be eaten, skin the fish first before applying your coating. By the way, there is nothing like a good pair of pliers for this procedure. It's worth having a pair in the car or in your camp toolbox. If you do go with fillets, you'll be pleased to see that the flour-egg-bread crumb approach does wonders to stretch a meager catch. In fact, you'll be surprised how much of the crumbs are consumed by the egg-coated fish. Make sure you bring more crumbs than you think you need when you'll be cooking fish this way!

A final tip on sautéed whole fish: You can always introduce a little extra flavor, even if only salt and pepper, by liberally seasoning the inside cavity of your fish. As mentioned, dill or tarragon (not both) is wonderful with most fish. I also use onion powder, paprika, and occasionally other spices inside the cavity of a fish.

Three super coatings for sautéed fish are buttermilk pancake mix, cornmeal, and oatmeal. Because it is so fine, I think pancake mix is tailor-made for very small fish such as bluegill fillets or small brook trout. Of all the fish coatings I know of, cornmeal seems to absorb the least oil. It, too, is quite fine and is good for small fish like perch or smelt. Oatmeal works nicely with medium-sized fish that have been made "pan ready"—entrails, head, and gills removed. If you try oatmeal and find you like it, here's a little tip. At home, grind some regular rolled oats in a food processor for a few seconds. You'll find that this finer oatmeal will adhere more easily to the fish.

When using any of these coatings, or some other one for that matter, be very careful not to let the coating burn. Golden brown is the precise color you want.

On some of our camping-fishing trips, trout amandine has become a tradition. It is at once exotic and simple, and as you probably know, any toasted nut takes on a sublime taste.

TROUT AMANDINE

4 trout, 10 to 12 inches
(smaller OK)
1 cup unsalted almonds, whole,
slivered, or sliced

2/3 stick of salted butter
2 T. lemon juice
1/4 cup flour, salt and pepper added

Gut and gill trout and wipe dry. Chop almonds if whole (you can put into a plastic bag and just pound with a skillet bottom). Sauté almonds in half of the butter. Cook till golden brown, but do not allow to burn! Add lemon juice. Stir, then remove this mixture from skillet. Keep warm. ✦Dredge trout in flour. In same skillet, heat remaining butter until frothy. Cook trout about 5 minutes or less per side. Serve hot with the almond sauce. ✦I like to bone the trout before spooning on the sauce. SERVES 4.

Poaching

By and large, poaching is a method to be matched with mild-tasting fish. Small trout from certain waters lend themselves perfectly to this gentle means of cooking, but it is the regal salmon that is perhaps most closely associated with poaching.

In a fancy city kitchen, a special elongated pan made just for poaching may well be hanging above the butcher block. But in camp, just pull out your largest skillet and fill it to a depth of about one inch with cold, pure water. If you wish—and I almost always wish—make a court bouillon to add flavor to the fish. An easy court bouillon recipe is just ahead, but if you haven't the ingredients or the time, use just water.

Make your fish pan-ready by removing entrails and gills. You can leave the head and tail on or remove them. Wipe the fish well and slip it into the simmering liquid. Keep the flame low as the liquid should just barely simmer. The French would say "shiver" to denote a stage just below boiling. Cover and poach for about 10 minutes, or 15 minutes for a larger fish. Do not turn the fish over during cooking. Using a spatula, remove the now tender fish to a platter. Remove the top skin. Cover tightly with foil to keep hot.

COURT BOUILLON

1 qt. spring or well water
1/3 cup cider vinegar
1 tsp. salt

Several slices onion (or 1/2 T. dry
minced)
1 small carrot, sliced

Combine all ingredients in a pot. (These optional spices/herbs may be added if available: one bay leaf, broken; 1 T. dried parsley; 1 tsp. dried thyme.) Simmer 10 minutes. ✦Place fish in a large skillet. Pour in only enough of the court bouillon so that it is an inch deep. Cover skillet and simmer until fish is opaque and flakes easily.

Now you can do one of two things. You can serve the fish right away with a hot sauce. Or you can serve the fish later, either cold with a sauce, reheated, or whatever. If you opt for a sauce, the classic finishing touch for poached fish, try to have it done at the same time as the fish. Here is an easy sauce for camp-poached fish. You should know that dry package mixes for certain sauces like hollandaise can be purchased in the supermarket, and are ideal for campers. Just be sure to bring the ingredients that have to be added to such a dry mix.

LEMON-PARSLEY FISH SAUCE

Blend 1 T. cornstarch into 3/4 cup cold water in a small pot. Add 1/2 tsp. sugar, 1/4 tsp. salt, 1 tsp. lemon juice, and the grated rind of 1 lemon. Cook, stirring, about 3 minutes until thickened. Add 1 tsp. dried parsley and a tablespoon of butter. Continue cooking just until butter melts. FOR 4-5 FISH DINNERS.

SPECIAL TARTAR SAUCE

Into 2/3 cup of mayonnaise, add 1 tsp. each of chopped sour pickle, capers, and finely chopped onion or shallot. Chill if desired. Good with any cold fish or shellfish. MAKES 1 CUP.

Deep-Frying

Deep-frying makes just about anything taste good, or better, including fish. Regrettably, either the fish or the coating on the fish will absorb at least some of the cooking oil, and guess whose cholesterol count it winds up in? True, you can and should deep-fry with unsaturated oil (many health experts recommend safflower oil), but great amounts of any kind of oil in the diet are not desirable. This is not a cooking method to use every day.

Either of these two batters can be used for deep-frying fish, as well as certain shellfish like clams and mussels.

BASIC DEEP-FRY BATTER

1 cup all-purpose flour	About 2/3 cup milk
1/2 tsp. salt	2 eggs, well beaten
Dash pepper	

Mix flour, salt, and pepper. Stir in milk gradually to make a medium-thick batter, then add eggs. Stir briefly. Batter should be a bit lumpy.

BEER BATTER

Beat 4 eggs very well. Slowly add 1 cup flour, stirring briskly. Add a generous dash of black pepper. Add beer slowly to make a medium-thick batter. You may use about 3/4-1 cup. If you make the batter too thin, it will not adhere well.

Here is a good opportunity to purge the cooler of any assertive-tasting fish. Nonetheless, mild, firm, white-fleshed fish also make for a good fish fry.

The key to deep-frying is temperature: 375°F is about right, but since you're not apt to have a thermometer in camp you'll have to feel your way along. Cast iron can't be beat for this method of cookery, since its heaviness will tend to hold a fairly constant temperature. I use my 10½-inch cast-iron skillet but iron deep fryers can be purchased. These take two forms: large, roughly oblong pans, and normal-sized pots with wire mesh baskets. The large oblong pans are superb if you'll be deep-frying on any regular basis for a large group. For up to about 6 or 8 people, my 10½-inch cast-iron skillet serves beautifully. The nice thing here is that occasional deep-frying in my skillet really helps to maintain that smooth, satiny finish.

After you've prepared your batter or other coating, heat oil of a depth sufficient to cover the pieces of fish. Don't commit to a whole batch—drop in one coated piece of fish and see if the fat is hot enough. The fish should instantly start to sizzle vigorously, with bubbles forming all around it. Further, it should turn golden brown quite quickly. If the fat is not hot enough, the coating will absorb too much oil and will not become crisp. If the fat is too hot, it will spatter menacingly and the coating will turn an unappealing blackish brown. Once you do have the adjustment on your camp stove just right, you'll almost certainly have to readjust for second and subsequent batches.

When you start deep-frying, you'll more often find that the fat is not hot enough. When you get to the second or third batch, you'll usually find that the fat has gotten too hot. Keep testing. It's just like making pancakes. The temperature is everything.

Always drain the cooked fish on paper towels, but don't pile pieces on top of one another. They'll get soggy. It's best to drain them only one layer deep, for maximum crispness. Use several paper plates if necessary.

I suggest that the fish should always be coated, although there is no law that says so. You can deep-fry small pieces, whole fillets, and whole fish. The net effect is pretty much the same, although the cooking time for a whole fish could be a bit longer. As for the actual coating, just flour or flour-egg-bread crumbs is fine, but I like to make a nice batter, such as the two presented above. Deep-fried fish should be served immediately after cooking.

Soups

The early morning scenery on Allagash Lake was stupendous. There were no mayflies visible that early, but there were some damselflies bouncing about. A few of the better fishermen in our group coaxed up brook trout in the 16- to 17-inch class on damselfly nymphs, and when we cleaned them they proved to be of a deep, pink color. Although not all trout are good tasting, these were superb, and the chowder our guide made from them was a one-pot meal nonpareil.

I would make chowder with any firm-fleshed fish that was mild or assertive tasting, but not strong tasting. Unless your friends find you shockingly prepared with a genuine fish stock brought from home, you'll simply have to make up a quick stock in camp if your chowder is to be flavorful enough.

The initial step is to tell your rod-toting pals beforehand not to remove the heads and tails of any fish they catch. These parts will figure heavily in the quick stock you will want to make. If you can, scale the fish. This will prevent unwanted scales from ending up in the finished chowder. (If scales do end up in your stock, just strain it through one or two layers of paper towel.) Then cut the fish into pieces, bone-in. After the fish pieces have simmered in water for about a half-hour, remove all the skin and fins and discard. Also discard the heads and tails, saving the cheek meat from the heads. Stir as little as possible so as to avoid breaking up the meat; the finished soup will then look much nicer. When the meat is finally removed from the bone after the initial stock-making, and added to the pot, also stir as little as possible. You want to end up with nice-sized chunks of fish.

My two original chowders are quite elaborate, but I have made each in a camp setting where good fishing was close at hand. I vary each of these considerably.

For some reason I can't explain, canned evaporated milk makes an excellent chowder. If the first two of these fish soups seem daunting, try the Easy White Chowder. All you need to bring into the woods fresh is an onion—and you won't lose much in flavor. Finally, I've included my original Easy Red Chowder.

DELAWARE RIVER CHOWDER (WHITE)

3 fish, 3/4 lb. to 1 lb. each, dressed, scaled, and gilled
5 cups water
2 slices bacon, cut up
1 small onion
1 stalk celery
1 medium carrot
1 medium potato

2 T. white vermouth or 4 T. white wine (opt.)
Fresh parsley
Dried thyme
Salt and pepper (white pepper is desirable)
3 cups milk + 1 cup light cream (or all milk)
Flour

Cut fish crosswise into pieces. Put pieces including head and tail into a pot with the water. Simmer gently for 30 minutes, covered. Remove fish, strain broth, and reserve. Discard heads and tails. Remove fish flesh from remaining pieces and return this now boneless meat to the strained broth off heat. Keep fish pieces as whole as possible. ✦ In a separate heavy pot or dutch oven, sauté bacon pieces. Add onion, celery, and carrot all diced to the same size. Add diced potato, vermouth or wine, 2 T. parsley, and the fish in its broth. Simmer 30 minutes. Season to taste with thyme, salt, and pepper. When stirring, avoid breaking up fish chunks. ✦Add milk and the cream if you have it. In a separate small cup, blend 4 T. flour into 1/2 cup cold water. Stir until smooth. Now pour this thickening mixture into the main pot. Stir well. More thickening can be added if desired. Cook another 10 minutes on low flame. Do not boil. Garnish each bowl with additional chopped

parsley. ✦Thyme is key to the recipe, but add slowly—it's a potent herb. SERVES 10 AS A SIDE DISH.

FIRST-ICE FISH CHOWDER (RED)

2 T. each butter and oil

2 small onions, chopped

2 carrots, chopped

2 stalks celery, chopped

2½ lbs. whole dressed fish (gutted and gilled), cut into pieces crosswise

6 cups premade fish stock

1 32-oz. can crushed tomatoes

1 can Campbell's tomato soup

4 sprigs parsley, chopped

Few dashes each powdered thyme, cayenne, garlic powder

Big pinch of sugar or to taste

1/2 tsp. caraway seeds

Dash turmeric (opt.)

Salt and pepper

6 oz. heavy cream (strictly optional—do not use milk)

For this one, make a good fish stock ahead of time, at home or in camp. Combine oil and butter in a skillet. Sauté onion, carrot and celery until softened. ✦In a separate pot, steam or simmer fish until done, about 12 minutes. Cool, remove flesh and reserve. Discard heads, tails, skin, and all bones and fins. ✦Heat the fish stock in a large pot, preferably stainless steel. Add sautéed vegetables, fish, tomatoes, tomato soup undiluted, parsley, and spices to taste. Simmer slowly 30 minutes. Adjust seasonings. Add cream as an enrichment, or omit. SERVES 10-12.

EASY WHITE CHOWDER

Gut, gill, and scale two 1½-pound trout (or equivalent) or other mild to assertive-tasting fish. Cut into 4 or 5 pieces each, crosswise, including heads and tails. Simmer gently in 3½ cups water, uncovered, about 30 min-

TOM FEGELY

utes. Remove heads and tails and discard. Remove other fish pieces and from these remove all bone, skin, and fins. Reserve meat. ✦Strain the broth through a paper towel to remove any remaining scales or small debris. Add the now boneless fish meat. ✦In a skillet, sauté a diced medium onion in 2 T. butter until soft. Add this to the soup pot. Then add a 10-oz. can of evaporated milk and a 16-oz. can of sliced potatoes, drained, plus salt and pepper to taste. Simmer gently 30 minutes more. ABOUT 6 SERVINGS.

EASY RED CHOWDER

Into a suitable pot, empty a 10¾-oz. can of Campbell's tomato soup (undiluted), a 14½-oz. can stewed tomatoes, and 8 ozs. water. Bring to a simmer and add 16 oz. (by weight) of boneless, uncooked fish meat, cut into chunks. Simmer slowly 30 minutes. Add a 16-oz. can of white potatoes, sliced, and simmer 15 more minutes. Chill and let sit 6 hours or overnight. Serve hot. ABOUT 5 SERVINGS.

Baking

One June we took a camping trip and encountered the worst blackflies we'd ever seen. Between the blackflies and the other bugs, it was not a trip where we felt like elaborate cooking.

One evening back at the campsite, already past 9 P.M., we took a pair of 17-inch landlocked salmon and baked them in the coals with a minimum of fuss. For each two people we took a sheet of aluminum foil and laid a gilled and gutted fish upon it. Then we sprinkled a little each of salt, pepper, and paprika on and inside the fish. Finally, we laid strips of very thinly sliced onions along the flank of the fish. Fresh lemon was squeezed over all. Then the foil was wrapped up and folded tightly and set directly on the coals. Each fish baked in about 20 minutes, and there wasn't a pot or dish to wash.

Baked fish in camp can be extremely simple, and it can also be quite a bit more complex. A beautifully baked, stuffed fish makes perhaps the grandest finale to a successful camp-to-fish trip.

Foil baking is already given some space in chapter 9. Towards the end of that chapter, I mention the hinged basket made just for grilling fish over coals, and I present one recipe for stuffed fish using that basket. Foil baking as just described is easy, but a genuine, charcoal flavor is just not a by-product of foil cookery. With the grilling basket, the fish is almost completely exposed to the heat and smoke, and since the grill has legs on two sides you simply turn the whole affair over when it comes time to turn the fish. It's a device that I wholeheartedly recommend to the fish-loving camper. It is bulky though, so I don't bring it on every trip.

Lacking such an implement, you can bake your fish directly on a greased grill. Here's where it really helps to bring your own grill, as discussed in chapter 1. The actual grates of the grill you find at the campsite may be spaced too far apart or they may be extremely dirty or rusty. Bring your own and you won't be vulnerable to these irritations.

With a cast-iron skillet, you can bake directly in the coals. Let those coals die down to the gray-ash stage. Grease the bottom inside of your skillet and place your fish on top. Season as desired, and add whatever condiments or vegetables you find in camp: bits of onion or carrot, canned or fresh potatoes, diced celery, fresh dill, whatever. You might want to parboil the vegetables, if they aren't canned, so they won't still be hard when the fish is done. Now, cover the skillet and set it right in the coals. Never set a very cold skillet directly on the coals!

Native brook trout from Maine's Penobscot River. After a day or so at camp, my camp kitchen becomes a cupboard as well.

When the fish is done, the bottom skin may be stuck to the skillet in spite of the oil you rubbed on. It may also be black. Don't attempt to remove the fish from the skillet if that's the case. Rather, serve it directly from the pan. Place a potholder or hot plate on the picnic table. Place the skillet on top of that. Remove the top skin of the fish and carefully lift off the flesh from the top half of the fish. Remove the vertebrae, when they start asking for seconds, and now you have the boneless bottom half of the fish to carefully lift off with a spatula. Left in the pan? The burnt bottom skin, which when dinner's over can be easily removed with a little boiling water and some gentle scouring.

A whole host of supermarket foods come packaged in aluminum-foil trays. Many other foods come in special plastic trays that are microwaveable and also heat resistant. You're making a mistake if you routinely pitch these. Should you end up with fillets at day's end, you can cook these delicate and easily-broken-apart prizes in such trays. First, set your grill so it's about 1½ to 2 inches from the coals. Melt a little butter in the tray. Add the fish fillets and the seasonings of your choice. Turn thicker fillets once during the cooking process. Sometimes I'll add a sprinkling of about two tablespoons white wine and a little lime juice to the pan. I've also been known to whimsically sprinkle on a little dried thyme or cayenne. Chopped fresh parsley is always welcome, and marries well with many other seasonings. Recently, I've been using Adobo, a Spanish blended seasoning.

You could also wrap your fillets in foil and place them on the grill over hot coals. Again, you could add a little white wine or my own favorite, white vermouth (the latter sparingly). For a really offbeat touch, splash on a little Pernod, but my God, who's got that in camp?

I admit, when you start adding liquid to your foil you're not really baking but steaming. But when you have a pleasingly mild-tasting fish, fillet or whole, steaming in a foil pouch is indeed credible. Just make sure you fold the foil so that there is room for the steam to develop. I like certain fish steamed, for example sea bass, but I feel it calls for some kind of sauce. The sauce described under poaching can easily adorn a steamed fish.

Last, but surely not least, fish can be baked in the reflector oven. The beauty here is that you'll get a genuine baked effect and perhaps a browned top, which not all of the preceding methods will yield. Stick to thin fillets is my advice, as a whole fish may take too long. Here, once again, it's hard to beat those little trays that come free with store-bought foods. Place your tempting little fillets, perhaps from perch, flounder, catfish, or bluegill, into the tray and add some butter. Season it the way you like it and set it into a preheated reflector oven for roughly 20 minutes. You can turn the fillets once but it's not strictly necessary. For a gratiné effect, sprinkle dry bread crumbs on top of the fillets. Crank the fire up as much as you can those last 10 minutes to try and brown the crumbs, a sometimes achievable effect. Cheese could also be melted on top.

ANN'S EASY BAKED FISH
ANN FENTON

4 fish fillets, or enough to total about 1 lb.	1/4 tsp. onion salt
	Dry bread crumbs (opt.)
3 T. mayonnaise	Paprika
1 T. lemon juice	

Butter a baking dish, put in fish. Mix next three ingredients and slather onto the fish. Repeat in layers if dish is small. Sprinkle on bread crumbs then paprika. Bake in reflector oven about 20 minutes or until fish flakes easily. SERVES 2.

Composed Fish Dishes

One of the most popular fish and shellfish dishes in America is a composed dish: The venerable and widely varied fish cake. "Cakes" can save the day, and the wasting of fish, when the anglers in your group have been lavishing your camp larder with assertive-tasting specimens.

FASTEST-EVER FISH CAKES

To 3 cups cooked, flaked fish add 1 cup bread crumbs from day-old bread, 1 tsp. onion powder, 1/2 tsp. salt, black pepper to taste, and one beaten egg. Form into cakes, press into dry bread crumbs, and fry in butter until golden. MAKES ABOUT 9.

Now let's shift the locale. Instead of chasing the wily and revered brown trout in pristine mountain watersheds, you find yourself at your shore-based summer camp. Each evening, bluefish have been ravaging baitfish pocketed against the jetty, and each dinner hour has you wondering just what you are going to do with this notoriously strong-tasting fish. Successful cookery here begins the instant the fish is killed.

All strong-tasting fish, which includes bluefish, tuna, mackerel, bonito, and some others, must be gutted and bled very quickly, and just as quickly gotten onto ice. The second key is to eat the fish fresh, preferably the day it's caught. If you do freeze an oily, strong tasting fish, try to use it within a month. (But I have to tell you that I'm not wild about this category of fish after it's been frozen.) Once you have those darkish, robust fillets lying on the butcher block, and the sea gulls outside seem to be daring you to try and make them taste good, there are three main things you can do. You certainly can barbecue them, using a feisty garlic baste. You can also smoke them, in which case they will probably be superb. But if the dark clouds of mid-November are threatening, and the sea is building to the rhythm of autumn's migrating fish, you may wish to stay inside your cozy little camp while the intrepid cast to the suds. In that case, make a composed dish of your strong-tasting fish, using other ingredients that will stand up to those fish.

A hinged grilling basket made just for fish. It has legs on both sides, so you simply turn it over halfway through the baking.

Here is a very adaptable recipe from my good Long Island friends Tom and Tina Schlichter. I have used it several times on blues taken from the mosaic of bays on Long Island's south shore, and have gone on to try it with other fish such as freshwater bass and striped bass. This Italian treatment is tasty and appealing, and is the right thing to do if you need to sublimate some off-flavors in your Pesce Du Jour.

DEEP-SEA PARMAGIANA
TOM AND TINA SCHLICHTER

2 lbs. fish fillets, fairly thick	1 T. water
1/2 cup all-purpose flour	1½ cups dry bread crumbs
1/2 tsp. salt	1/2 cup cooking oil
1/4 tsp. garlic powder	1½ cups mozzarella cheese
1/4 tsp. oregano	1 16-oz. jar tomato sauce
1 egg	1/4 cup parmesan cheese

Combine flour, salt, garlic powder, and oregano in shallow dish or pan. Break egg into a second pan. Add water to egg, and beat thoroughly with a fork. In third pan place bread crumbs. Dredge fish in flour mixture, then dip in egg mixture, being sure to moisten both sides. Press fish into bread crumbs. In large skillet, heat oil over medium heat. Sauté fish, cooking three minutes per side or until golden brown. ✦Place fish in a baking tin. Cover with mozzarella cheese, then tomato sauce. Sprinkle with parmesan cheese. Bake in a dutch oven or camp-stove oven set at 350°F, about 20 minutes. SERVES 6.

Shellfish

Some of the most beautiful and scenic campgrounds in America are located at or near the shore. Because of heavy development in coastal areas few of these could really be considered remote or wild. But whatever the specific locale, there's scarcely anything so wonderful as waking up in a tent to the roar of a good, building surf.

Shellfishing and shellfish cookery have been passions of mine for a long time. The Atlantic coast is my native shore, and the ocean is never far from my thoughts. I must visit it often to fish, sunbathe, swim, clam and crab, and—yes—camp.

It was hard to choose just a few recipes for this section and harder still to omit some important information on the proper handling of shellfish. The space in any book is simply finite. There are many good books on this topic and putting your nose into a few of them is advisable if you're new to the game of gathering and cooking crustaceans and bivalves. These delicious creatures are highly perishable, and no one needs a camping trip tarnished by food poisoning. Above all, keep them cold and alive till cooking commences!

Here's an easy and appetizing soft-shell crab recipe, followed by two superb recipes using the meat of the blue claw crab in its hard-shell stage.

SOFT-SHELL SAUTE FRANCAISE

4 small soft-shell crabs
Flour seasoned with salt and
 pepper
2 eggs, beaten

Butter
Juice of 1/2 lemon
2 T. dry white wine

Dredge cleaned crabs in seasoned flour. Dip in egg. Sauté in lightly browned butter about five minutes per side or until nice and crisp. Add lemon juice and wine to the pan, to form a sauce. Bring to a simmer, stir well and serve. Makes an excellent sandwich (hot or room temperature but not cold), especially if topped with lettuce and tartar sauce. SERVES 2.

CRAB DIP

7/8 cup mayonnaise
1/2 cup sour cream
1 T. chopped parsley
1½ cups fresh crabmeat
1 T. sherry (opt.)

1 tsp. lemon juice
Salt and pepper to taste
1 tsp. chopped chives (freeze
 dried OK)

Combine all ingredients. Chill thoroughly before serving. It will be better the next day. Serve on very thin crackers or with thinly sliced crudités.

GUNNINGS FAMOUS CRAB CAKES

GUNNINGS CRAB HOUSE, BALTIMORE, MARYLAND

In a large flat pan, spread out 2½ lbs. fresh blue crab lump crab meat. Shake over this 1/4 tsp. salt, 1½ tsp. freshly ground pepper, and 1½ tsp. Old Bay Seasoning. On top of this, spread 1½ pkgs. Saltine crackers, well crushed. In a separate bowl, lightly beat 3 eggs and add 4 T. mayonnaise and 3 T. Dijon mustard, plus liberal dashes of Worcestershire sauce. Add this mixture to crabmeat mixture and gently mix the whole thing together. Form into cakes, broil four or five minutes or until golden.

This red cocktail sauce can be used for dipping shrimp, on top of raw clams, and even with certain fish dishes (breaded and fried fish sticks, for example).

TOM'S SPICY COCKTAIL SAUCE
TOM SCHLICHTER

1 cup catsup	Dash celery salt
3 T. horseradish	5-7 drops Tabasco sauce
Dash garlic salt	1 tsp. fresh lemon juice

Mix together all ingredients and stir thoroughly. Chill at least 1/2 hour before serving on raw shrimp, oysters, or clams. Increase Tabasco for a hotter sauce. ◆Bottled horseradish loses its potency extremely fast after the jar is opened. A good sauce can be made only with a fresh bottle.

Mussels can be gathered by hand by almost anyone who is lucky enough to be camping near seashore areas. No equipment is necessary. Clams—both soft shell and hard shell—can also be had for free by the shore-based camper, although here a shovel or clam rake is often needed. In some places, even oysters can be rather easily gathered by hand.

Here is one recipe each for these three shellfish delights. When gathering any shellfish, especially bivalves, be keenly aware not only of what laws might exist regarding harvest, but also what laws or advisories might be extant regarding coastal areas that are off-limits due to pollution.

HALF-SHELL MUSSEL DELIGHT
TOM AND TINA SCHLICHTER

Blend 1 tsp. curry powder per 1/2 cup of mayonnaise and chill. Dip chilled, steamed mussel meats into this mixture and return to shell. Serve cold, arranged on a bed of lettuce if possible.

WHITE CLAM SAUCE

2/3 cup olive oil	3 T. minced fresh parsley or 1 T.
1 T. finely minced garlic	dried
1½ cups chopped raw clams,	Freshly ground black pepper
drained	Pinch red pepper flakes
1 cup clam juice	

Combine oil and garlic in a skillet. Cook over low flame until garlic is barely golden. Add clams and clam juice and cook only 2 minutes, stirring. Add the parsley, freshly ground pepper, and red pepper flakes and cook 2 more minutes. Remove from flame. Cover, let set 10 minutes, then serve over linguine. Garnish with additional parsley. ◆You can use freshly opened hard clams with their own juice, adding bottled clam juice if necessary to get up to 1 cup. Or, you can use minced fresh clams (not pasteurized), available in many seafood markets, plus bottled clam juice if necessary. ABOUT 6 SERVINGS.

OYSTERS BENEDICT

2 dozen oysters, shucked (retain
  juice)
6 slices white bread
6 slices Canadian-style bacon

Hollandaise sauce, from package
  mix
Ingredients called for on
  Hollandaise package

Toast bread lightly and place on warm serving platter. Lightly fry bacon in 10-inch skillet. Drain on absorbent paper. Place bacon on toast. Pour oysters with juice into same skillet and simmer 3-5 minutes until edges curl. Remove oysters with a slotted spoon and place on bacon. Pour hot sauce over oysters. Serve immediately. ✦Fresh, unpasteurized, shucked oysters are available in many seafood markets. SERVES 6.

Chapter 14
GAME MADE GREAT

Game cookery in camp can and should go well beyond the token deer liver and onions. When fortune shines on one hunter, the kill can give strength and fortitude to the others who must still venture high into the ridges or deep into the swale to fill their own tags.

Spit cookery has always been a difficult thing in the outdoors, but now there is a rotisserie made just for cooking over coals. Run by a battery, it's called a Camper Q Rotisserie. Still, the more usual options for game cookery will be sautéing or pan broiling, braising or stewing on top of a stove or in coals, and roasting either in foil or in a dutch oven. Pot Roasting is really braising, and would be included in that category.

There are so many types of game animals found across America that it would be impossible in this book to do justice to all of them. So what we will do is talk about some techniques and principles that have broad application and that many game cookbooks give too little space. When you do get to the actual recipes in this chapter, you'll find that many will be appropriate for different kinds of game.

People have written entire books about the care and handling of game. In the limited space I have here, I'll touch on only a few of the most important points.

Gut your game immediately, no matter who might have told you otherwise. After death, the innards of the animal will putrefy fast enough without a load of buckshot complicating things. You must get them out right away, both to keep the meat sweet and to cool it quickly.

There is no real need to actually wash out the cavity of the animal in the field, but you can take some ferns or other soft vegetation and wipe the cavity out. If there is snow on the ground, take as much as you need to fill the cavity then leave it there for a few minutes. It will rapidly cool the meat and when the snow is removed the cavity will also be much cleaner. Then take a stick of the appropriate size and prop the cavity open. With a bird like a pheasant or grouse, a small stick will suffice. With a rabbit or similarly shaped critter, you may have to use two sticks. With a big game animal, you'll need to use a longer, stronger stick.

Now sit down for a minute. Admire the game, pet your dog, reload or do anything to kill a few minutes. Especially if you had no snow to stuff the animal with, these few minutes will help to rapidly cool the carcass. If you're small-game hunting and the animal must be put into a coat or vest pocket, beware that you shouldn't keep it there too long if it's a hot day (above 50°F). Better to carry it out on your belt. Or, make a trip back to camp and put the bird or whatever in a plastic bag and then on ice. You can also put the tightly sealed bag into any type of clean, cold water (for example, a stream) until better refrigeration becomes available.

Back at camp you can hang the game overnight if you wish but only if the night-time temperature goes down to at least the high 30s. It isn't necessary to hang game, so a safer approach would be to skin or pluck the animal immediately upon getting back to camp. A small game animal can be cooked right away. With big game, you can excise a tender piece as we'll discuss. If you do have ice in camp, put the game on it as soon as possible. I like to wrap fish or game in wax paper first; then I put it in a plastic bag. You might like to use freezer paper or foil. Then again, in camp, you might have to use whatever's there. In any event, if you put the game on ice, try to use a double plastic bag as coolers are known to get sloshy. If you replenish the ice continually, the game will keep for three or four days with no problem. Longer than that, and you'd better either consume the game or head back to civilization to get it into a freezer. It really all depends on the temperature. After 25 years of hunting, I know instinctively whether I can hang game and if so, for how long. Until or unless you develop this intuitiveness, either consume the game in camp or get it frozen, smoked, or otherwise preserved relatively quickly.

Let's look at the primary camp-cooking techniques for game, and try to isolate the principles involved. As I hope is the case throughout this book, those principles should form a basis for many spin-off recipes of your own creativity.

Braise: The Foolproof Method for Game

By an easy margin, braising is my favorite camp technique for wild game, and I use it only a little less in the city kitchen. Nothing's foolproof, you say? True. But here's why braising comes closest.

Braising means cooking in a small amount of liquid. It usually is done with meat, but vegetables and even fruits can be braised. The old reliable and popular beef pot roast is the most familiar example of a braise. In camp, you can braise two ways: in your dutch oven set in the coals, or on top of a stove in a heavy skillet or legless dutch oven. Either way, there are advantages versus other cooking methods.

PENOBSCOT GROUSE

2 grouse
Flour
Butter and oil
Paprika
1 can cream of mushroom soup, undiluted
2 small carrots, chopped

2 T. chopped fresh parsley or 1 T. dried
Dash cayenne
Rosemary to taste (opt.)
2 chicken bouillon packets dissolved in 16 oz. water

Split each grouse in half lengthwise. Clean, removing any shot damage or traces of blood. Cut into several pieces each, bone-in. Breast can be boned if desired. Lightly flour meat. Sauté until golden in butter and oil in a cast-iron skillet. Sprinkle on paprika. Add all other ingredients. Taste, add salt only if needed. Cover and cook about 25 minutes on low flame. Serve with mashed potatoes. ✦Cream of celery soup could also be used. SERVES 2-4.

NOVEMBER 4TH GROUSE

2 grouse
1 stalk celery with leaves, chopped
1 small onion, finely chopped
Butter
Bread crumbs

2 T. flour
1 cup sliced mushrooms (wild ones may be used)
Salt, pepper, paprika

Skin both birds. Bone out the breast on each side. Carefully slice each breast half end to end. You now have 8 thin cutlets. Cover and set aside. ✦Clean and cut up rest of bird pieces. Cover these with 2 cups water. Add celery and half of onion and simmer uncovered 30 minutes. Remove meat and reserve for a next-day snack. Continue heating if necessary to reduce stock to half. Strain and reserve. ✦In a heavy skillet, melt 4 T. butter. Dredge cutlets in this, then in fine bread crumbs. Return cutlets to same pan and sauté up to 5 minutes on a side till golden brown. Remove and keep warm. ✦Melt 2 more T. butter in same skillet. Add flour slowly, stirring till smooth. Add reduced stock, stir well. Add rest of onion, mushrooms and seasonings. Simmer 10 minutes. Serve over cutlets. SERVES 2-3.

Long, slow cooking in a moist medium will eventually tenderize anything this side of shoe leather. Any hunter knows that it's not always easy to assess the relative toughness or tenderness of a game animal before cooking, so if in doubt, a braise is a safe choice. As long as you keep adding liquid as necessary to keep the pot from drying out, it's only a matter of time before your meat will be tender. Keep checking. Cut off a sliver if it's a large piece of meat. Pop a small whole piece in your mouth. It will get there.

Another big advantage of braising is that it's a good way to deal with shot-up meat. With a roast, which you want to keep whole and nice looking, undesirable sections with heavy shot damage can remain. But with a braise, just use your knife as much as you have to. If your erstwhile roast ends up in four pieces, no problem. Just slide them into a cup and a half of bubbling liquid and it will matter not.

A braise can also be a one-pot dish. Throw in the vegetables of your choice, including potatoes if you like, and you end up with only one pot to clean. If it's seasoned cast iron, you'll only have to wipe the pot.

A braise, by nature, lends itself to combining different types of game. Not all game will marry perfectly, but some will.

Braising is much less heat-sensitive than either sautéing or roasting. A venison steak or chop cooked one minute too long can lose its charm. Similarly, a roast that's cooked without liquid had better be tender going in or that dry heat will turn it into what my friend Bob once called a dish of mine: Curry of Boot.

Finally, a bubbling braised dish needs to be watched less carefully, and in camp, where distractions are rampant, this forgiving quality can often save the cook's hide.

A typical piece of meat for braising would be a boneless shoulder roast of venison. Roll it in flour and brown it in some hot fat; that's an essential step in the braising process. The flour is optional, but will add body to the gravy. If you're shooting for a nice, dark brown gravy, brown the meat very well, turning it so all sides get that way. At this point, I like to add the chopped onions and a tiny bit more butter or oil, and then cover the pot to let it all steam together for five minutes. Then I'll uncover the pot, add whatever other vegetables I want, and add the liquid. In camp, you have to be flexible most of the time. If you have only water, that's fine. If you have a bit of venison stock you've brought from home, use that to replace all or part of the water. Canned beef broth or dried beef broth

If you're going to burn wood in camp, there are three things you really need: an axe, a chopping block, and a tarp to keep the wood dry.

reconstituted in the prescribed amount of water can also replace some of the water. This stuff is salty, though, so watch out! For a typical roast of two to three pounds, I'll start with about a cup and a half of liquid total. No pot or dutch oven is completely steamproof, so I will expect to have to add liquid—perhaps even a couple of times—as the cooking progresses. Red wine can be used in place of part of the water, say a quarter- or half-cup.

Penobscot grouse, a one-pot meal prepared here in my 10-inch iron skillet (recipe on p. 161).

When it comes to stews and braises, I'm not a big one for cutting up the vegetables too finely. The bigger the chunks, the more the flavor of the vegetables comes through. I cut a small onion in half, a carrot in three pieces, a yellow turnip in large chunks, a leek in several pieces, potatoes in about four pieces each. And those are the vegetables I use most frequently. Again, what you have in camp is what you use. Sometimes you'll have to use canned or freeze-dried vegetables. If you have leftover cooked vegetables, don't hesitate to throw them into the pot, but wait until the meat is nearly cooked before so doing. If you like your vegetables crisp like I do, cook the meat at least halfway through before adding the vegetables. I like to add chopped fresh parsley when I have it. When the meat is browning, I usually sprinkle on some paprika, salt, and pepper. You may like other spices, perhaps onion powder or garlic powder.

Gravies are one of those things that define the skill level of the camp cook. Keep tasting that pot liquid towards the end of the cooking. Is it flavorful enough yet? Remove the cover to reduce it as necessary so as to concentrate the flavor, or add some Kitchen Bouquet, Gravy Master, or other store-bought product designed to enhance gravies. To thicken, mix two tablespoons of flour in some cold water in a separate cup. Stir vigorously until smooth, then tip into the pot. Otherwise, if you add flour directly to the pot you could end up with lumpy gravy. Special superfine flour, like Wondra, can be added directly and lumping should not occur. If you happened to only have cornstarch use half as much as you would flour. Gravy should always be served very hot. If necessary, reheat it, even if it's inconvenient to do so.

With game birds and most small game animals, braising is not that much different. Instead of venison stock, use a game-bird stock if you have it (see discussion ahead). Also, substitute chicken broth for beef broth. The flour is again optional. With these light-fleshed animals, it is not advisable to brown the meat deeply. Just get it to a light golden brown and add the vegetables and liquid. The ticket is to be creative, and see how well you can do by using what's at hand. That's the real challenge of camp cookery.

Stewing has many of the same qualities as braising. With stewing, the meat is nearly or completely immersed in the liquid medium. The difference between these two similar methods might not always be dramatic, but I usually prefer braised game meat to stewed. For one thing, the individual ingredients seem to maintain their own character and flavor, yet those flavors do mingle together in the juices or gravy that results. With both braising and stewing, you can brown the meat first. But with a braise, the meat (often left in one large piece), especially red meat, seems to retain a bit more memory of the browning process. I want to say crispness, but it's really a combination of taste and texture. And texture is important. A braise made from a slightly tough cut of moose, deer, or elk will be just a little bit chewy, and most people like that texture, witness the great popularity of the good old American beef pot roast. That's a good reason not to squander a real tender cut on a braise. The tougher cut will turn out better by this method. With beef, by the way, no other cut makes as good a pot roast as flank steak (see p. 92).

BAREBONES VENISON STEW

Flour

2 lbs. cubed venison or elk or
  moose (tougher cuts OK)

Oil

5 small onions, peeled

4 carrots, peeled

3 medium potatoes, peeled

3 beef bouillon cubes

Seasonings to taste

Flour the game meat and shake excess off. Sauté in oil in a large, heavy iron skillet until brown on all sides. Do in batches if necessary so as not to crowd meat in skillet. ✦Cut onions in half, add to skillet with 1/2 cup water. Stir, cover, cook 10 minutes. Chop carrots and potatoes coarsely, add to skillet with bouillon plus 2 cups more water. Stir, cover, and cook on lowest flame of your camp stove about 50 minutes. Add salt only if necessary (the bouillon is salty) plus pepper and any other seasonings you like (a few dashes each of cayenne and garlic powder would be good). Cook 20 minutes more or until meat is tender. ✦If desired, thicken gravy as follows: mix 4 T. flour with 1/3 cup cold water. Stir till smooth. Tip into skillet, stir well. Cook five minutes more. ✦Canned vegetables may be used in this recipe. SERVES 4-6.

There is a definite gray area between braising and stewing, but in camp nobody argues about semantics. The underlying trick is to make your gravy or sauce flavorful and seasoned just right, and of the right consistency for what it's supposed to be. Nothing makes a camp cook into a camp chef like a well-done gravy. Just spoon that satiny smooth brown gravy over the mashed potatoes and watch the eyes of the people at the picnic table. If their eyes light up, you're well on your way to being a bona fide sourdough.

Sautéing

As stated elsewhere, I am using frying and sautéing interchangeably in this book, despite the technical distinction.

I reserve sautéing mainly for tender cuts of red meat. That usually means big game. After numerous disappointments, I now usually braise, stew, or occasionally roast small game. Or, I render it into small pieces, often precooked, and then make salads, patés, burgers, sausage, meat loafs, and so on.

The two big-game cuts usually used for panfrying are the loin (along the back) and the rump (upper part of the hind leg). The loin can be boneless whole, bone-in whole or cut into rib, loin, and shoulder chops. The rump can be cut into steaks either boneless or bone-in, depending on your preference, or into roasts or cutlets.

The heavier the implement, the better the sauté. Regardless of the metal used, sides that slope inward somewhat are helpful. First, get the meat to near room temperature; cold meat sticks much more. Take the chop or steak with the end fat still in place and rub that fat on the inside of your heated pan. This may be all the fat you need. Otherwise, add a little oil. When the pan is hot but not smoking, toss in your meat and do not cover. Never crowd meat in a pan! It won't brown as well. Turn the flame to medium high. Season with coarse sea salt after turning. Sprinkle on any other seasonings you like. Get the meat to a nice golden brown color but don't blacken it. Unlike true charbroiled meat, meat cooked to the black stage in a pan will not be appealing. For true panbroiling, get the pan quite hot and use no fat at all. In a hunting camp we go to, our old host and cook, Biscuit, used to really have us thinking that he broiled all our meat. It tasted that good. But he panbroiled every bit of it in old cast-iron pans. As discussed in chapter 8, you can buy cast-iron skillets with ridges made expressly for panbroiling. The ridges, of course, keep the meat out of the fat, and this promotes the crispness that is part of the allure of broiling and charcoal grilling.

FILLET OF SQUIRREL
NICK SISLEY

Like most mammals, including deer and cattle, the squirrel has a very tender strip of meat along the top of the backbone. This is the honored "fillet mignon" of larger animals, but it is no less distinctive from the humble squirrel, which has two such strips. With a small sharp knife, remove the fillets from as many squirrels as you have. Sauté in butter until just cooked. Sprinkle on a tiny bit of sea salt if you wish. That's all there is to it! It's a simple and elegant dish that should be served with a somewhat reserved wine, perhaps a simple salad of lightly dressed greenery, and boiled new potatoes with parsley. The rest of the squirrel, by the way, should be reserved and can be used in stew or some other composed dish.

I like panfried venison with mustard on the side. If it's a cut off a boneless loin, or a small boneless steak from the rump, I like to slap it between two slices of bread and make a sandwich. I slather mustard on top, and I use all kinds. One of my favorites is Pommery mustard. For a different taste sensation, place two cooked strips of bacon on top of your meat sandwich. You could also add a bit of crisp lettuce. A small sweet pickle, radish, or scallion makes an appropriate garnish, but this is a garnish that you eat.

For extra flavor, rub your steak with a little bit of Kitchen Bouquet shortly before cooking. If you've a sneaky suspicion that your meat might be a little tough, sprinkle on 100 percent natural meat tenderizer a short while before cooking. Pierce the meat deeply with a fork as you do this.

With just a few more ingredients, you can embellish your sauté. If fresh vegetables are not in camp, open a can of small, skinless, white "Irish potatoes" and heat them sliced or halved right in the pan with the meat. You could also add a few tablespoons of chopped wild leeks (see chapter 21) or wild mushrooms. Naturally, presautéed onion slices will match up with almost any fried meat. An interesting addition to the pan is thin slices of carrots, especially in combination with the onions. When I mix vegetables, I like to cut them about the same shape and size so they cook in the same amount of time.

WOODCOCK A LA DANFORTH

3 whole woodcock	3/4 tsp. sugar
Oil	2 T. Marsala
Butter	3 T. game stock or water
1 medium-large onion, chopped fairly fine	Flour seasoned with salt and pepper
Several dashes Worcestershire sauce	White bread
	Scallions for garnish

Remove breast meat from birds. Cut each side of the breast in half lengthwise. Cut off both legs as a unit and then divide in half. You now have 6 pieces for each bird. Rinse and put on paper towels to dry. ✦In a heavy skillet, sauté onion in 1 T. each of butter and oil. Add Worcestershire and stir. Cover and simmer 15 minutes until onion is soft and light brown. Sprinkle on the sugar. Turn heat to high for one minute. Add Marsala and game stock (or water) and swirl pan to deglaze. Immediately remove from heat and remove contents of skillet to bowl. ✦Dredge woodcock pieces in seasoned flour. Over medium flame in the skillet you just used, add a little each butter and oil. Sauté woodcock pieces until lightly browned. Do not overcook; about four minutes on each side is fine. Add onion mixture. Meanwhile, toast very lightly 6 slices of medium-thick white bread (Pepperidge Farm "Toasting White" is perfect; or use a homemade white bread). Serve woodcock pieces in sauce over toast. Garnish with scallions or radishes. MAKES 3 APPETIZERS.

If you have a little wine, do this: Sauté the steak or pair of chops uncovered till nearly done, preferably with some sliced onions. Turn the heat to high, assuming you're using a camp stove. Add about one-eighth cup wine, stir energetically for just three seconds, then very quickly cover the pan. Immediately set the heat back to medium-low. After 30 seconds, remove the cover and stir to fully deglaze the pan and you will have a wonderful little gravy for your meat. It will be all the better if you applied a little bit of Worstershire sauce to the meat before the cooking.

The most common small game animals in this country are rabbits, hares, quail, squirrels, pheasant, grouse, dove, woodchuck, and raccoon. There isn't a one of these that can't be fried, but as I've said, my preference leans to braising with most of these meats. Frying and deep-frying are high fat methods that I've greatly cut back on, but many game cookbooks will provide recipes along those lines for small game animals you bag yourself.

Roasting

Roasting meats in a dutch oven is gone over in chapter 8. Red game meat can usually be substituted in those recipes calling for beef. Naturally, anything you braise or stew atop a camp stove can also be done in a dutch oven set in the coals.

You can spit-roast a tender cut of game over the hot coals, using the device mentioned at the start of this chapter or a makeshift spit fashioned from a stick. You'll need a pretty good pile of the coals if it's a large roast. Perfect for this purpose is the inside tenderloin, two flaps of extremely tender meat found inside the chest cavity of a gutted deer. These should be cut out right after gutting, before glazing occurs. Wrap them tightly in plastic wrap to keep the air out till supper time. Just thread the tenderloin, or minitenderloin as some call it, onto a green stick and cook over the coals. The legendary deer hunter Larry Benoit of Vermont speaks about making a moonlight snack of the tenderloin when dragging out a big buck after dark. He brings a little salt and bacon grease into the woods for just this happy occurrence. There really is no better cut of game meat in camp since no outside cutting of the deer need be done. If you are set up for butchering in camp, a boneless loin of venison, or a half of one, would also be ideal. Because its shape is fairly uniform, it will not be so apt to turn on a makeshift spit, if that's what you're using. Its diameter will also be small enough that the cooking time will be reasonable. Should you choose to roast a section from the rump, try to make it not too large a one. If your coals die down before the roast is done you're in trouble (in less trouble with charcoal briquets, since you can always toss a few more to a fading pile).

If you'd like to take a nap or steal an hour for any purpose, wrap the roast tight-

In a more elaborate camp, gamebirds like these grouse can be roasted on an electric spit. The strips of bacon will help to keep them from drying out.

ly in a double layer of foil and place it either in the coals with the coals somewhat piled up around the sides, or on a grill very close to the coals. With the former method, resign yourself to the fact that the outside of the meat could get pretty black, and that this may happen before the inside is even done. With the grill method, you can turn the meat every so often and the outside of the roast should turn out pleasingly browned if the foil is tight around it. Using the grill, you can shorten the cooking time by making a little tent of aluminum foil over the whole affair. Small rocks can be used to hold the foil down over the roast and onto the grill.

ROAST PHEASANT WITH BRANDY
L & L PHEASANTRY

6 oz. mushrooms (canned OK; if fresh, sauté then measure 6 ozs.)
1/2 tsp. salt
1/2 tsp. oregano or marjoram
1/4 tsp. pepper
1/2 tsp. chervil (opt.)
3 cups day-old bread cubes
1/2 cup orange juice
2 oz. brandy
2 whole, well-cleaned pheasants
Bacon slices

Fire up about 25 briquettes and swab your dutch oven with some oil. In your mixing bowl, combine the mushrooms with the spices and bread cubes. Combine the orange juice and brandy and pour this over the bread mixture. Toss. Stuffing should be moist but not soggy. Stuff the birds. ✦Place 14 coals under a 12- or 14-inch dutch oven. Put birds in oven and drape each one with a few slices of bacon. Replace lid and put remaining coals on top. Roast about 1 hour. Remove birds to a serving dish. Warm some brandy, pour over the birds, and ignite immediately. Serve with green peas and warm bread. SERVES 6.

MARINATED DUCK
STEPHEN KAMINSKY,
THE NORTH AMERICAN HUNTING CLUB WILD GAME COOKBOOK

2 ducks, dressed and plucked
1/2 cup soy sauce
2 T. sugar
1/2 cup dry red wine
1 small onion, chopped
1 tsp. ground ginger
2 cloves garlic, minced
2 bay leaves, crumbled

Split ducks lengthwise and place in a stainless steel or plastic vessel. Combine all other ingredients and pour over ducks. Marinate overnight or 10 hours, turning occasionally. Place duck halves in a pre-heated dutch oven and pour the marinade over. Cover oven and bake until ducks are cooked just rare (test after only 30 minutes). SERVES 2-4.

While out fishing and hunting with friends and acquaintances, especially while ice fishing, the discussion will invariably turn at some point to fish and game cookery. I'm always very curious about how other deer hunters butcher their deer—it seems as if no two people have the exact same approach. One thing I've noticed is that few sportsmen I meet cut roasts, believing perhaps that they'll be too tough or too gamey or possibly too bland or uninteresting. I've almost never had tough venison, and I've eaten everything from young does to old bucks. I cut at least two or three roasts off a deer: at least one shoulder roast for pot roast or sauerbraten, and at least one rump roast for traditional roasting. If we're lucky enough to hang two deer, I'll sacrifice the loin chops from one and cut a loin roast.

Cooked to medium rare, venison roast can be served with a pinch of coarse sea salt and that's all. But if you have individuals in camp who balk at the comparative plainness of a roast, then maybe a rich, brown gravy will win them over.

To make a proper gravy, you need drippings. Cooking with a rotisserie won't provide any, unless you fashion a drip pan, something that could be a little intricate in a camp setting. Your best shot at making a real gravy in camp is the dutch oven.

It's worthwhile to look at the constituents of a good gravy. It will consist of fat rendered from the meat and/or added, drippings from the meat which will include some blood, some thickening agent (usually flour), water, and a bit of salt. If it needs to be darkened, a small amount of Kitchen Bouquet or other gravy enhancer can be used.

With a properly trimmed venison roast, you may not end up with enough liquid fat and without the fat you may not get enough browning. So do this. Heat your dutch oven in the coals. Add a bit of oil, about two tablespoons. Now flour your roast and brown it well in the oil. Turn it several times so it's well browned all over. Lay two strips of bacon over the roast. Cover and roast about 1 to 1½ hours, or until done. Towards the end, add a few tablespoons of water to loosen the burnt-on drippings.

Barbecued ribs are one of those dishes where a hinged grilling basket really shines. These are venison ribs, which I parboil for tenderness.

Remove the roast to a warm place and add a big chunk of butter to the oven. Now, sprinkle on about two tablespoons of flour and, using a large wooden spoon, blend it into the fat, stirring well to incorporate as much of the browned bits stuck to the oven as possible. When smooth and pasty, add about a half-cup of water. Stir again and add about another half-cup of water. From one average size roast, you should have enough drippings to be able to make 1½ to 2 cups of gravy (that's assuming you use the bacon and add the butter). A good rule of thumb is that you can thicken one cup of liquid into a gravy consistency with about two to three tablespoons each of flour and fat.

Sprinkle on a little salt and taste the gravy. Add a little pepper if you wish. Cook the gravy for a total time of about 10 minutes. If it's feasible, strain it, but in camp that's not mandatory. If you were smart enough to roast four or five halved onions along with the roast, just leave them in the oven and incorporate them into the finished gravy. Make every effort to serve the gravy piping hot.

If you wish to do a tender beef roast in the dutch oven, the gravy-making process is not much different. With beef, though, you won't need the bacon and you may not need to initially flour the roast (though you may be pleased at the net effect of it).

If you still feel intimidated by gravies, turn to page 65, where a simple and nearly foolproof one is presented.

Besides gravies, sauces of all kinds can be served with roasts. In fact, if sportsmen took the time to learn a bit about sauce making, game roasts might well become more popular. Two sauces easy enough to make in camp are just ahead.

Small game animals and birds can be roasted too, but as discussed there is more risk of ending up with tough meat. One solution is to learn to gauge the age and relative tenderness of the game you have in hand. There are little ways to tell, which if you don't know, can be learned from hunting books, other game cookbooks, and experienced hunters.

RED CURRANT SAUCE

In a small pot, heat 1/2 cup port wine. In this, melt a 10-oz. jar of red currant jelly. Add a pinch each of nutmeg and cinnamon and a dash each of salt and pepper. Add 1/2–1½ tsp. prepared horseradish (depending on its potency) and, optionally, a few thin slivers of orange peel. On low heat, reduce to about half. Good with gamebirds, but especially good with a roast of red meat such as venison. ✦This sauce will quickly regel. Warm again before using.

MUSHROOM-GIBLET SAUCE

In 1¼ cups water, simmer the giblets (neck, gizzard, heart, and liver) from two small gamebirds or one large gamebird. If available, add to the pot any of these in combination: few celery leaves, bay leaf, pinch of thyme, parsley, thin slices of onion. Cover pot loosely. After about 30 minutes of gentle simmering, strain the broth and discard any herbs or vegetables. Remove meat from necks and discard bones. Use only that part of gizzard containing no food matter. Chop giblets and reserve. ✦Stir the strained broth into 1 cup warmed white sauce (see p. 139) to which you have already added 1/2 cup sliced, cooked mushrooms. Add the chopped giblets plus salt and pepper to taste. Serve over your carved, roasted game bird. ✦Two tablespoons of sour cream may be added last to enrich the sauce. MAKES ABOUT 1¾ CUPS.

A big key to ending up with tender wild game when using any dry-heat method (sautéing, roasting, grilling, broiling) is to cook it till just done and no more. In spite of the occasionally very tough old specimen, most small game will be palatable even when cooked by dry heat if you don't overcook it. Always remember that wild fowl is just nothing like today's domestic fowl, which is incredibly fatty and very difficult to overcook. Wild waterfowl should be cooked only to the rare stage. If you've had tough duck you've probably had overcooked duck.

Soups

A soup is often nothing more than a thin stew, although the ingredients may be cut more finely. Some people who say they like thick soups really like stews. I remember that my grandmother hated thick soups. To her a soup was a broth with small bits of meat and vegetables sometimes present. Since I like both soups and stews, I'm more concerned with flavor than degree of thickness, and most of your camping guests will also be very obliging in this regard. But since we've already gone over stews and their first cousin, braises, let's assume here that we want our soups to be comparatively thin and brothlike. The steps involved are a little bit different than with stews.

If it's a soup involving meat, initial treatment of that meat may be the first consideration. For a true soup, don't flour the meat, though you certainly can brown it very lightly if you wish. With game birds, you can boil the heart, neck, and gizzard in about a cup of water and use the resulting flavorful broth in your soup. Eat the heart, liver, and—in some cases only, gizzard—as an appetizer, or toss the heart and gizzard into the soup pot. I would fry the liver like chicken livers, floured and with a little butter, salt, and pepper. Game-bird livers range from delicious to inedible, depending, I presume, on what the critter's been snacking on. To get back to your small-game soup, as you've done with the giblets, you can parboil the meat with or without aromatics like carrot, celery, celery leaves, onion, or bay leaf. A half-hour should do it. Reserve the cooking liquid and bone the meat. That cooking liquid and the giblet liquid, if any, constitute a basic stock which can form the foundation for your soup. Now return the meat to that medium, add the vegetables of your choice, and add a bit more water and/or dry chicken-bouillon packets. Keep tasting it till it's got the punch you want. All this speaks to the underlying, most fundamental principle of soup making: You must balance the amount of liquid you use, or end up with, with the quantity of flavoring ingredients you have at hand. To put it another way, you can't make grouse soup with one grouse and a gallon of water. Stocks and stock jellies of course help, but these are not usually available in camp. The stock you use is usually a quick one that you prepare on the spot and essentially as just discussed.

Red meat-based stocks are also wonderful. I make venison stock every year with cracked bones, but this is a little beyond what most people are going to do in camp. If you do want to try and make a nice little venison (or other red-meat) soup in camp, use beef bouillon, canned or reconstituted, as your base. For the actual soup, use a tough cut like a shank, shoulder, or flank. If you camp a lot and deer hunt a lot, make a true venison stock at home, with a good quantity of cracked bones, and freeze some of it in one-pint containers until camping season. Then just bring them along to flavor your stews, soups, braises, and even gravies and sauces.

With every deer, you'll get four shanks. The shank is the bottom of the leg, just above the hoof, and is usually about eight inches long. I've found that a shank perfectly makes a nice soup for three. Here's how I do it.

TRACKER'S VENISON SOUP

1 venison shank	1 can (13¾ oz.) beef broth or
Butter or oil	venison stock
2 small carrots	1/3 cup uncooked brown rice
Handful mushrooms	Salt to taste
2/3 cup yellow turnip (opt.)	Dash each garlic powder,
1 med. onion	Worcestershire, cayenne
2 stalks celery	

Trim shank of excess fat and cartilage. In large pot or dutch oven, brown well on all sides in butter or oil. Chop vegetables and add to pot. Add broth and 3 cups of water. Simmer about 40 minutes. If desired, remove shank from pot, cut off meat, and return boneless meat to pot. Add 3 cups more water and the rice. Add seasonings to taste. Cover and simmer 30 minutes more. You want to end up with about 5-6 cups of soup so leave cover off to reduce to that amount if necessary. Thicken with a flour-water mixture if desired. I like to slip in a tablespoon or two of white vermouth if I have it. SERVES 3-4.

Here's another tip or two for game-bird soup, which I happen to go for. If you buy the theory about true soups being thin, you really don't need a lot of meat in them. Thus, you can get a main meal out of your hard-won game bird and still have your soup. Breast-out that nice pheasant, grouse, or trio of quail. Wrap the breast meat and keep it cool till you're ready to use it. Now you have a carcass with, truthfully, not a heck of a lot of meat on it. Toss it in a pot with some good clean spring water or natural water and some celery leaves and simmer gently for about 40 minutes. After that step, I like to remove the entire carcass, carefully remove all bone, chop the meat a bit and eventually return the now boneless meat to the soup. I like just about everything without bone in it, when I can have it that way. The two exceptions are T-bone steak and venison rib chops.

Finally, noodles can be added directly to most soups. I recommend small or thin-cut noodles like orzos or fine egg noodles for game-bird soups. With red-meat soups, I prefer to cook up some thicker egg noodles and add them to the soup pot just before serving.

Composed Dishes and Accompaniments

Under braises, we talked about that method's accommodating nature when it comes to shot-up meat. Don't fret about meat with shot damage. You're not a hunter till you've spit out a few BB's at the dinner table, though it's only polite to warn your nonhunting guests about that possibility. But if that old rabbit or dove or woodcock was really centered in your pattern, carefully cut out and around the shot part and salvage every morsel you can. Game meat is sacred, it deserves no less. Now, though, what you have may not even be appropriate for a braise. Not to worry. You can make a delicious salad, which, when served with lettuce and garden tomato on homemade sourdough bread, makes a lunch that's tough to beat.

RABBIT SALAD

Combine 1½ cups diced, cooked rabbit (about 1 cottontail) with 1/4 cup mayonnaise, 1/8 cup sour cream, and 1/2 tsp. each onion powder and poultry seasoning. Serve on a sandwich or on a bed of crisp lettuce or watercress. ✦Will work equally well with many other small game animals, including most white-fleshed game birds. With rabbit, in particular, be very careful to remove all tiny shards or splinters of bone!

By the way, I never soak red game meat due to shot damage. I cut around it. However, I will soak rabbit, hare, or game-bird parts overnight in very cold salted water. This will drain out most of the blood and does not seem to adversely affect the taste or look of the meat.

BASIC BREAD STUFFING

4 cups bread cubes	1/2 T. Bell's seasoning or other
1⅛ cups finely chopped celery	poultry seasoning
1⅛ cups finely chopped onion	2 T. white wine
1/2 stick sweet butter	

Unless bread is day-old, leave on table a few hours to stiffen. Sauté celery and onion in butter until golden. To this add seasoning, then wine. Stir. Pour over bread cubes, toss. At this point the bread will probably be too dry. If I have it, I'll add a few tablespoons of stock (fish stock if stuffing is for fish, game stock if stuffing is for game). Otherwise, a little water or additional wine can be used. Now test stuffing by squeezing it together. It should just barely hold together. ✦Can be used for stuffing game birds, poultry, or fish, and is referenced in several other recipes in this book. ABOUT 6½ CUPS.

You have a wide assortment of savory possibilities to choose from when selecting game-dinner accompaniments. Besides the three recipes which conclude this chapter, here are some other possibilities.

Any tart jam or jelly, either as is or melted down, is an appropriate accompaniment for rich red meat like venison or bear. Red currant, blackberry, and gooseberry preserves all are very fine. Preserved lingonberries go very well with sautéed or roasted white-fleshed game birds.

Lightly sautéed apple slices, along with French fries or shoestring potatoes, are superb accompaniments for roast duck.

Red cabbage is the perfect vegetable for dishes like venison sauerbraten, or even game sausages. The slight piquancy of Brussels sprouts, steamed and buttered, makes them an excellent side dish with most game casseroles.

Wild rice goes well with virtually any game dish.

FRENCH FRIED ONION RINGS

Peel 2 large onions, slice, and separate into rings. Combine 2 unbeaten egg whites, 1/2 cup milk, 1/2 cup flour, good dash of salt. Beat until smooth. Dip rings in batter. Fry in deep fat 60-90 seconds on each side or until golden brown. Serve virtually immediately. Not good served later or reheated. SERVES 4.

WHITE TURNIP WITH CREAMY PUMPKIN SAUCE

4 cups white turnip, diced	1/2 cup half and half
2/3 can pumpkin puree	1½ T. light brown sugar
1/8 tsp. ground cloves	

Cut turnip into thick slices crosswise, then peel. Dice, cook in lightly salted water about 12 minutes or until just tender. ✦In a separate pot, combine the other ingredients and stir well till smooth. Serve hot over turnips. Excellent as an accompaniment to turkey, wild duck, or wild goose. SERVES 4.

BROCCOLI STIR-FRY

In a bowl, combine 1/2 cup canned low-salt chicken broth, 2½ T. white or sherry cooking wine, 2 tsp. cornstarch, and 1/3 tsp. dried thyme. ✦In an iron skillet or wok, heat 1½ T. oil (peanut or sesame oil would be ideal) to hot. Stir-fry one 10-oz. pkg. frozen and just-thawed chopped broccoli, about 3 to 4 minutes. Pour broth over, and stir until mixture thickens, about 3 minutes. Stir, cook 1 minute longer. SERVES 2-3.

Chapter 15

CLEANUP MADE EASY (EASIER?)

I burn most of the fully burnable, nontoxic, nonrecyclable garbage that accumulates in camp. I surely do not have a fire going all the time, even in a fixed or base camp. But around mealtime, I will sometimes make a small fire even if it's not needed for cooking. If I have to burn some paper towels or potato peels from breakfast, I need only give a huff or puff and the flames lick right up. If I see more garbage coming, I toss on a few sticks to build the fire slightly. Naturally, where the wood supply is clearly limited I would build fires of as short duration as needed. But I don't waste a lot of wood in any case. It's very possible to keep a fire going at a snail's pace, even if that means only a few cherry-red coals ready to kick the fire up quickly when necessary.

The specific tangible benefits? One, no unsightly garbage accumulates in the fire pit; it is quickly burned. Two, less trips to the garbage station, if you're in a campground. Three, if you're off backpacking, the more you burn the less you have to take out. Four, no matter where you are, the less garbage there is hanging around camp the less problem with flies and other insects. Five, by minimizing food smells in camp you decrease the risk of drawing in bears, raccoons, skunks, and other raiders.

My next best cleanup tip also isn't about soap. That tip is: When it comes to camp cleanup, an ounce of prevention is worth a pound of cure.

Each year, Americans create a tremendous amount of garbage that has to be toted away by someone else. Often, this volume of garbage is simply testament to a profligate society. Other times it just means that we don't know how to recycle our garbage effectively; we're really just starting to catch on to recycling. Yet in camp, where eliminating garbage is a far more acute problem, especially for backpackers, the best approach is to plan not to make much garbage in the first place.

Now, you may only visit drive-in commercial campgrounds, where you just walk over to a garbage pail to dispose of your refuse. But what if you someday camp off the road? What bad habits do you not want to get into?

Bottles are the worst. They can't be crushed, they're heavy, and they must be taken out, never buried. Avoid bottles whenever possible. Cans are better, but avoid relying on them too heavily. They're nearly as heavy when full, but while they can be partially burned and crushed they then display sharp edges which makes packing them out hazardous, not to mention dirty. And they do have to be packed out.

Many foods that come in a tin can can be transferred to a zip-locking bag. Repackaging is discussed in chapter 18. Some say that plastic should not be burned, as it creates toxic gases. When no garbage can is available, try to rinse used plastic bags and then store them in another, larger bag for transport back to where disposal facilities are available. Plastic bags can and should be reused when possible.

With vegetables, you might take freeze-dried or frozen instead of canned, that way the little pouches can later be burned or toted out, as you wish. With beverages, you might consider the fruit drinks that come in leak-proof, waxed-paper cartons. These, too, can be burned afterward. Consider not only the types of food containers but the foods themselves. With steaks, for example, a bone-in cut will only add weight and the bone will be difficult to burn. Why not bring a boneless steak instead? Another example is fruits. Some fruits have pits that must be discarded or burned, and they may not burn too easily. But why choose these when you can bring fruits like apples, oranges, or pears where the soft waste parts can be easily burned?

Things You Can and Should Burn
1. All fruit rinds, peels, etc.
2. All or virtually all vegetable skins, peelings, etc.
3. Most nonrecyclable paper and cardboard
4. Most table scraps, including boneless meat and fish without heavy bones. Burn fish heads and large pieces of meat only in a very hot fire.
5. Unfinished hot or cold cereals
6. Bacon or sausage grease, or other grease (beware flare-ups)
7. Leftover pancake batter
8. Most soft foods, like stale muffins

Things You Cannot Burn and Must Pack Out
1. Glass of any type
2. Aluminum foil (will be useful in camp even though you can't burn it)
3. Cans (but can be charred to sanitize and soften for crushing)
4. Styrofoam in any form
5. All plastics

It should be apparent that some of the burnables named will burn more easily than others. Adjust the size and intensity of the fire as necessary in anticipation of what garbage needs to be burned. Don't burn things unless they will burn completely. Don't leave unsightly, partially burned garbage in your fire pit. In sensitive wilderness areas, avoid fires, make as little garbage as possible, and carry out everything.

Still No Soap

This tip has to do with water. How easy the cleanup job turns out will be directly determined by the water situation. If there is a tap at the campground or other place where you're staying, be reasonably near it. If you're off the road, but have found a natural water source, don't be farther from it than necessary. On the other hand, be careful of regulations that might limit how close you can camp next to bodies of water. In the backcountry, be an ethical, low-impact camper and try to minimize your affect on fragile watersheds.

One mistake campers often make is that they bring too small a vessel or vessels to hold their water. For example, all they might have along is a two-quart

In a fixed camp, two rubber or vinyl nesting wash basins are essential: one for washing and one for rinsing. During the day, place dirty dishes and utensils in a basin pending cleanup later on.

canteen, which runs out so quickly at cleanup time that they have to make constant trips to the water spigot or to the lake or stream. At campgrounds, I bring both a five-gallon water can and a two-quart canteen. I usually fill the can only once in the morning and it lasts two days. At a hike-in campground I stayed at recently, the five-gallon hard plastic can would have been too bulky and heavy when filled. There we used a two-gallon canvas bucket to good effect. In any case, I tap directly from the large water vessel, and also use it to refill the canteen, which serves primarily as my drinking water.

Burn all fully burnable table scraps. If they are too large to burn, bury them at least one foot deep, but try to avoid this option if at all possible in the backcountry. In a commercial campground you can clean the plates right into the nearest garbage can, but always check to see if there is a compost pit available first.

In a backpacking situation, the best procedure for cleaning up is this. Take some clean water from your water source and heat it. Clean your utensils by the method you prefer, but do not just fling away the dirty water. Rather, walk at least 50 yards away from your campsite and away from any drinking water source and bury the water in a small pit. Use your entrenching tool to cover the pit so it appears natural. At this stage, if you have clean utensils but they have not yet been rinsed you can do one of two things: You can heat some more water to the boil and pour it over the washed utensils. Or, if this is not practical or there is not time, you can take the washed dishes down to the edge of the stream or lake and give them a final rinse. If you end up with rinse water you don't have to fuss with burying it if it looks reasonably clean and is almost soap-free. Just walk away from your site and pour it into the dirt.

You must remember that soap does not sanitize cooking or eating utensils. Soap is merely an emulsifier, which means that it holds grease molecules (and the dirt that clings to them) in a suspension until it is swept away by the dishwater in which the soap has been placed. To really sterilize utensils, wash them in very hot water with a little soap and then pour boiling water over them as a final rinse. A super way to handle the final rinse is to place the cleaned but not rinsed utensils in a mesh bag of the type that certain vegetables come in. Some of these are one-gallon while some are larger. They are also made commercially just for campers. Then, if you have a big enough pot or other vessel, pour some very hot water into it and dip the utensils, bag and all, into the water. The now sanitized utensils thus do not have to be handled; they can just be hung in the bag until next needed.

Before even starting a meal, have your five-gallon can or other large water vessel already filled with water. When you're finished cooking with your wood fire, say just before supper time, heat a gallon or so over what coals remain. Next to the fireplace, have two wash basins, one for dirty dishes and one for rinsing. As dirty dishes or silverware accumulate during the cooking or during the day, toss them into the wash basin. It gets them away from the eating area and keeps them all together. Right after the meal, pour the water you've been heating over the fire on top of the dirty dishes after pouring or squirting on a little dish soap. Now, if you're still busy eating or fixing dessert or coffee, the bulk of the dishes are already soaking in hot, sudsy water. By the time someone gets to them—never the chef!—they will be much easier to clean. As each dish is washed, remove it from the wash basin and put it into the rinse basin or into the mesh bag if you're using that method. As I mentioned, I like to use boiling water for rinsing when possible.

Minor Cleanup Tactics

In the chapter on cooking for groups I mentioned how to encourage guests to see after their own utensils. This applies to small groups as well as large ones. If you're doing the bulk of the cooking you're contributing enough. Ask each person to bring his or her own plate, knife and fork, and cup. They will be inclined to wipe them off after dinner and take them back to their own campsite so they don't get lost. This means fewer dishes and silverware clogging up your own basins.

Cast iron should not be scrubbed vigorously nor soaked in soapy water. Care and cleaning of cast iron is discussed thoroughly in chapter 8.

Pots other than cast iron or those with nonstick finishes require less tender loving care. Eating dishes seldom have to be scrubbed, but pots often do, and here we get into the subject of abrasives.

First, you should always try to use as little soap as you can. If water is limited, you may not be able to completely clean a heavy soap film away, and soap residue may well make

A three-wash-basin system for dishwashing: hot soapy water, then hot clean water, then hot clean water again for the final rinse. Ideally, the last rinse should be boiling hot.

you sicker than the substances it's intended to remove. To be able to cut down on the amount of soap you use, follow these simple guidelines: Clean vessels and utensils as soon after cooking as possible, use soapless cleaning pads when possible, use lots of boiling water when feasible.

At the campground, my favorite type of cleaning pad is a sponge with an abrasive surface on one side. Some manufacturers call this a scrub sponge. Often, I find that I can clean pots quite well with hot water and this abrasive pad. It works best, by far, when the pot and the food remnants in it are still warm. The day will come, though, when you've burned some stew or chili into a tenacious coating that resists most cleaning efforts. For such cases, I do like to have along a few standard soap pads. They are tough to beat with badly burned pots or situations where there is a heavy grease residue. Soap pads rust very quickly after use, often, regrettably, before you've used the soap you paid for. An economy trick is to just tear or cut the pad in half. This goes for soapless steel wool as well. Another type of scouring pad is one made of fine, copper wire fashioned into a sort of loose ball. This often works on very badly burned pots when even a steel-wool soap pad won't cut it. Finally, if the pot just won't come clean, gently boil some water in it. In minutes the food should loosen and be easily scrubbed away. In the most severe cases I have found a stainless-steel (soapless) scrub pad to be the only answer. This will actually start to gouge your aluminum pots so it's a last resort for sure. Better to pay attention to what you're doing and not burn the pot that badly in the first place.

I always try to use what is called biodegradable soap, at campgrounds and while backpacking in particular. Experts say such soap is not completely harmless to the environment, so I never use any soap flagrantly.

In certain places where biodegradable soap seems to be an unnecessary precaution, you can use the same liquid dish soap you use at home. This is concentrated and goes a long way. All you need for a weekend camping trip is a few liquid ounces, which you can transport in a small bottle.

I've already trumpeted about how it's best to avoid making a lot of garbage in the first place. You can avoid other types of unpleasant cleanup, too. For example, any time you camp where there are picnic tables use a cheapie plastic tablecloth. It is nonporous so it rarely stains, and food wipes off it quickly and cleanly. Spill some food on wood, by comparison, and you often have a mess on your hands. Wood will not only absorb the food as you try to cloth it away, but it will absorb odors that will invite over such persona non grata as yellow jackets and ants. The disposable type of tablecloth may last only a weekend or two; this kind you may not even have to clean at trip's end, just toss it. But I use a somewhat better one, which lasts a season, and which needs to be cleaned thoroughly before it's packed away. Whatever your choice, do bring a tablecloth, and make sure it's plastic.

Immensely useful to have along on any camping trip are plastic bags in different sizes. I routinely leave several sizes in a box that stays permanently in my car. I'll have some that are one gallon in size and are perfect for storing food and a host of other things. I might also have a few each of four gallon, eight gallon, and thirteen gallon. Finally, I make sure to have at least several of a size that would line a garbage can—generally, 26 gallons and heavy duty. Many times, I've gotten to a campground and the can was missing a liner or the attendant just hadn't replaced it yet. Also, sometimes I find that the garbage can nearest my site is full or too far away. Then I'll simply prop open one of my own bags and I'm thus prepared for the situation. In the outdoors, even at a very civilized campground, don't count on things always being there. Be as prepared and self-sufficient as possible.

MIKE BLEECH

Part Two
LIGHTWEIGHT CAMP COOKERY

Way back on page one of this book, I explained how many of the ideas, techniques, and recipes presented in Part One—General Camp Cookery—would have substantial application to a backwoods kitchen. Part 1, in many ways, is for all campers.

To a more limited extent, the material to follow here in part 2 could be of service to the campground goer, or even to the owner of that little cabin in the woods described on page one.

For example, if you camp primarily where the vehicle is only paces away, you still may shrink from the thought of extensive cooking (and extensive cleanup) outdoors. In that case, these simpler recipes and procedures might seem less daunting to you.

In spite of this reciprocity between the two parts of this book, part 2 is most definitely a section of specialized information aimed primarily at the backpacker.

We live our whole lives with literally tons of personal property at our disposal, and when it comes time to reduce that to forty-three pounds it can be quite a shock. To dealing with that shock, a goodly part of part 2 is dedicated.

Depending on where and when you camp in the outback, safety can be a big factor. So, one's pack is first and foremost the repository for a good shelter, a snug bedroll, and just a little more than enough clothing to keep you warm. To also eat well, you have to have a well-honed system and a deft hand at embellishing what meals you are able to put together given the weight restrictions.

Ingenuity, resourcefulness, adaptability—these are the attributes of the accomplished backwoods chef. But it all starts with good planning.

Chapter 16
GENERAL TIPS AND MENU PLANNING

I doubt there is a more organized outdoor group than backpackers. I tend to be quite organized, so ounce-by-ounce planning came easily to me. But I have some true, shoot-from-the-hip outdoor amigos who wouldn't any more write up a checklist than they would make their bed first thing in the morning. These spontaneous souls, though, still get their acts remarkably together before a backpacking trip. True backwoods travel demands organization, as any challenge-the-wilderness neophyte has learned after one or more miserable experiences.

Meal-by-Meal Planning

I indicated somewhere in part 1 that I usually have some general idea of what I'm going to cook on a campground trip. It is only with this general sense that I am able to bring from home the various spices, condiments, and other things I will need (buying duplicates of things like mayonnaise or relish or onion salt at the campground store, especially for only a two- or three-day trip, is just a waste of money). Yet on most camping trips near the car or near civilization, I let the menu pretty much unfold in its own way.

You can't do this on a backpacking trip. You just won't be able to carry enough provisions to allow you to wing it three times a day. Yes, some flexibility is always possible, but virtually all skillful backpackers plan their trail cooking meal by meal. Start with a written menu for your trip at least two weeks ahead of time. It's amazing how fast time slips by. If there are some things on your menu that are going to have to be mail ordered, then you should prepare your menu two months or more ahead. Otherwise, if there is a good backpacker's store near you, two weeks should be enough.

If when you write your menu you are very specific, what spices and condiments you need will become obvious. You don't necessarily have to list these, but if you have a food checklist separate from the actual menu—a good idea—you might just as well include honey, salt, dry mustard, and so on.

As I write this, it is late April. One month hence I will be taking a three-day back-packing/fishing trip in my home state of New York. Here's the menu. (Note that I usually keep backpacking lunches quite simple, and often skip them completely.)

Friday 5/19

Lunch
    Cheese and crackers

Dinner
    Fruit juice
    Venison chops
    Fresh green salad
    Corn (from dry)
    Fresh bread
    Cookies

Saturday 5/20

Breakfast
    Coffee
    Fresh eggs
    Dried fruit
    Fresh bread
    Fruit drink

Lunch
    Gorp (a mix of raisins, peanuts, etc.)

Dinner
    Trout amandine
    Sweet hot cider (from dry)
    Vegetable medley (from dry)
    Tomato rice soup (from dry)

Sunday 5/21

Breakfast
    Coffee
    Cream of wheat cereal with dried fruit
    Pancakes (from dry)
    Maple syrup (from dry crystals)

Lunch
    Cheese and crackers
    Fresh birch tea
    Honey (dried crystals)

This menu will serve to make several points. First, I consider this to be a reasonably healthy menu. The venison, brought in frozen, is quite lean. The cheese is natural Cheddar. The crackers are natural whole wheat from the health food store. The cookies I make myself, and I replace sugar with honey and molasses. The freeze-dried foods I choose are labeled as all natural (see chapter 20). I always buy organic eggs. The fruit drinks are natural and come in paper containers for easy disposal.

Note that I list trout on the menu. The general wisdom is that you never count on fish or game you might procure. Let it be strictly a bonus, the cautious urge. But if we don't catch any trout on this trip, I make a point to always keep an extra freeze-dried meal in the pack. An important asterisk to this: The trip in question is not a strenuous one. On long, arduous trips, or ones taken in winter, the best advice is to plan not to skip any meals and in fact to bring extra provisions.

It's standard procedure and smart to plan to use the bulkiest items early in your trip. This is reflected in the first three meals listed. By the way, if you relish some fresh meat, bring it frozen wrapped in aluminum foil and a plastic bag and it should be fine for at least a day. Except in the hottest weather, it won't even thaw out for a half-day or more. It is axiomatic that the best backpacker's meals fall on the first day. Fresh is best, so push your less exciting dried stuff to the later stages of the trip.

Hunting for and using wild edibles is part of camping for me. On the last day of the trip I plan to make birch tea (see chapter 21) which is a certainty since I know there is black birch where we are going. Although not listed, I'll also look for wild leeks and toss them in with the venison chops. The good thing about wild edibles is that many types are there in the same spot year after year. Certainly, trees will be.

It's best to plan your food meal by meal and, often, one package per meal.

Backpacking checklist Date **6/18** Trip *Trout, Mud Ponds*

Main Equipment

✔	96	Backpack
✔	64	Tent
✔	64	Sleeping bag
✔	16	Ground pad
✔	18	Outdoor kitchen
✔	8	Stove
✔	12	Fuel
✔	32	Camera
✔	12	Frypan
NO	2.5	First aid kit
✔	28	Cook set
✔	9.5	Saw
✔	9	Mini kit
✔	5.5	Grill
—	—	
—	—	

✔	15	Canteen, empty
✔	2.5	Small towel
NO	4	Sunglasses
✔	2.5	Parachute cord
✔	1.5	Toilet paper
✔	2.5	Flashlight
✔	.5	Paper towels
✔	1	Insect repellent
✔	1	Compass
✔	1	Butane lighter
✔	2	Trowel
✔	1.5	Mirror
✔	1	Map
✔	--	Plastic bags
—	—	

Total ozs **413**   Lbs. **26**

Clothing

✔	58	Boots
✔	32	Sweat shirt
✔	20	Wool jacket
✔	16	Mocassins
✔	12	Rain parka
✔	22	Pants
✔	16	Belt with knife
✔	12	Flannel shirt

✔	6.5	T shirt
✔	5.5	Underwear **2**
✔	3	Hat
✔	7	Socks **2**
—	—	
—	—	
—	—	

Total ozs. **210**   Lbs. **13**

Less worn **7**

Actual **6**

Special gear

✔ **16** *Pack rod set*
✔ **48** *Light waders*
✔ **16** *Wading sneakers*

—	—	
—	—	
—	—	

Total ozs. **80**   Lbs. **5**

Total lbs. less food **37**

Approx. food this trip **6**

Total **43**

Weight Considerations

Generally, cookware and food are among the more adjustable items in your back-pack. The weight of your pack, tent, bedroll, stove, and fuel are pretty much fixed. Your clothing will also be pretty much fixed, although determined by the season. Because of this, I work backwards when determining how much my food can weigh.

A man of average build and good physical condition can hike several miles a day with 45 pounds if his pack is well fitted. A woman of similar description can carry 35 pounds. Now there are all kinds of things that can alter these figures up or down: age, experience, conditioning or lack of, and many others. For the sake of this discussion, let me say that while I have carried 50-55 pounds, I shoot for the 45-pound figure. I camp mainly between spring and fall when the weather is reasonably good, and with a little cutting I can often get the figure down to 40 pounds. That's better if you're climbing mountains. I once traveled hut-to-hut in New Hampshire's White Mountains, where I heard that one of the hut work-ers—a college-age man—routinely carried 100 pounds of garbage up a hill several times a week. For the merely mortal, let's take that figure of 45 pounds and see how we're going to use it.

I thought it would be useful to present my entire backpacking checklist. This will enable me to show how my cookware and food fit in with my gear.

In chapter 1, I present some general tips on creating and using checklists. With my backpacker's list, I follow the same concept but here I leave room to ink in the weight of all items.

This is, as noted, my master checklist. It is the only formal list I use. I do not have similar forms for menus, food lists, and so forth. Those I simply write long-hand as a trip approaches. But from this master list I make photocopies and use one for each trip. As you can see, I leave room for the date and place of the trip. I always save these for future reference.

Since the main equipment varies hardly at all from trip to trip, I have typed in the weights of all the items on the original. Similarly, I have typed in the weights of all the clothing items. I find that this varies little, too, although I may add or delete a garment as weather dictates. I should note that the clothing includes items worn. To get the weight of my pack, for baseline comparisons, I just deduct the appropriate amount, in this case seven pounds (clothing plus boots).

Under each of these two subheadings, Main Equipment and Clothing, I leave room for additions—the blank lines. If I wish not to take an item listed I write "No" next to it. On this trip you can see I plan to add no items but I do plan to delete sunglasses and first-aid kit (often when I make deletions it is because someone else on the trip will have the item or items). Usually I can finalize the Main Equipment and Clothing sections of the list two weeks in advance. The weights are listed in ounces, so I divide by 16 and place the weight in pounds in the lower right-hand corner. In this case, the main equipment and clothing total about 39

Author's backpacking checklist, as used for an actual trip. See discussion in text.

pounds, less seven for clothing worn equals 32 pounds. Then I move on to the section titled Special Gear.

This could be fishing tackle, hunting equipment, photo accessories, field guides, or whatever. On this trip it will be fishing and as you can see I will be bringing three separate items that will weigh a total of about five pounds. Now I have a total weight of 37 pounds. Shooting for the 45-pound figure, that leaves me eight pounds for food, more than what my food will weigh. When this situation arises, I can either go with the lighter pack, or consider what little luxury I can tuck in. This may well be a small bottle of Drambuie or some other cordial. I also like to bring fresh bread or rolls when I can fit them in. I might even look at the fishing equipment list and see what else I'd like to bring that might make my angling efforts more fun or productive.

By the way, the general wisdom is that backpackers should plan on carrying two pounds of food per person per day.

Seasonal Considerations

I've already indicated that the winter camper must pay more attention to food and drink. You expend more calories in winter, largely because your body uses great amounts of fuel just in trying to keep you warm. For example, an average male who burns 2,500-3,000 calories a day in summer could burn 4,000-6,000 during very strenuous winter hiking or expeditioning. This poses a dilemma: He must bring more clothing and yet he also must bring more food (or more calories). One

You need a system for backpacking. Food and cookware are often best stored in a pack's outer pockets.

TOM FEGELY

approach is to delete all fresh food and drink and rely strictly on dried foods. What usually happens, though, is that the winter pack simply gets heavier, and often by a hefty degree. The upshot is that winter campers must take a far more serious approach to what they're doing. Here are a few of the more important and better known tips for winter backpacking food needs.

The trail snacks that you might skip in summer should most surely be added onto your trip menu. Keep them as lightweight as factors dictate, but keep them. For a quick energy boost on the trail, carbohydrates are what you want. That's because carbos, namely starches and sugars, are very quickly assimilated into the bloodstream and the body starts to metabolize them almost instantly. In the metabolizing or burning process, both energy and heat are released, the heat being a big bonus in wintertime. Candy bars, chocolate, cookies, sugared dry fruits, and hard candies are commonly relied upon quick-energy foods. If white sugar is anathema to you, buy or better yet make trail snacks that incorporate honey instead of sugar. Some carbos make better trail snacks than others. For example, chocolate is assailed by some health-food experts. You'd be well advised to explore that topic via the books that discuss nutrition for backpackers in more detail.

This is not to say that you should skip fats and proteins in winter. These food groups also fuel the body, but they are metabolized more slowly so energy is yielded over a longer period of time. Eating some protein at the evening meal could help you sleep warmer that night.

Some outdoor writers claim that increased salt intake in winter will help to keep you warm. This theory holds that lack of salt dehydrates the body, and draws blood towards the body core and away from the extremities—toes, fingers, ears—where frostbite is most likely to occur.

Alcohol to excess is always a taboo in the backcountry, but it is especially unwelcome in winter. Alcohol constricts your blood vessels, making you colder.

To sum up, winter camping requires a higher overall caloric intake and much more general attention to meal planning. Think of winter camping as a survival contest, almost a different activity from summer camping. Then approach it with the respect it deserves.

In summer, you may need fewer calories and you also may have somewhat less of a need for a carbo rush from quick-energy foods. Nonetheless, the expected fair weather can lull you into a complacency that can be dangerous. At most latitudes, the real problem lies in spring and fall: the unpredictable seasons. Summer may indeed be euphorically pleasant, while in winter you will be soberly prepared. But in spring and fall you can let your defenses down. As proof, hypothermia most often occurs not in true winter conditions but when the air temperature is between 35°F and 55°F. My advice is that you approach spring and fall backpacking with the utmost thoughtfulness.

In high summer, water may be a larger concern than food; see chapter 18. There are some food concerns, though, beyond the dilemma of perishability, and one of them is salt. I don't carry salt tablets but I do bring salt and I use it more liberally in summer. I don't go hog wild, though, because I have a slower than normal metabolism and I do not sweat profusely. No two people are the same, but in general you will need some salt in summer to replace the salt lost through the skin. Fortunately— or unfortunately—salt is a common ingredient in most processed foods.

Some General Considerations

It's wise to consider your backpack meals within the framework of your planned activities. As an example, one good rationale for simple lunches is that you just may be too busy at midday to cook. On the other hand, the trail ahead may be one of many hours, so there could be an impetus for a relatively fast breakfast. I'd say, though, that the worst meal to skip is breakfast, and the second worst, lunch. In winter, all meals are important; a good dinner, as already mentioned, helps keep you warm.

Prepackaging is a vital part of planning backpack meals and menus. This discussion, though, is relegated to chapter 18.

Accomplished woodsmen develop systems, because something that has worked before will work again. As an illustration, you might want to allocate all your cookware to one part of your pack and all your food to another. If there is no other wisdom to this, at least you will always know where to find things, even in the dark. Both my food and cookware go into outside pockets on my backpack. This way, if something leaks or an egg breaks, the chances of my clothing being glopped up are minimal. When I get to the campsite, however, I make a change. With my sleeping bag and tent and other things out of the main compartment of my pack, I now use that compartment for food storage. I'll take the stuff sack that the sleeping bag came in, or possibly the one that houses my cookset, and place all the food in it. Then at night, when it comes time to hang the food to thwart the critters, the food is together and I don't have to go rummaging around in the dark. If we move on to a new site, the remaining food will go back into the same outside pockets.

Home preparation can be valuable, even before prepackaging. For example, if a lengthy or much-anticipated trip is in the offing you want to do everything you can to see that nothing undermines your vacation. You could, for one thing, practice pack: load your pack fully to see if everything fits and if there is room left for anything. You might also plan in detail your departure day, since such days can be critical. Will you be picking up some last minute fresh foods on the way, and if so, will there be a store en route and will it be open? When you're leading a group, such details can make or break the whole group's trip.

Do your shopping for the trip ahead of time—way ahead. It's certain that if you go to the backpack store on the day before your trip they will have just sold their last freeze-dried meal. Or their last stove of the type you wanted. Or their last canister of butane. Do it now. If it's something that requires testing, for example a new stove or a complex procedure, also do that in advance.

One of the biggest mistakes outdoor trippers make is that they plan on buying something on the way. Country stores are great, and I find them as charming as the next person. But when I get in my car to leave for a backpacking trip I like to have nothing to pick up en route. When my companions are scurrying around look-

A minimum-impact fireplace. A small bed of coals are contained within the two logs, which also serve to support a small pot. As long as you constantly watch your fire, you may not need many (or any) rocks for containment. In any case, try to keep rocks far enough from the fire so flames can't blacken them.

have nothing to pick up en route. When my companions are scurrying around looking for this or that necessary item, I can luxuriate in the fact that I have 45 minutes to take a nap on the grass outside the store. It doesn't always work out that way, but I try. By all means, if you do plan to pick up food or cookware, try to make it the less critical items on your checklist.

Bringing the right cooking implements and correctly transporting your food and water are essential parts of the planning process. The next two chapters contain information that should be considered long before you anxiously pull up to the spot marked Trailhead.

Chapter 17
STOVES, COOKSETS AND OTHER TOOLS

There are three primary types of backpacking stoves: those that use gasoline, those that use liquid petroleum gas (LPG), and those that use any one of several different fuels. There are also two secondary types of lightweight, single-burner backpack stoves: wood and liquid alcohol (as opposed to jelled alcohol like Sterno).

Here are the essential considerations when purchasing such a stove:

1. How the stove meshes with your personality and particular camping style
2. Ease of operation
3. Portability (packability may be more accurate)
4. Dependability
5. Safety (These stoves are very safe, but when you're far from civilization, any product or product feature that could possibly hurt you should be looked at.)
6. Speed/fuel efficiency
7. Stability
8. Adjustability

Item 1 is probably most important. If you have a mechanical bent, you might love the traditional gasoline stove that needs to be primed and tended. If you hate fussing and mechanical procedures, you might better stick to an LPG stove. If you're a real lightweight fanatic, you'll look to the lighter stoves in any category. If perfect silence in the outback is not something you thrive on you might like what Colin Fletcher called "the homey roar of the Svea" (a type of gasoline stove).

Ease of operation is self-explanatory, but most often would refer to exactly what you have to do to get the stove lit.

Portability centers around the concern of weight (backpacking stoves range from

The venerable Svea gasoline camp stove, above. The windscreen being placed on serves double duty by securely holding a pot of the right size. The Sigg Tourist cook set is made for use specifically with the Svea. Below is the Bluet butane single-burner stove: extremely simple to use and quite light in weight.

about five ounces to about two pounds) but it can also refer to the shape of the appliance and its fuel tank and fuel lines if these are separate.

Dependability means just that, but frequently refers to how the stove performs in cold weather.

Safety is always a consideration when you're dealing with flammable substances.

Speed is extremely important. Most backpackers want to eat as quickly as possible when base camp is reached. A backpack stove's primary reason for being is to boil water. How fast it does that is really what it's all about.

Stability refers to how well the stove sits on the various surfaces a backpacker is likely to encounter. It also refers to how stable the pots and pans the stove must accommodate will be on top of that stove.

Adjustability refers to how much—and indeed whether or not—you can set back the flame from full-burn to simmer speed.

Which Type is for You?

GASOLINE STOVES. Most backpacking stoves that use gasoline require a pure type of gasoline typified by the familiar Coleman Fuel. As with the larger camp stoves discussed in part 1, some backpacking stoves now can burn ordinary unleaded gasoline.

The hottest, quickest, single-burner stoves are found in this category. Not only are they fast to boil water, but they're very dependable in cold temperatures, something not true of all LPG stoves. These stoves are efficient, meaning that you get a lot of burning time per unit of fuel. There are no empty canisters to haul back as with LPG stoves (but if the stove has a separate tank, or if you bring a fuel bottle, that can add up to quite a few ounces).

There are two types of gasoline stoves: those with a pumping mechanism and those without. Many serious backpackers prefer the pump-type gasoline stoves although some think they're not the most dependable due to the (small) possibility of the pump mechanism failing. Nonetheless, with a pump stove you have all the attributes named in the above paragraphs, but you save the priming and tender loving care that is required of gas stoves of older design. We get back to personality here. Gadgeteers might actually like to carry a little service kit, an eye dropper, and possibly a special stove primer. These same traditionalists might also not mind waiting a minute or two to actually have a flame you can cook on.

LPG STOVES. Since we're hot on the trail of ease-of-operation, that's the big selling point here. An LPG stove is one that burns propane, butane (the two are not interchangeable), or a butane-propane mixture. The main advantage of stoves in this category is that you turn a valve, light a match, and you're in business. No priming or pumping. Most of these stoves burn quite hot, and thus fast, but not quite as hot on average as the gasoline stoves. These stoves offer good adjustability, and usually simmer very well.

The disadvantages are several. They are known for poor performance in cold weather, meaning, generally, temperatures below the freezing point (but read on). These stoves are less efficient in that the ratio of burning time to fuel bulk is not as favorable as with gasoline. And, you have those bulky containers to haul out at trip's end. With LPG stoves, the heat diminishes somewhat as the fuel level in the canister drops. This is not true of gasoline stoves. Very significantly, with LPG stoves you cannot gauge the fuel level as you can with gasoline. This might prompt you to bring an extra (heavy) canister that you may not need. This can be somewhat gotten around with butane, since half-canisters that stack together can be purchased.

The cold weather hex of the LPG backpack stove has been attacked by the entrepreneurs of the trade. Now, stoves that burn a butane-propane mixture are said to work perfectly as well in very cold weather as gasoline stoves.

By the way, single-burner propane stoves are relatively uncommon. Propane requires a heavier gauge metal fuel tank than does butane, increasing weight, and that's the main reason why butane is the more common choice for LPG backpack-stove designers.

MULTIFUEL STOVES. This animal is really more a gasoline stove than anything else, but there are several different designs from several different manufacturers. The obvious advantage is that, if you travel, you can almost always find some fuel or another that will work. For example, the white gas that is easy to find in the United States is not widely available in other parts of the world. On the other hand, kerosene—which most multifuel stoves can accept—is internationally available. Some of the stoves in the popular MSR line burn any of white gas, leaded gasoline, unleaded gasoline, aviation gas, deodorized or regular kerosene, Stoddard solvent, #1 diesel fuel, or stove oil. That's quite a choice.

Depending on the particular fuel you use, spills can be a big problem. Some of these fuels are dreadful smelling, and one mistake culminating in a leak can about ruin your trip. No such worry need plague you with LPG stoves.

ALCOHOL. I don't think there are many backpackers who would rely solely on an alcohol stove on any strenuous trip. In fact, one prominent backpacking author states that she has an alcohol stove, but uses it mostly to keep the coffeepot hot on the patio!

Alcohol stoves do not burn nearly as hot as either LPG or gasoline counterparts. Alcohol can be a particular nuisance in extreme temperatures. In cold weather, it can be hard to light and you may have to heat the stove to get it going. Conversely, in hot weather, alcohol can burn too hot, although in that eventuality you can cut it with about 10 percent water to slow it down.

Other than that, an alcohol stove is dependable in the sense that it is painfully simple. It has no moving parts to fuss or worry over. It's just a container of fuel in some kind of housing. And, certain alcohol stoves are among the lightest backpacking stoves. The European-made Trangia stove is well regarded, and the price tag is currently $19.99. Its weight is only 6 oz. You can purchase the Trangia with a .8 liter pot, 5½-inch lid/frying pan, windscreen, and handle for only $24.99. This set weighs 11.6 oz.

WOOD STOVES. I don't know about you, but the reason I'm buying a backpacker's stove is that I don't want to worry about whether or not there is wood available at the campsite. That's just what you have to do with this somewhat anamolous critter. True, you don't need much wood to fire it, but what if you're in the desert, or high in some alpine meadow where wood is all but nonexistent? Or what if it has rained for three days, and all the wood—all of it—is drenched? Most woods smoke to some degree, and that just about precludes using the stove, ever, inside your tent (even the vestibule). In the three-day rain scenario, the wood in the stove will smoke in the extreme, and it may keep going out.

I look at this type of stove as more a curiosity than anything. But in honesty, I have not tried it so you should get other opinions before you finally decide against this category of backpacking stove.

Stackers, Windscreens, Etc.

Now you have your stove, and soon I'll try to help you select a couple of functional pieces of lightweight cookware. But there is an intermediary consideration that is most important.

Wind is brutal on backpacking stoves. Keep it out of the wind as much as possible, and that will help it burn hotter. Besides this, avail yourself of the windscreen if one is made for your particular type of stove. It may cost a few bucks extra, but will be worth it. Sometimes, the windscreen is actually part of a contrivance that also helps to keep pots stable. Indeed, with some stoves there is a whole system that includes stove, windscreen and/or stacking device, and/or heat exchanger, and then one or more pots that nest into or are otherwise integral with the stacking unit. When this is the case, strongly consider purchasing the whole system (assuming they do give you a choice). With such a design, you may find pot stability to be excellent, and you have the added benefit of not having to search around for pots that will work with your stove.

If no integral windscreen is available for your stove, a simple folding metal windblock, usable with any backpacker's stove, is available and costs only a few bucks.

Lightweight Cookware

If the stove you select offers no system as just described, you'll have to look in a few speciality stores to see what collection of cook pieces jive with your stove and your camp cooking aspirations. The discussion that follows is geared around the most common backpacking situation: You're cooking for one or two persons. If your group is typically larger, you may want a bigger set of pots and pans. Heed this warning, though: Backpacking is a very personal expression, and you may find that the others in your group-to-be do not want to eat the way you eat. Before you buy a larger than usual backpacking cookset, be certain that you really will be preparing meals for more than two people on a regular basis. And that the others will be helping to tote some of the other gear, since you'll be hauling an oversize cookset.

The size of the pots is really the big thing. Give this choice a lot of thought.

When I got my first set, I bought one of the smallest, lightest cooksets I could find. That one weighed only about a pound, and included two pots of one quart and .8 quart, plus a bowl and a lid that is supposed to double as a frypan. At only one quart, the largest of these two pots turned out to be just a little small for me, though if weight is really critical you'll probably require a set of approximately these specifications.

The "frying pans" that come with many backpack cook sets are notorious. Often, they are nothing but pot lids and these usually make lousy skillets. You can bring a separate, real frying pan as I do (when I can), but if you're shopping for a cookset it would be best to get one that includes a frying pan that actually can be used as such.

My second kit was made by Mirro, weighs one pound 12 ounces, and I've settled into it. It includes the following:

My backpacking cook set: two pots, a straight-sided skillet, and a plastic drinking cup. I add a 7½-inch plastic plate to this.

1. 1½-quart pot
2. 1 quart pot
3. 2 lids for pots
4. 2 cups
5. 1 straight-sided 8-inch frying pan (not just a pot lid)

The photo above shows what this set looks like taken apart. I like the fact that the frying pan is functional. I find the pots to be adequate in size, and I like the fact that it is stainless steel, which I prefer to aluminum. In some cases, it's nice to have a 1¾- or 2-quart pot, but you have to make sacrifices somewhere. As you can see from the photo, both pots and the frying pan have fold-out handles that are coated with some type of vinyl material. This obviously means that you can't allow the handles to perch directly over hot coals. Some backpacking pots and pans lack handles completely, which means you will have to purchase one of those little pot holders sold by every camping store and camper's catalog. It's always good to have one of these anyway.

Why, you might ask, do I carry a separate frying pan when my cookset includes a pretty decent one? In fact, I only do so when weight permits. My separate frying pan has sloped sides and is just so useful for so many things.

A very lightweight telescoping grill (right). As below, tie your funnel to your fuel bottle if at all possible. Bottom photo shows the little pot grabber every backpacker should have.

Further, it features a nonstick finish which I like a lot for backpacking. As an example, it makes much nicer eggs. The folding handle on this pan is convenient because it reduces bulk and also because it lets me nest a 7½-inch plastic plate under the handle. If I can't bring the separate frypan because of weight, I will still bring the plastic plate since I detest eating off metal. In this eventuality, the plate by itself fits into the stuff bag that houses my main cookset. By the way, the plate I use was free as it came with a "Le Menu" frozen dinner. I also use these very hard, durable, heat-resistant plates for car camping.

Other Accessories

I find the grill I carry to be extremely useful when cooking over wood fires. In the discussion in chapter 5 on cooking with wood, I talk about a two-log fire being a good one if you don't have a grill. Straddling a pot or pan across two green logs (with the hot coals in the center) will work sometimes, but the backpacker's grill weighs only five ounces and saves headaches. The one I have telescopes from 13 inches long to 20 inches long. Naturally, if I plan not to cook over wood at all I omit this item on my checklist.

Even the most Spartan backwoods kitchen should have some odds 'n' ends gadgets and containers to make the cooking chores go forward. My "Outdoor Kitchen," made by Outdoor Research, really helps to organize and centralize the small stuff. It's a little compartmented pouch that folds in half and then zippers shut. It includes:

1. 2 Lexan knives
2. 2 Lexan forks
3. 2 Lexan spoons
4. 1 can opener
5. 1 wire whisk
6. Scrubber sponge
7. Two 1/2-oz. plastic bottles

8. Two 1-oz. round bottles
9. Two 2-oz. squirt bottles
10. 1 mini pancake turner

This is the compact set, which weighs 14 oz. The deluxe set that this company offers is a little more elaborate and weighs 21 oz. These are off-the-shelf weights before anything has been added to the containers.

I modified my compact set slightly. First, I removed the Lexan knives. I wear a very good belt knife whenever I go into the woods and that is the only knife I need. I also added a set of measuring spoons, which are included in the deluxe set but not the compact set. I did this because I sometimes like to bake and it pays to measure when you're baking. On each trip I add to my kit a few steel soap pads, cut in half. These go into a very small zip-locking bag before going into my Outdoor Kitchen.

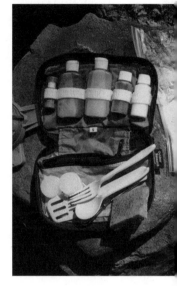

This set makes sense to me. In the little vials and bottles it includes I carry spices or condiments, plus oil, honey, and maple syrup. If you choose not to buy such a premade unit, devise something yourself that centralizes at least some of your cooking gear. Otherwise you'll have too many small objects floating around your pack and begging to get lost. Remember: Think "Ultimate Containers."

There are an endless number of gadgets for the camp cook, and a few new ones appear every season. I'll highlight here just a couple of the more interesting ones.

First is a tiny oven meant for use over a single-burner stove. Called a "Bakepacker," it has become quite popular though I have not tested it yet. It comes in both standard ($15.99) and lightweight ($13.99) models. Now, a number of prepared foods including baking mixes are made just for the Bakepacker. These include honey corn bread, chocolate cake, apple muffins, and others. Besides the Bakepacker, at least one other lightweight baking device has surfaced in the most recent catalog. It is called the "Outback Oven," and it too comes in two models, and has its own premixes.

The Outdoor Kitchen, made by Outdoor Research. Top photo shows it open, bottom photo, zippered shut.

Paper towels are next on the list. In truth, I'd like to bring a whole roll on a backpacking trip, and on a one-week trip I just might. But for a short few days I can only fit in a few dozen and I'm always glad I have them along. Rip them off the cardboard core, fold them up tightly, and they won't take much space.

Plastic bags are almost as useful as paper towels. One of their primary uses is for hauling nonburnable garbage out of the woods. They also, of course, can be used for storing food in camp. I don't have aluminum foil listed, but I sometimes fold up a good wad of it and tuck it into one of the plastic bags. Into the largest plastic bag go all the smaller ones, plus some ties. The sizes I like to bring are 1 quart (preferably zip-locking), 1 gallon, 4 gallon and 8 gallon. I may also tuck in some very small "sandwich" zip-locking bags.

The larger sizes can be used to carry clothing when necessary. For example, on a recent trip, we got hit with murderous thunderstorms and hail on the last day. When we packed up to go home that afternoon, just about everything we had on was wet. It was nice to have plastic bags to tote out the wet clothing. Also, plastic bags ensured we had a dry set of clothes to change into for the ride home. Bring several plastic bags in different sizes—you won't be sorry.

Camp cooking is a personal expression. If you feel that you need to bring other things, then maybe you do. Still, cookware is a good place to trim ounces. It's far better than cutting out an extra sweater or an extra package of soup, either of which could go a long way towards sustaining you in a bad situation far off the road.

Chapter 18
TRANSPORTING FOOD AND WATER

One time a close friend of mine led two others into a mountain area for a November deer hunt. His companions were younger than he, and in exceptional condition, but they had never winter camped before. When they left the trailer at the base of the mountain, my friend told them exactly how much water they would each need to bring, but they ignored his admonishments. They figured they'd find it on the mountain, and besides, who gets thirsty in winter?

Water probably was on the mountain, but they made no particular effort to seek it out first thing as my friend suggested. Each member of the party struck out on his own the first morning, but by the end of that day the two without water were climbing the walls they were so parched. When they all met at camp near suppertime, my friend naturally shared his canteen, but by the next morning there was none left and the two men were so drained that they didn't care to start hunting around for a spring seep. They ended up walking out of the woods the second morning, making for a broken, and very disappointing hunting trip.

Another good friend of mine leads a group backpacking into another mountain area every October. One time I asked him how he knew where the water would be. It turned out he had driven up the weekend before for the express purpose of checking on water availability; he had some maps and a report of a good spring or two. Since it is a good three hour trip from his home, he essentially made a one-day trip just to ensure the success of the upcoming three-day trip. Fanatical caution? My friend was just being a conscientious trip leader. Water is that important. In the first of these episodes, the inexperienced winter campers made two common mistakes: assuming there would be water available, and underestimating their need for water in winter. Campers of all kinds, of course, make many other errors in judgment in regard to our life-sustaining liquid.

An average person doing strenuous hiking should plan to consume at least six glasses or 1½ quarts of liquid a day. Since most backpackers take in dry mixes of

I take either a one-quart plastic bottle or a two-quart canteen on backpacking trips, depending on circumstances. The former weighs about half as much as the latter. The cloth-covered canteen has value. Dip it in water every so often, hang it up to dry, and the resulting evaporation will somewhat cool the contents.

one sort or another for beverages (though one guy I know, Maury, always brings in a six-pack of Coke!) most or all of the six glasses will be in the form of water or flavored water. Six glasses is just an estimate. Certain individuals in some circumstances may well need more.

Planning a backpacking trip, then, should include the planning of water needs. If you're going into a new area, an excellent starting point is a topographical map. Topos depict virtually all streams, ponds, and lakes and sometimes they even show natural springs. Importantly, the topos usually indicate which streams are permanent and which are intermittent (know that prolonged droughts can turn the former into the latter). Some guide books are also very specific about water sources, and these days there are guide books for most of the popular hiking and recreational areas in America. Other backpackers can be helpful too, as can be local people, especially those who work in outfitter shops in proximity to the area of your destination. Finally, there are a number of unusual ways to obtain water, most of them difficult and all of them out of the scope of this book. This could prove to be an extremely important survival skill some day, so putting your nose into a couple of survival books would be highly recommended.

There are a couple of ways to obtain water (in one form or another) that do not require elaborate condensation sheets or their ilk. On one trip I was on, a group on a site near ours found ice in a cave and used it to replenish their coolers. The date was June 30th. On another trip, in spring, we couldn't find running water right off. But by climbing up about 500 feet we found some lingering patches of snow and melted that down for drinking water. Both these tricks work increasingly well as latitude increases.

Transporting Water

Water weighs 8.3 pounds per gallon, and indeed, in certain arid areas an individual may have to tote in a gallon. Except for expeditions that would be the rare exception, though, since you'd have to sacrifice so much gear to make room for that much water. Where I backpack, water is never a problem, so I rarely bring in any. When there is some doubt about how quickly I will find water, I will take in a fresh quart which weighs only 2.1 pounds. If the doubt is greater, I'll bring in my two-quart canteen fully filled, and know that I'm good for better than a day.

Vessels for transporting water are several in type. For a short day-hike, I like a one-quart plastic bottle which is lightweight and usually adequate. The wide-mouth kind is best in case you want to mix something in the vessel. For overnight camping, my personal choice is a two-quart round metal canteen with a cloth coating. Empty it weighs only 14 ounces, and even if I don't always want two quarts I have that option when needed. I like my drinking water cold, and the cloth really helps. Just dip the whole canteen (prefilled) into a cold stream or lake, hang it up in the shade, and evaporation will help to cool the water inside. And, since the metal is a better insulater than plastic, water will stay cold longer than in a lighter plastic bottle.

There are a few other types of water vessels. One is a compressible plastic model that folds up flat for easy storage or transportation but expands to two gallons, depending on the model, when full. This is nice for storing water in a backwoods camp since you have to make fewer trips to the water source.

Another is made out of a stretchy, rubberlike material and, when full, looks like a balloon hanging upside down. This is even more compact than the just mentioned plastic model, but since it has no real cap it's not the easiest to use.

Purification Methods

All surface water found on location should be purified, with the exception of clean, white, fresh snow (the purest form of water) which can be eaten as is or melted down, or clean ice.

Boiling is a foolproof method if you boil it long enough for the altitude you are at. To be certain of killing all potentially harmful organisms, boil water for five minutes at sea level (some say two to three minutes is enough). For every 1,000 feet of elevation, boil one minute longer, since water boils at a lower temperature the higher you go.

Boiled water can taste quite flat. That's because much of the oxygen has been boiled out. To reoxygenate it, pour it back and forth several times between two clean vessels. Its taste will often improve if left uncovered overnight.

When boiling is not possible or convenient, filtration is the method I prefer. The modern camper has portable filtration devices to turn to that never existed in days of yore. There are two types: those that use filtration plus one or more chemicals, and those that use strictly filtration. I recommend the second type.

The most problematic waterborn infection in the world is giardiasis, the name of a disease caused by the protozoan organism *Giardia lamblia*. For that reason, when water purification methods are discussed these days, a particular method's effectiveness with *Giardia* is usually at the top of the discussion. This is probably a good thing, since *Giardia* is known as being a tough little beast, not easily destroyed. Destroy (or filter out) *Giardia* and you have also destroyed (or filtered out) most though not necessarily all other pathenogenic organisms.

Giardia has two principal life stages: trophozoite and cyst. In the first stage, the organism is 12-15 microns in size. In the second, it is only 8-12 microns. Thus, you should purchase from a dependable, established manufacturer a filtration unit that filters down to no more than a few microns, just to be on the safe side.

The straw-type filters are questionable. Here, you can just dip your mouth down to an appealing little brook and sip through the straw of the unit. Some of these use a 10-micron filter along with iodine.

Perhaps the most serious filtration unit you will currently see among the popular camping catalogs is the Katadyn Water Purifier. This unit incorporates a high quality ceramic filter that filters down to 0.2 microns, more than adequate for *Giardia,* other protozoans, fungi, and parasites. The Katadyn produces a quart in a minute, plenty fast enough for a backpacker's needs. It measures 10 by 2 inches and weighs 23 oz. That's pretty heavy, but for a group of two or more, where weight is being shared, it is not unreasonable. It costs $219.99 at present and comes in a zippered carrying case. A replacement filter for it costs $124.99.

In looking at a popular camper's catalog before me, I see five other types or brands of water filtration units. Clearly, campers and especially backpackers are moving in the direction of filtration versus the older tablet method. Just to look at one other model in the filtration category, General Ecology makes the popular First Need Water Purification System. This unit costs only $47.99 at present; a spare filter costs $24.99. It claims to strain down to "0.1 microns, 0.4 microns absolute"—whatever that collection of words means—but that is still more than enough for *Giardia.* A little more cumbersome than the Katadyn unit (but lighter—only 14.5 oz.), the First Need features a special bracket which holds both the pump and the purification canister. It claims to filter a pint in a minute.

It should be noted that with some filtration units, including the two just discussed, more than just disease-causing organisms may be filtered out. The better units claim to also filter out asbestos fibers, toxic chemicals such as herbicides and pesticides, and so forth. This should not be looked at as a good reason to let down your guard regarding contaminated water. Not all harmful chemicals will be eliminated.

The other main category of water purification is the tablet method. Here, you introduce a chemical, in tablet or crystal form, that is strong enough to kill the bugs but (ostensibly) not strong enough to hurt you. Being an avid skeptic of man's flagrant use of chemicals, I have now switched over to the filtration units and would not use these tablets unless I had no other choice.

Two chemicals are used: chlorine and iodine. The most popular tablet using chlorine is the widely available Halazone tablets. You add the prescribed number of tablets to your water vessel, shake it, and let it sit, usually for about 30 minutes. One guide I tripped with brought along Clorox bleach and used an eyedropper to

MIKE BLEECH

A semi-collapsible plastic water jug is the right ticket in some camps. This one holds five gallons.

add two drops to a quart of water. If you do use chlorine-based tablets, remember that their shelf life is limited. Pay heed to the date on the package. Some experts contend that chlorine is not 100 percent effective against *Giardia* in the normally recommended doses, and is less effective overall than the other chemical popularly used for water purification: iodine.

One big advantage with iodine-based formulations is that the taste of the water seems to be less affected. (Nonetheless, if a chlorine-treated vessel of water is allowed to sit uncovered for several hours most of the chlorine taste will dissipate.) Another plus to iodine is that shelf life is less critical. It also has excellent solubility (true of the tablets but not iodine crystals). Most experts who do use or recommend tablets versus filtration state that iodine is the better method overall. Still, to destroy *Giardia* effectively you must follow the manufacturer's directions carefully. Two variables usually discussed in the literature that accompanies these tablets (or crystals) are "contact duration" (waiting time before you drink) and water temperature. Generally, the colder the water the more difficult it is to kill pathenogenic organisms.

Remember that with the tablet method, you must kill any little bugs that happen to be hiding on the neck or cap of the water vessel you are using. This is why the tablet makers suggest that you allow a little of the treated water to slosh up onto the threads and neck of the water bottle or other vessel.

Giardiasis is a formidable malady, worthy of all this consideration. A friend of mine had this disease, and he went through agony with it; it left him with some damage of the colon. With this in mind, it would seem to me that one would have to have a pretty good reason not to use a portable filtration unit these days, when using or planning to use surface water.

There is a final thought on this subject. If the water is a little bit murky, most manufacturers and experts recommend that you increase both the dosage and the contact duration. Don't even consider doing this without reading the directions on the tablet bottle, though. Iodine in a large enough dose can be fatal.

Transporting Food: Prepackaging

On a backwoods trip, nothing makes the cook's job easier than water close at hand. But the second most important aid is prepackaging. Actually, there are two facets to this process: repackaging and prepackaging.

The aim of repackaging is to take your store-bought food from its original package and get it into something leakproof and lighter in weight. While doing this, you will also divide the food into portions, one meal to a package. Keep in mind that the ultimate goal as you do this is to make meal preparation as fast and easy as possible once you get into the woods. For example, if you want to make oatmeal, you can combine "instant" rolled oats, evaporated milk, sugar, and raisins or other dried fruit and place these in a plastic bag one meal to a bag. When you get to your campsite, you then simply add boiling water to your mix. With camp baking, this kind of prepackaging can be especially useful since mixing and measuring on your hands and knees ceases to be romantic after about the first meal. If you're packing into a base camp, perhaps one that's used intermittently through the season, you might want to keep there a "starter barrel." Such mixes usually incorporate either flour or cornmeal, and include the leavening (usually baking powder), salt, and sugar. Normally made in bulk amounts, such a starter can be used to make biscuits, breads, pancakes, and other items. You may only have to add some shortening, perhaps a fresh egg or two, and some combination of water and/or milk. These starters do save time, but will only have application in certain fixed base camps.

It's hard to beat those zipper-lock plastic bags. They are good for all dry mixes and I will even use them for such semisoft foods as peanut butter, butter (if it's not too hot), cream cheese, and various spreads. Be sure to label all packages— it's best to do this meal by meal. For example, you might mark your dry oatmeal mix "Breakfast Day 1" or "Breakfast Friday." If final preparation of your prepackaged foods requires directions you might forget, you'll have to include that on the package. Some trail chefs just insert a little piece of paper into the package. My approach is to stick a strip of masking tape onto the outside of the package (plastic bag, most often) and write on whatever I need to know: add 2 eggs, add 2 cups water, add 1 cup milk, boil 10 minutes, whatever.

I definitely think there is some justification for cans on a backpack trip. True, they are heavy and must be packed out, but they are certainly leakproof and meals like "fresh" chili or beef stew provide a nice break from freeze-dried. Importantly, these canned foods are nonperishable. If you want to avail yourself of supermarket canned goods but really hate to lug around those cans, a good trick is to remove the contents and freeze it in a zip-locking bag. For the first day, and possibly longer, the contents may be firm enough not to leak and cold enough not to spoil.

The frugal backpacker may be amazed at what he finds on supermarket shelves, since "compact" foods, including, of course, freeze-dried, are proliferating. Fortunately, many of these compact foods come in containers suitable for backpacking, so no repackaging is needed. There is more on this in chapter 20.

There are several other types of containers all backpackers should know about. One is the high-quality plastic containers which come in a wide array of sizes and shapes. One well-known brand name is Nalgene. Since they are heavier than plastic bags, I use them mostly for liquids or very runny foods that might leak from a plastic bag. I don't rely on these plastic containers too heavily, but it's nice to have a few different sizes for when the need arises. In their smaller sizes, these plastic jars or bottles are very useful for transporting relatively small amounts of condiments such as relish, ketchup, and oil.

The smallest pill-size plastic bottles are useful especially for bringing in very small amounts of spices. Or, if you wish to go the other way to the more elaborate, backpacker's shops have nifty little containers that carry two or more spices at once, for example salt on one side and pepper on the other. Personally, I carry most or all of my spices and condiments in my "Outdoor Kitchen," described in chapter 17.

Use your imagination and your ingenuity and you will come across free containers to transport foods into the backcountry. A good friend of mine showed me some very tiny bottles he had gotten from his dentist. False teeth come in them! They're perfect for carrying minute quantities of anything, and let's face it, if you only need one gram of curry powder why bring in four ounces of it?

Transporting Difficult Foods

The best way I know to carry fresh eggs is with a hinged plastic case made expressly for that purpose. I have a 6-egg carrier but there are also 12-egg models. One lesson I learned the hard way with these carriers is that extra large or large eggs may not fit properly into them. Test yours out at home. If it doesn't close easily, the eggs could break. However, if you stick to medium size eggs I don't believe you will have any problem. To be even safer, place the entire egg case, eggs and all, into a zip-locking plastic bag.

Semisoft foods often pose a dilemma. Here I'm talking about butter, peanut butter, mayonnaise, certain soft cheese, and the like. As I've stated above, such foods can sometimes be nicely toted in plastic bags. But if the temperature is too high, such foods could melt and no plastic bag unless sealed with heat is totally leakproof. The other horn to this dilemma is low temperatures. If you place your food (especially butter) in a squeeze tube made for backpackers, it will be difficult to squeeze out in cold temperatures. You'll have to use your judgment as to when a tube is going to work better than a bag or bottle. If you do use a tube, you want the kind made just for backpackers. It opens fully at one end for insertion of contents, and is held closed by a type of clip. As you use up the contents, you squeeze the tube as if it were toothpaste and push the contents upward. This is almost always the best way to go with things like peanut butter or jelly.

Heat-sealed plastic bags will be leakproof unless they're punctured. Thus, a heat-sealing machine would not be an absurd extravagance for a serious backpacker.

Perhaps the best way to handle all the various spices and condiments you might want to have along is to save up the little prepackaged ones that constantly come your way from fast-food places, delicatessens, and diners. It seems there is very little they haven't been able to put into these tiny, one-portion packages, and since they are air-tight they are not generally perishable (a real big consideration with mayonnaise). Among the free condiments of this genre that I've used are salt, pepper, mustard, sugar, jelly, relish, coffee, mayonnaise, table syrup, honey, ketchup, lemon juice, and I keep coming across new ones. If you start squirreling these away in October, guaranteed you'll be covered for all your backpacking trips the following season.

Almost everyone likes to bring in a little fresh fruit or vegetables when possible. These foods are central to any healthy diet. Most of this is best carried in plastic bags. With some foods, like peppers, tomatoes, onions, corn, squash, beets, you can cut away all the nonedible parts at home to cut down on weight. Pits, seeds, and tough or stringy parts should all be removed from most vegetables. With many vegetables and fruits, however, this procedure is not advisable because oxidation (browning) will quickly occur. Some things you just have to bring in whole. I believe raw, fresh, and preferably organically grown fruits and vegetables are so important that you should try to bring some and sacrifice elsewhere.

Food Storage in Camp

You're set up next to a tumbling, crystal clear brook, in an idyllic little glen right out of Rip Van Winkle. With tent pitched, and other primary chores seen to, you and your companion strike out for a nearby peak on a quick overnighter. When you return the next morning, though, your little piece of paradise has all gone sour. Not only have the critters been into everything, but they've chewed through one backpack and one storage bag to get at those great-smelling freebies. At least three of your five day's worth of provisions are scattered in half-bitten pieces around the campsite and if that isn't bad enough, an unexpected hot day the day before has spoiled another meal's worth of rations. There's nothing to do now but clean up the campsite and face a shortened trip—or unexpected hunger pangs.

Proper food storage in camp centers on two main concerns: perishability and animal protection. Let's look at perishability first.

Though you may not believe it, dealing with food perishability is more of an art than a science. The factors are never quite the same in two different camps, and like so many aspects of camp cookery, instinct must prevail.

When your food will spoil in camp is a vector of time and temperature. If your meat was frozen it may take a day to thaw and many more hours to get to a dangerous temperature. Conversely, meat brought in at room temperature could start to spoil in as little as a few hours. Personal experience might tell you that food at room temperature can go a pretty long time without turning bad, but remember that in camp you must be extra careful about such things. No one wants to get sick away from home, where cold comfort and medical assistance are just not to be had.

Hanging food to thwart the animals is something you should almost always do in the backcountry.

That warning notwithstanding, some people worry more than they have to about food spoilage. A good example is butter. In temperatures ranging from the 50s to the 70s I have never had a problem with butter spoiling. If you're still worried, though, you can always tote along margarine which spoils much more slowly. Clarified butter, easily made yourself or available from backpacker's sources, is said to be nonperishable.

In the chapter on game cookery, I talk about this instinct of knowing when a food is going bad. There are tips in that chapter for feeling your way along in that area. Here now are some specific tips for keeping foods cool in camp.

The single most important thing to avoid is absorbed heat. You often hear two temperatures given: in the sun and in the shade. Did you ever stop and wonder how the temperatures could differ when it's all the same, ambient air? The reason is that a thing left in direct sun absorbs heat and its temperature climbs. Some things, because of their color, texture, and degree of opacity, absorb more heat than others. But your aim is to avoid direct sun completely. In part one I admonished you to find a campsite with more sun than shade. While backpacking in summer, you should seek out a site with at least some shade.

The temperature difference in and out of the sun is just amazing. Avoid the sun, but avoid in particular leaving glass or plastic containers in the sun, which will bake your food and possibly render it poisonous with amazing speed.

Another tip is to use a shiny but opaque material to wrap food in. This will somewhat reflect the sun's rays versus a black material which will absorb and retain heat.

You probably don't have to be told to use a cold stream or lake to keep your food cool. In tidal waters, though, beware of a rising tide. In streams, try to place rocks on top of anything that might wash away. If you're upstream of camp trout fishing one day, and the skies open up, your lunch may wind up 100 miles downstream, perhaps near your mother's house. There is no such thing as a completely

stable water level. Also be thoughtful about what types of packages might leak if you're cooling them in the nearby water source.

Out there in the woods it's you against the critters, and unless you enjoy thumb wrestling to help you forget about food, you better take precautions to keep the animals at bay. They can and will steal your food, they will chew through all types of valuable gear to get at the food, and they can even take a bite out of you if a poorly timed confrontation occurs.

Here is an overall game plan that I've found to be effective. When I get to the campsite I first pitch my tent and lay out my bedroll inside. I usually remove some clothing from the pack as well. I then take the stuff sack the sleeping bag was in and place it in the large part of my pack, which I leave outside and covered with a large plastic trash bag at night and when rain threatens. Before dark, but after dinner, I put all my well-wrapped food in this sack and now it's ready to be hung for the night. There will be no food in my pack or tent the smell of which might encourage late night critter gnawing. If there are several in your group, each can do this, to keep the food separate, then all the food bags can be hung together in one communal bag or stuff sack. Naturally, all the food items should be in their own packaging so they can't leak all over your stuff sacks. Toss a rope over a tree branch and hang the bag 10 feet off the ground. As dexterous and intelligent as raccoons and bears are, it's unlikely they will be able to get into provisions so hung. Some outdoor experts say to hang food 12 feet where bears are common. Suit yourself there, just make sure in bear country that no food is inside with you in the tent. Bears have great noses and if something smells good inside your bivouac you may wake up to the commotion of a very bad dream.

Some experts opine that in bear country, food should be hung 50 yards away from the tent area at night.

To avoid drawing animals to your campsite in the first place, burn all burnable garbage right away and don't leave dirty dishes around camp. It's the smell of food that will bring them in, so don't tantalize them any more than necessary.

More than one person I know has had a pocket of his backpack chewed into. I've never had, but one night something, possibly mice, chewed up three pockets on my fly-fishing vest. I'm not sure what they saw in this Velcro-and-cotton snack, but maybe I left some candy inside.

No matter how careful you are outdoors, sometimes nature is going to win.

Chapter 19

INGENUITY FOR THE BACKPACK CHEF

In a backwoods kitchen it's tough to beat ingenuity and resourcefulness, even though stoicism might be the number one attribute for all backpackers. If I've seemed to have come down too hard on the little tricks that make for such nice photographs and sketches in handbooks, then perhaps I will somewhat redeem myself in this chapter.

For the backcountry chef, ingenuity really centers on two things: working around the conditions you encounter, and simplifying wherever possible. How will you cook if it rains? How will you cook if it snows? What if it's extremely buggy? Or cold? Or hot? For every obstacle, there are little ways by which the chef can cope. This comes from experience and a good sense of anticipation (foreboding?). As for simplifying, do this: use fewer ingredients, make fewer dirty dishes, stick to meals that are done in 20 minutes or less, and bring some fully prepared foods from home. And, oh yes—keep reading.

More Tricks with Foil

Some of the most esteemed camp cookbooks on my shelf devote an entire chapter to the use of aluminum foil. Indeed, it often seems there is no end to the uses of this material. In chapter 9, there is much rambling about the uses of foil in a general camp setting. Some of those techniques can surely be imported to the backwoods kitchen. Here are some other ways that aluminum foil can keep you from being foiled by the constraints of a 40-pound pack.

Most obviously, you can bake potatoes in the coals. So, be sure to bring one of the toppings presented on the next page.

MEXICAN POTATO TOPPING
HELLMANN'S MAYONNAISE

Bake 8 foil-wrapped potatoes in the coals. To 1/2 cup Hellmann's mayonnaise, add 3/4 cup prepared hot salsa, drained, plus 1 cup shredded Cheddar cheese and 1 cup refried beans (available in cans). Mix well. Serve over cooked and split potatoes.

CHEDDAR-BACON POTATO TOPPING
HELLMANN'S MAYONNAISE

Bake 4 foil-wrapped potatoes in the coals. To 1 cup Hellmann's mayonnaise add 1/2 cup shredded Cheddar cheese and 1/4 cup crumbled cooked bacon. Serve over cooked and split potatoes.

Popcorn can be popped in an on-the-spot foil pouch. Be sure you make the pouch large enough that the corn has room to expand. Directly below, a reflector oven has been fashioned from foil, sticks, and wire. In bottom photo, heavy duty foil is molded around a can to create an impromptu drinking cup.

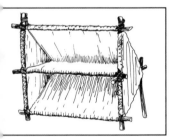

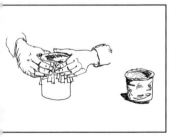

You can make some camp popcorn very easily. Take a 15-inch square of foil and use your fist to form a pocket in it. Add a tablespoon of oil and two tablespoons of popcorn. Fold up the top. Now take a piece of string or wire and dangle the pouch from the end of a stick. Each kid (and this will turn everyone into a kid) pops his own corn over the campfire.

If you lack a pot cover, foil makes a great substitute. Rip off a length of the foil and place it over the cooking pot. Using your hands or a frypan or other implement, push down the edge to form an effective seal. By the way, even if you do have a lid for your skillet or pot, adding a foil gasket can make for an even tighter seal. This can be good insurance against all the liquid in your implement steaming out on you while you're distracted with something else.

Here's wishing that the weight of your pack allowed for the bringing of a lightweight reflector oven. If not, you can fashion one out of foil, sticks, and wire, as shown in the drawing. You're still not out of the woods though, for what will you bake your goodies in? In chapter 9 I talked about a baking tray. That's too cumbersome to backpack in so use foil instead. If it's something like biscuits or my own favorite, Royal Raisin Scones (see p. 96), you can just place them on a double sheet of greased foil then insert the whole sheet into the reflector oven. But for things like cake or corn bread, you'll need a pan. Simply use a pot, skillet, or even a dish to help you fashion one out of foil. Press and mold the heavyweight foil (perhaps doubled) into the implement and voila: an instant baking tin, one that doesn't have to be washed.

Filtered sun made this campsite in New York's Catskill Mountains a pleasant one. Each site in this area had an ad hoc fireplace and logs for sitting. It's best to just use what you find in areas where use is moderate to heavy.

LO-CAL BUTTERMILK HERB DRESSING
In a jar, combine 1 cup buttermilk, 1 T. Dijon mustard, 1 tsp. minced fresh onion, 1/4 tsp. dried dill weed, 1 T. chopped fresh parsley, and a large dash of cayenne. Shake well. Chill overnight. Bring to camp to serve over some wild or domestic fresh greens. Only 5 calories per tablespoon. MAKES 1 CUP.

CURRY DRESSING
In a bowl, combine 2/3 cup corn oil, 3 T. white vinegar, 1 T. curry powder, and 1/4 tsp. white pepper. Whisk until smooth. MAKES 2/3 CUP

If you happen to have any kind of tin can along, you can fashion a drinking cup for that lost soul who has forgotten his. Just mold the foil over the can, turn it upside down, and twist the leftover edges of the foil into a little handle.

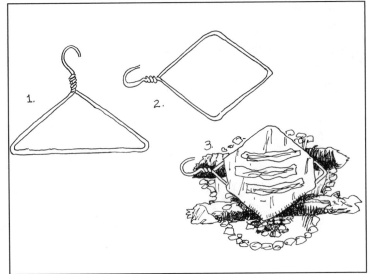

A coat hanger can be shaped as desired and then covered with foil to improvise a variety of extemporaneous cooking implements. Below, a simple pan has been fashioned with foil alone.

Besides baking, such on-the-spot tins have other uses. Cook fresh vegetables (or heat canned or frozen ones) in them over a grill or straddled across a two-log fire. They'll come out a little different tasting than by the steaming method described in chapter 9, and perhaps you'll prefer them this way. Whenever you use one of these foil tins, and you fear food sticking to it, lay a strip of bacon down on it before the food is set on to cook. Or, use a little oil, or vegalene.

If you bring the compact grill I describe in chapter 15, wrap foil around it and use it to fry over the coals. It's yet one more way to avoid dishwashing. If you have any breadstuffs, you can warm them on your little foil pan above the coals. Anytime you warm bread directly in the coals, triple the foil and watch it carefully so it doesn't burn.

Corn baked in the coals is an exceptional treat, although this is more a technique for a campground or base camp. A good two hours before mealtime, soak your unhusked ears of corn in a big pot of water. Now, start a fire and build up a good bed of coals. Place the foil-wrapped but still unhusked ears right on the coals. Be sure to turn them every so often. The water trapped in the husks will turn to steam and cook your corn beautifully. The edges of some of the kernels should turn a golden brown color, which only enhances the flavor and the effect. The corn should be done in 30-40 minutes.

For maximum efficiency and to keep out the dirt and ash, foil packages cooked in the coals should be sealed very tightly.

The food can be placed on either the shiny side or the dull side of the foil. Either way, taste will not be affected. If you face the dull side of the foil out, heat will be absorbed a little better making for slightly shorter cooking times.

No need to pack in foil in its bulky, rolled form. Pull off as much foil as you think you'll need for the trip and fold it compactly. It will weigh very little and tuck nicely into almost any available nook in your pack.

If you can bring along a folded coat hanger (weight, about one ounce), the sleight-of-hand performable with foil will be even more impressive. By simply bending a part of the hanger into a rough circle you have a rigid rim to make that little drinking cup or pot work all the better. The other end of the hanger can be folded back on itself to make a handle. With a little imagination, you'll find other tricks you can do with the combination of this flexible wire and the aluminum foil.

You don't have to go through the substantial toil of fashioning a reflector oven from foil and sticks. Rather, you can simply use the reflective qualities of foil to bake or otherwise cook something. For example, you could take some foil and wrap a big square of it around some sticks (which can be lashed together with string or wire). Now place the item to be cooked between your wood fire and the mounted square of foil, or on the side of the fire opposite the foil reflector, whichever works best.

SARDINE SPREAD
King Oscar Sardines

At home, drain one 3¾-oz. can sardines. Combine sardines with 3 oz. softened cream cheese, salt to taste (or omit), 1 tsp. horseradish, dash onion powder, and dash Worcestershire sauce. Bring to camp in a suitable vessel. In camp, use the mixture to spread on crackers or to fill fresh celery sticks. A spicy, high-protein trail snack.

SARDINE SURPRISE
King Oscar Sardines

In camp, open two 3¾-oz. tins of sardines and mash with the oil. Partially hollow out 2 large ripe tomatoes and fill with the sardine mixture. A little grated cheese can be sprinkled on top. ✦These can be cooked in foil in the coals, especially if the tomatoes are hard, but cooking is not strictly necessary.

Remember, finally, that aluminum foil is not burnable and every scrap of it must be packed out.

Stick Cooking

Bannock is bread at its most basic. It can consist of only flour, water, and salt, although most of the recipes I've seen include some leavening, and sometimes other ingredients. Bannock is as much a part of camping as wood smoke and you should know how to make it. Bannock on a stick is one of those romantic little camp tricks that appears in every outdoor manual, but it is practical, easy, and draws a smile every time.

To bake bannock on a stick, strive for just the right consistency. Form the dough as usual, then cut it into strips about 1¼ inches wide. Take a smooth, green, hardwood stick and roll and press the bannock around it. Each diner holds his own stick over the fire.

To cook bannock in a pan, the easier of the two methods, just mix the ingredients and press the resulting dough into a skillet or one of those ad hoc aluminum foil pans discussed earlier in this chapter. Where I am able to use my cast-iron skillet I find it bakes the nicest bannock. You can set the pan in the coals, but this will probably burn the bottom of the bread. I try to use a grill or otherwise prop the pan two inches or so above the coals. I've also cooked bannock on a camp stove.

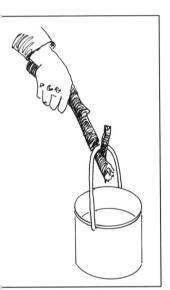

After 15 minutes or so, you'll need to flip your bannock. A clever ploy here is to use two cast iron skillets. Just turn the first pan over and let the bread slip out onto the second pan; then cook about another 15 minutes. If you don't have a second pan of a large enough size, turn the pan over onto a plate and then slide the now-stiff bread back into the same pan.

Actually, there is a better way, when you are in fact cooking with coals. Cover the skillet and cook the bread until it's about two-thirds done. Then remove the cover and tilt the pan to the coals or flames. This will complete the cooking and promote browning.

I always grease the skillet well before putting the dough in. Also, I always flour the dough. These steps thwart sticking.

Each of my own bannock recipes was created to work perfectly in my 10-inch cast-iron skillet. When pressed into the pan, it will be ¾ or 1 inch thick. It should rise a good half-inch.

Bread-on-a-stick (right), as tantalizing as it is convenient. The real trick to making bannock in this way is to get the dough to just the right consistency. Above, a forked stick makes a convenient pot lifter.

JACKPINE BANNOCK

3 cups unsifted flour
1 T. baking powder

1/4 tsp. salt
2½ T. melted bacon fat

Combine flour, baking powder, and salt. In camp, add the bacon fat. Stir with a wooden spoon. Add water slowly until dough is soft. You may use about 6–8 oz. Gather the dough together in the bowl, turn onto a floured surface, and knead until smooth but a little sticky. Flour the dough, place in a lightly greased 10-inch cast-iron skillet, and press the dough down so it just touches the sides of the pan. Prop the skillet about 2-3 inches above some coals. Cook 15-20 minutes. Flip over. Cook 15 minutes more. MAKES ONE 10-INCH ROUND.

SWEET BANNOCK

3 cups all-purpose flour
1/3 cup sugar
1/8 cup powdered milk
1 T. baking powder

1½ tsp. cinnamon
1/4 tsp. salt
3 T. oil

Dry ingredients can be mixed at home. In camp, add oil and stir well. Slowly add water, about 6-8 oz., to make a relatively dry dough. Turn out onto a floured surface and knead for 60 seconds. Press into a cast-iron skillet. Prop over hot coals. Cook 20 minutes then flip loaf. Cook 20 minutes more or until golden on both sides. MAKES ONE 10-INCH ROUND.

A single small fish or a small game animal can also be cooked on a stick. Cut a forked stick from dead wood and sharpen the ends of the two prongs with your knife. With a fish, insert each prong into a flank of the fish. With a small mammal the head will be missing but a similar arrangement can be used. With a small game bird, make the fork of the stick smaller and insert the entire fork into the cavity of the bird. Using your fingers, press the barbs of the fork into the inside of the breast meat of the bird. A small fish will cook quickly, a small game animal, truthfully, will not. You'll have to use some rocks to prop up your stick so you don't have to kneel by the fire for 45 minutes or more. And of course even if you do this, you will have to turn your deliciously browning prize from time to time.

BACKPACKER'S FISH SAUCE

At home, soften 4 T. butter or margarine. Mix in 1 tsp. lime juice and 2-3 tsp. chopped fresh dill. Place in a backpacker's squeeze tube. In camp, squeeze out onto hot, just-cooked fish and it will melt and form a sauce. ✦In hot weather, if the tube might leak, use a small sealed bottle or canister. FOR 3 FISH DINNERS.

With smaller pieces of meat, a shish kebab may be in order. Just cut a smooth (preferably hardwood) stick with your knife and skewer on the small hunks of bone-free meat. Add fresh or canned vegetables if you have them.

Kebab cooking is spotlighted in chapter 6. The only difference here is that you're using sticks instead of steel. See that section of chapter 6 for some tempting marinade recipes and kebab combinations that could easily be toted back into the bush.

The "dingle sticks" that appeared in all the old camp cookbooks are beautiful to look at, but usually, not at all easy to devise. Dangling (or is it dingling?) a pot usually implies cooking over flames, and I've already made my case against that in chapter 5. I'd much, much rather tote a lightweight grill and cook in a more stable way over coals.

Still, there are some other neat things you can do with sticks. For example, cut a stick but leave a four-inch fork at the end. Use this to toast a slice of bread over coals. If you've forgotten your pot gripper, and lack a potholder, a stick can help you lift any pot that has a bailing handle. Just cut a strong stick in such a way that the stub of a broken branch can grab the handle on the pot.

Substitutions

It seems to me that making do with what you have back in what Bradford Angier liked to call "the farther places" is the essence of woodcraft. Like it or not, on the trail you will often do without. But if you're clever, you can do with something equivalant. Perhaps this list will help:

1 cup milk	=	4 T. powdered milk + 1 cup water
1 cup milk	=	½ cup condensed milk + ½ cup water
1 cup milk	=	½ cup evaporated milk + ½ cup water
1 cup milk	=	⅓ cup instant nonfat dry milk powder + 2 tsp. melted butter + 1 cup water
1 cup sour milk	=	1 cup sweet milk + 1 T. vinegar
1 cup plain yogurt	=	1 cup buttermilk
1 cup light cream	=	½ cup coffee lightener + 1 cup hot water
1 cup heavy cream	=	¾ cup coffee lightener + 1 cup hot water
1 tsp. baking powder	=	¼ tsp. baking soda + ½ tsp. cream of tartar
1 cup pastry flour	=	1 cup bread flour less 2 T.
1 square chocolate	=	¼ cup cocoa
1 T. cornstarch	=	2 T. flour (for thickening)
1 T. dry minced onion	=	1 small onion
1 small clove garlic	=	⅛ tsp. garlic powder
¼ tsp. dried herb	=	1 tsp. fresh (an approximation)
1 tsp. dried oregano	=	1 tsp. dried marjoram
1 tsp. dried mustard	=	1 T. mustard

1 cup beef or chicken broth	=	1 cube or packet + 8 ozs. water
1 cup honey	=	1¼ cups granulated sugar + ¼ cup water
½ cup tartar sauce	=	6 T. mayonnaise + 2 T. sweet pickle relish

Doctoring

As important as clever substitutions can be in a backwoods kitchen, judicious "doctoring" can be just as important. Backpacking recipes (especially those made in camp) are almost always simplified, and often flavor is lost along with the deleted ingredients.

As often as not, doctoring in camp means little more than adding a pinch of this or that. Here's where a basic command of cooking will serve you well. What spice or other flavor enhancer will go with what kind of food? It takes experience.

A pinch of salt or sugar (sometimes both) can really wake up a meal, especially a freeze-dried meal. A bit of butter can also make a magical difference. In the realm of spices and herbs, parsley, thyme, and bay leaf reign supreme; paprika, curry powder, and onion powder are also very versatile. Coarse sea salt is worth bringing as is sesame salt; both are extremely versatile. If you like to bake, bring some whole or ground poppy seeds, as well as some orange extract. Ground cardamom is very expensive but, like poppy, helps to punctuate the tastes of many baked goods. Pure extract of vanilla or almond are yet other important flavorings for desserts and other goodies, and because each is so concentrated you only need to bring a minute amount.

A green stick can be used to make a backcountry shish kebab. Two forked sticks set into the ground can be used to prop the whole thing a desirable distance from the coals. A forked stick (middle) can be used to easily cook a small fish over the coals. Even a gamebird can be cooked on a stick, though cooking time will be long enough that you'll need to find a way of propping the stick over the coals. The log reflector is not for back-country situations.

Here are some other "doctor's tips" for the backcountry chef:

- Add a small amount of any citrus juice to perk up many dishes.
- Add grated citrus rind to many baking mixes.
- Add a pinch of cinnamon to beef, venison, or lamb stew.
- Use dried onion flakes for more "body" than onion powder or minced onion. These work nicely in chilis.
- Add chopped leftover bacon or sausages to pancake batter. Pancakes thus made make good lunch treats.
- Add a dash of cayenne to perk up many dishes including meat dishes and many types of salads.
- Add a dash of freeze-dried chives to any egg dish.

- Add a tablespoon or two of bacon drippings to many soups, including fish and clam chowders.
- An overripe banana can be mashed and added to a biscuit mix and many bread mixes.
- Jelly can be melted to make a quick sweet sauce.

HALF-HOUR CORN BREAD
AUNT JEMIMA'S

To 2 cups self-rising cornmeal mix add 1/3 cup powdered milk. Bring this to camp in a tightly sealed plastic bag. In camp, add to this mixture a mixture of one beaten egg, 2 T. oil or melted butter, plus 1⅓ cups hot water. Stir well. Pour into a skillet and bake over a camp stove or over hot coals. Could also be done, in a skillet or baking tin, in a reflector oven. Should take 30 minutes in a reflector oven, less in a skillet placed on a stove. ONE ROUND.

APPLE CRUMBLE

1/3 cup flour
1/2 cup powdered milk
1/2 cup brown sugar
1/4 tsp. salt

1 tsp. cinnamon
1/4 cup butter or margarine
5 cups sliced apples

At home, combine flour, powdered milk, sugar, salt, and cinnamon. Place mixture in plastic bag. In camp, soften the butter or margarine; use fingertips to blend into dry mixture until crumbly. Slice wild or domestic apples until you have 5 cups (tart apples OK). Spread apples in a round cake tin or directly in your dutch oven. Cover with crumb mixture. Bake for about 25 minutes until apples are tender. SERVES 6.

Chapter 20

SIMPLE TRAIL FOODS AND RECIPES

The two grizzly old trappers were unshaven, unkempt, bone tired, but loaded down with prime, rich, Hudson Bay beaver pelts. They met in late afternoon at their base camp on the shores of a wind-blown lake, and immediately set about to fix some grub.

The first trapper reached into his ancient leather spice bag: ground coriander, miso paste, and turbinado sugar. He looked to be well prepared. Meanwhile, the other trapper already had going a cheery flame.

"Is that the new MSR XG-IV iso-butane model?" the first trapper said.

"Yup," the other replied. "Boils water in 4.24 minutes even at minus 18°C. Superlight, too—only 18 ounces counting the integral windscreen and heat exchanger."

"Neat," the first trapper said. "Whatayer fixin' tonight?"

"I thought I'd make this here packet of freeze-dried radicchio-lentil salad. I've got some dehydrated bok choy that should make a good side dish. Got some chia seeds to go on top, too—hey, you got any walnut oil?"

"Something better," the first trapper said. "Tahini, fresh-pressed at the health-food store in Mooseluk. It tends to separate, but it's good on most any backwoods dish, fer sure."

"By the way, whatayer fixin' tonight?" the second trapper asked.

"Bootstrap stew," the first trapper grinned through broken front teeth. "Freeze-dried beef with buckwheat groats, tamari sauce, and a pinch of sun-dried tomato."

"By golly, that sounds good!" the second trapper said. "And I've got something t' wash th' whole thing down," he added slyly.

The first trapper looked over with great interest. "Apricot Perrier—that's wonderful! Is that the new recyclable plastic bottle?"

Ah, wilderness! But whatever happened to the good old camp days, and should we even care? Camp cooking has changed. But nutritionally and spiritually speaking, how far has backwoods cooking really come?

Let's set the table for those old trappers as it might really have been set a hundred years ago.

In an old cast-iron skillet, one trapper sets to sputtering a hind quarter of beaver, not wanting to waste any part of the animal. At the same time, the other trapper cuts up some potatoes that he and his wife raised on their own dirt farm in southern Canada. They were grown in pure, sweet soil before pesticides were even known. These spuds are an important part of the provisions of the trip. Later, they'll gnaw on sweet pemmican and a satchel of blackberries that they gathered along the way. Unnatural foods and processed foods are unknown to these men. Also, they never overeat. Their bodies are hard and lean, and they burn more than 5,000 calories per day, day after day. Their bodily functions (read: metabolism) are so much more highly tuned than those of the modern city dweller that virtually anything they eat is processed quickly and efficiently. They wear leather. Their canoes are cedar. Their packs are wicker. They burn only wood and have no butane canisters to later dispose of.

Are they really doing that badly?

Now let's set the table for a pair of modern day backcountry travelers. The first pulls out a freeze-dried meal that was manufactured in a gigantic factory in Japan two years earlier. His companion pulls out a noodle soup that is even more highly processed, but that is instantly ready to eat upon the introduction of hot water. Instead of the food being toted in an old leather satchel, it is brought in cellophane, foil, and plastic—all of which is environment-unfriendly. Their clothing, tent, backpack, and sleeping bags are all synthetic and also not biodegradable. Ditto their stoves, fuel bottles, and plastic water bottles. As they chalked up two more peaks in the day just passed, they walked by at least a dozen wild edible plants, but either didn't recognize them or else didn't have time to gather them—so much to do on such a short backpacking trip.

Who is eating better? For that matter, who is living better?

I suggest that the modern backpacker could learn a lot from the old camp ways. He should look to the past and retain what was good about those ways while rejecting those foods and those ideas where there was so much room for improvement.

HONEY-BUTTER SAUCE

1/4 cup butter   1/4 cup honey

2 tsp. cornstarch   1/4 cup lemon juice

Melt butter in a saucepan. Stir in cornstarch until smooth, then stir in honey and lemon juice. Cook 5-6 minutes on low flame. Excellent over fried chicken. **MAKES JUST OVER 1/2 CUP.**

CHEESE SAUCE

2 T. butter

2 T. flour

1 cup canned chicken broth

1/2 cup powdered milk

1/2 cup shredded Cheddar cheese

1/2 tsp. salt

Dash pepper

In a pot, melt the butter and stir in the flour. Add broth, stir till smooth, then vigorously whisk in the powdered milk. When smooth, gradually add the cheese, stirring constantly, until thickened. Add salt and pepper to taste. Use on broccoli, cauliflower, asparagus, or in many other ways. **MAKES 1 CUP.**

Here, then, is a good place for me to offer some hopefully constructive philosophy on how today's backwoods roamer might eat a little better:

1. Bring in as much fresh, unprocessed food as possible, to be eaten on the first day of the trip.
2. Become much more acquainted with grains, which are cheap, light, varied, and can often be eaten without cooking—which preserves nutritive values at the same time it eliminates cooking chores.
3. Use water filtration devices that rely solely on filtration and that use no questionable chemicals.
4. Live off the land a little. If you do choose to eat flesh foods, do a little fishing and hunting where it's legal, and the meat you will enjoy will probably be much purer than any supermarket meat. Surely, you will appreciate it far more.
5. Become an expert on wild edible plants, and munch on them slowly and leisurely as you stroll through the woods. Also bring them back to camp, and use them as substitutes for some of that expensive freeze-dried fare.
6. No matter how much you love to cook—and personally I do love to cook—let raw foods (fruits, vegetables, and grains) form a substantial part of your diet. Eat less on the backpacking trip in favor of healthier foods. Learn to soak and sprout grains to soften them so no cooking is necessary.
7. For protein, look less often to freeze-dried meat dishes and more often to seeds, nuts, and legumes, and a bit of wild fish and game if you're so inclined.

Now, having said all this, it's impossible not to discuss freeze-dried and dehydrated foods, since virtually every backpacker will utilize these foods to some degree. Freeze-dried foods made for the camper are very light, easy to prepare, and almost unspoilable. Besides the fact that most are highly processed, though, they are expensive, and more bland than fresh foods. With some brands or specific meals, they will contain ingredients that health-conscious people will object to. This latter concern can be somewhat gotten around by sticking to those brands that

Save all those little sealed, one-portion condiment packages that come your way day after day. They're nonperishable, and perfect for backpacking.

advertise as being "all natural," now a very important (perhaps even dominant) category in the backpacking food industry. As far as the taste goes, there is a sameness to this type of food, though some meals will taste better than others. As to cost, there's not much you can do but comparison shop and look for the odd sale at your local camp-supply store. Most people only backpack a few times a year so, in truth, price shouldn't be a big issue.

Relatively little needs to be said about these freeze-dried foods made just for campers. Usually you just add water, stir, and sometimes, heat or cook for a short while. With some, you can eat right out of the pouch the meal comes in, reducing dishwashing to about zero. With others, you may have to combine two pouches (for example the vegetables and cheese sauce). Occasionally, the addition of a fresh ingredient such as milk or butter will be indicated if not required. Very frequently, you may be able to doctor your meal in some way, and this is an important art in the realm of backpacker's food preparation (see chapter 19). Almost always, you can add a sprinkling of one spice of another to perk your freeze-dried meal up. But in a great many cases, you need do nothing but add water and then either eat as is or cook for a short time, usually less than 30 minutes.

TWENTY-MINUTE RAISIN SCONES

1 cup all-purpose flour	1/4 cup raisins
2 tsp. baking powder	3 T. butter
2 T. powdered milk	1 egg

At home, combine flour, powders, and raisins in a bowl. Cut in butter until mixture resembles coarse crumbs. Pack this into a zip-locking bag. ✦In camp, add the egg and enough water, a little at a time, to make a not-too-thick dough. Drop in good-sized mounds onto your baking tray. Bake in reflector oven or backpacker's oven until golden. MAKES 6.

These meals are somewhat analagous to tents: A tent that the manufacturer rates to sleep four will usually sleep two fairly comfortably. Similarly, a freeze-dried meal purporting to feed four may feed only two. It's true that sometimes the portions are reasonably generous and adequate. But unless you're a very light eater, you should consider this factor in your planning.

Here are some freeze-dried meals or dishes currently available, along with their suggested retail prices and serving size produced.

Country Chicken Soup	2½ cups	$2.49
Garden Minestrone	2½ cups	$2.49
Sweet & Sour Shrimp	22 oz.	$5.49

Chicken Paprikash	22 oz.	$4.99
Beef Burgundy	22 oz.	$4.99
Shrimp Cantonese	22 oz.	$5.49
Spaghetti in Mushroom Sauce	26 oz.	$4.20
Cinnamon Apple Pancakes	13 four-inch cakes	$2.99
No-Cook Chicken & Rice	24 oz.	$3.95
Cajun Rice with Chicken	24 oz.	$5.99
Chili with Beans	16 oz.	$4.30
Hash Brown Potatoes	16 oz.	$2.60
Hot Apple Cobbler	12 oz.	$2.15
Peaches & Cream	12 oz.	$2.20

This is just a small sample of what is available from the half-dozen or so manufacturers who make most of this type of trail food. Shown here are serving sizes in volume measure, not weight. Most of the uncooked main dishes weigh between 3½ and 8 oz., with 5 oz. being about average for a meal that claims to feed two. Soups, snacks, and such weigh between 2 and 5 oz. each on average.

Other Lightweight Specialty Foods

Most of the freeze-dried foods listed above are either complete meals or side dishes. There are other types of specialty foods for the camper, though. These would include condiments, sweeteners, and snacks.

BACKPACKER'S HOT COCOA

1/2 cup powdered milk	Big dash cinnamon
1/6 cup cocoa	Dash salt
1/4 cup sugar	1/2 tsp. vanilla extract (opt.)

At home, combine all ingredients except vanilla in a plastic bag. In camp, heat one pint water. Slowly stir in dry mixture, using a whisk if possible. Add the vanilla and serve. SERVES 2.

As is true with the freeze-dried meals just listed, these adjunct camp cook supplies can often be gotten through mail-order catalogs specializing in camping as well as at the local camp-supply store. Here are the ones I'm most familiar with:

Honey crystals
Maple syrup crystals
Dry whole milk
Chocolate survival bars
Tomato powder and tomato flakes
Beef jerky
Dry eggnog

Dry spiced cider (one of my favorites)
Dry Gatorade
Potato flakes and other vegetable flakes
Pinto beans
Brown rice
Backpacker's butter
Pemmican
Sesame-lemon meal packs
Coconut-almond meal packs
Dial-A-Spice
Vegelene pan coating

All these little extras are light in weight and inexpensive. When programmed into your master cooking plan for the weekend they take up but little space and brighten the menu considerably.

Simple Foods from the Health Food Store

I wasn't the first person to wander into a health-food store along with the hippies of the '60s. But a long time ago when I started long-distance running I gravitated to healthier food and have been concerned about healthy foods ever since. My diet is very much a compromise, but it's one that includes a lot of food bought at a half-dozen health-food stores where I like to browse. The newer generation of camp cooks speak often about the goodies you can find in health-food stores, and I add my voice to that chorus enthusiastically.

WHOLE WHEAT SOY PANCAKES
AXCELL, COOKE, AND KINMONT, *SIMPLE FOODS FOR THE PACK*

2 cups whole wheat flour | 2 tsp. baking powder
1/2 cup soy flour | 1 tsp. salt
1/2 cup wheat germ | 2 T. oil
1/2 cup milk powder

At home, combine all ingredients in a zip-locking bag. In camp, empty into a bowl or pot. Slowly stir in enough water to make a batter consistency, about 3 cups. Let rest 10 minutes. Cook on a lightly greased griddle or pan. SERVES 6-8.

Health food is simple! That's really the whole point of it, and also the reason why it's especially suited to the trail.

Few foods are more popular with backpackers than peanuts and peanut butter. Here you have a powerhouse of calories and protein with no cholesterol and yet a taste that few can resist. In the health-food store, they will often grind you a pound of fresh peanut butter that will actually cost less than the more processed stuff in the supermarket. Many items in health-food stores are very expensive, but fresh-pressed peanut butter seems to be one of the real bargains. It goes far, too, since it's such a concentrated food. Buy a box of whole wheat, low-fat crackers and you've got your primary snack food for a weekend in the woods. A little hint: A dab each of honey and peanut butter on a cracker is a sensation.

BUCKWHEAT DROP BISCUITS

Sift or combine 1 cup flour, 1 cup buckwheat flour, 2 T. sugar, 1 tsp. salt, 1 T. baking powder. Cut in 4 T. butter or shortening. Bring to camp in a plastic bag. In camp, add enough water to make a soft dough. Drop in mounds onto your baking sheet. Bake in your reflector oven about 15-20 minutes. ✦If you make the dough quite soft, just firm enough to mound up, these will be extremely light biscuits. MAKES ABOUT 10.

FANCY STEWED FIGS

From home, bring about 20 dried Mission figs in a plastic bag. In a separate bag, bring a small orange and 1/3 cup nuts. In camp, place figs in a pot, barely cover with water, add 3 thin orange slices, and simmer slowly about 30 minutes until liquid is reduced to half. Toast the nuts in butter in your frypan. Spoon over the stewed figs. ✦A combination of pecans and walnuts would be good. ✦For next-day use, warm both the figs in the remaining sauce and the nuts before serving. SERVES 3.

Don't limit yourself to just peanuts and peanut butter. There is almond butter, sesame butter, cashew butter, and others.

Better health-food stores will usually have a good selection of whole grains, and that's good because grains are packed with nutritional benefit, inexpensive (amazingly so in bulk), and virtually spoil-proof. They are also relatively light, and with the necessary addition of water a small amount goes a long way.

CAMP OATMEAL SUPREME

1 cup 5-minute oatmeal	3 T. brown sugar
1/2 cup powdered milk	1/4 cup dried banana chips,
1/4 cup golden raisins	broken up

At home, place all ingredients in a plastic bag. In camp, bring 2 cups water to a boil. Stir in the oatmeal mixture and cook 4 minutes, stirring. Cover, let sit 5 minutes. ✦I use the sugared banana chips, the crunchy ones. SERVES 2-3.

CALL OF THE WILD KASHA
WOLFF'S BUCKWHEAT PRODUCTS

1 7-oz. can tuna, drained	2 T. chopped green pepper
3/4 cup cooked kasha	1/4 cup mayonnaise
2 hard-cooked eggs, chopped	1 T. mustard
1/4 cup chopped celery	2 tsp. lemon juice
1/4 cup chopped onion	

Make this delightful nutritious medley at home. Combine all ingredients and chill at least a few hours. For a great trail lunch, you could use this mixture to fill whole wheat pita pockets. Also good served on lettuce, with tomato wedges and black olives. ✦To greatly reduce the cholesterol, omit the eggs and substitute plain yogurt for the mayonnaise. SERVES 4-5.

TRAVELER'S POLENTA

At home, blend together 1 cup cornmeal, 1/2 T. sugar, 1/2 tsp. salt, and 1½ cups powdered milk. Place in a plastic bag. In camp, heat 3 cups water, add 2 T. butter. When this is simmering, slowly pour in dry mixture, stirring constantly. Continue to stir until mixture thickens. ✦There is controversy as to how long to cook cornmeal mush. Over direct heat (as opposed to with a double boiler) it tastes fine to me after 20 minutes. ✦This somewhat sweet, rich polenta is ideal as a fast breakfast porridge. SERVES 4.

An appendix to this book, "A Grain Primer," discusses the different types of grains at length. As far as I'm concerned a bowl of oatmeal tastes good any time of the day, even though it's true that grains in their cereal form are most often eaten with breakfast.

Many health enthusiasts argue that cooking (high heat) destroys certain nutritive elements in food, for example vitamins and enzymes. I can't vouch for the scientific accuracy of this, but common sense and intuition prompt me to include a lot of raw foods in my diet. Fruits are all good raw; so are a great many different vegetables. But unknown to many, and unpracticed by all but a few in our society, grains too can be eaten raw. Just be sure that they were processed (rolled, crushed, whatever) without heat. Otherwise, you defeat what you're trying to do.

Here are two no-cook recipes. The first incorporates a small amount of raw potato. Chew all raw-food meals extremely well and eat slowly.

SPECIAL SALAD
MURRAY GRUBER

At home, place 2 cups salad greens (your choice) in a plastic bag. In camp, add a few thin slices or thin slivers each of raw, peeled potato and sweet potato. Also bring from home a light vinaigrette dressing. Dress salad just before eating. ✦To enhance this or any other green-based salad, sprinkle on some Durkee's "Natural Blend Seasoning For Vegetables and Salads," an excellent all-around spice blend for the backpacker. SERVES 1.

MURRAY'S NO-COOK OATMEAL SOUP
MURRAY GRUBER

Overnight, soak 1/3 cup rolled or steel-cut oats in a combination of 1/4 cup water and 1/2 cup skim milk. Do not drain. In morning, add half of a small, raw carrot sliced thin and a small handful of raisins, plus a bit more milk depending on how much liquid was absorbed. ✦You can substitute certain other whole or cracked grains. You could also use a prepared whole-grain cereal like Wheatena in place of the oats. SERVES 1.

Many of the prepared but minimally processed grains discussed in chapter 10 can be eaten raw, and they can be delicious. As examples, I soaked Cream of Rice and Cream of Wheat (separately, on different mornings of a camping trip) in soy milk and skim milk respectively. In each case, I put about ⅔ cup liquid in with about five tablespoons of the cereal the night before. The next morning I merely sliced on some banana or peaches—no heating whatsoever. The result, each time, was not only tasty and extremely fast but refreshingly different.

Rolled oats or steel-cut oats can be soaked overnight, with an eye to a change-of-pace breakfast dish. Raisins, maple syrup from dry crystals, brown sugar, and other things can be sprinkled over or mixed in just as you might do with hot cereal.

Quite clearly, these are simple and ideal backpacker's meals, since the grains won't spoil and are light in weight, the other ingredients are wholesome and also light in weight, and there is no cooking whatever to do.

Take-Along Trail Snacks & Light Meals

This is one of the best ways to avoid the highly processed trail food that used to hold backpackers in its spell. As I've said elsewhere, the overwhelming majority of backpackers go out for two to four days, notwithstanding the longer trip that any backpacker might occasionally take. This being the case, you can almost always indulge yourself for the first three or four meals with healthy, minimally processed foods made at home and brought along in some kind of secure container. Included within this section are some ideas along those lines. This being principally a technique book, you will not find dozens upon dozens of trail recipes, either make-at-homes or ones made at camp. But you certainly shouldn't ever be without recipes. Most backpacker's cookbooks are primarily composed of recipes, and by buying just a few of these books you will have hundreds of recipes at your fingertips. Increasingly, these will be "all-natural" or "lightly processed" recipes. If anything, you might have a hard time finding more traditional camp recipes, since camp cookbooks seem to no longer be written by the sportsmen who wrote almost all of these books in decades past. In any case, see the bibliography for some of the excellent and thoughtfully compiled backpacker's cookbooks you have to choose from.

HUMMUS

At home, press 1 clove of garlic and combine it with 1½ cups canned chick peas, 1/4 cup sesame tahini, and 1/8 cup lemon juice. Mash well, or use a blender or food processor. Place in a backpacker's food tube. Excellent on-the-trail spread on crackers.

MURRAY GRUBER'S TRAIL SNACK

At home, combine in a plastic bag 6 fresh dates, 1/8 cup whole walnuts, and 4 sprigs parsley. The slight tartness of the parsley is a wonderful comple-ment to the sweetness of the dates. SERVES 1.

Lightweight and Easy Desserts

If it's true that it takes resourcefulness to churn out a tasty entrée off the road, it's doubly true with desserts. Sure, you can carry in simple sweets like cookies or brownies. But made-in-camp desserts are as tempting as they are challenging. Here are several.

'PACKER'S MOCK PECAN PIE

In a pot or bowl, combine 1½ cups cold water and 1/2 cup powdered milk. Stir well until dissolved, then add one 1-oz. packet instant butterscotch pudding. Beat well. As pudding starts to thicken, spoon into tartlet shells (little pie shells, available in 6-packs in supermarkets), sprinkle with chopped pecans (which can be pretoasted in a skillet for heightened flavor). ◆Leave the tartlets in their original tight packaging until mealtime, lest they crum-ble on you. MAKES 6 SMALL TARTS.

S'MORES

1 bag of marshmallows   1 package mini chocolate bars
1 box of graham crackers

Let each camper roast his own marshmallow on a stick over the campfire. When done, it goes between two graham crackers into which a piece of chocolate has also been inserted. The hot marshmallow will melt the choco-late and make a tasty dessert sandwich. To simplify, use chocolate-covered graham crackers and omit the chocolate bars (not quite as good).

PORCUPINE LEMON PIE

At the supermarket, purchase a regular or vanilla-flavored graham cracker pie crust. At home, remove the crust from its foil pan and crumble it. Store it in a plastic bag until the morning of your departure. ◆In camp, beat 1 egg yolk in your largest pot. Stir in half of a 14-oz. can sweetened condensed milk, plus 1/4 cup lemon juice. Chill well if possible. ◆Take the crumbled pie mix-ture and spoon some into each backpacker's cup or small bowl. Spoon some of the cooled egg yolk mixture over each serving. ✦Due to the threat of salmonellosis, use only grade A uncracked eggs, freshly purchased. Do not use the topping the next day unless you can keep it cold. SERVES 4.

QUICK CHOCOLATE TART

At the supermarket, purchase 6 small "tartlet" pie shells, chocolate flavored if available. In camp, combine half of a 3.9-oz. package of chocolate-flavored instant pie pudding, 1/2 cup cold water, and 1/2 of a 14-oz. can sweetened condensed milk. Beat very well with a small whisk or a fork. Let sit 5 minutes. Fold the pudding mixture into the tart shells. Chill if possible before serving. MAKES 4-6.

Chapter 21

GOODIES PLUCKED FROM THE WILDS

"Hey Cappy, where you goin'?"

"I'm going to the store," I answered.

"Good—hey listen, you want to get me a quart of milk?"

"I'm sorry, they don't have that at the store I'm going to."

Hard looks. Bad thoughts. Appeasement will come later in the form of a wild-berry cobbler.

The shadbush and wild dogwoods had long since blossomed along the banks of the upper Delaware River, but the flowers of spring had given way to a succulent, early summer surfeit. I parked just off the old dirt road and started walking the train tracks downstream.

On the bluff overlooking the river, the single set of tracks had broken only a fifteen-yard-wide strip in the forest canopy, but it was enough to have nurtured a miles-long cornucopia of berries. It was early July and the blackcaps (black raspberries) were dangling side by side with the much more delicate wild raspberries. Garnering an honest quart led me well down the tracks, but this was all the better since I was able to look at some new trout water.

Earlier that day, I had been lucky enough to take a fine rainbow trout of 17 inches. I worked this into a creamy fish chowder (chapter 13), and followed that first course with venison stroganoff. When my four fishermen guests bit into that wild-berry cobbler—especially since we'd gotten some vanilla ice cream to go with it—their eyes started to roll like King Kong's. I have to admit, its taste was amazing. Later, when a fresh evening breeze rode upstream just before dark, it sighed through the butternut and helped to spread a perfect languor through the group, who were now gathered around the fire telling tales and sipping brandy.

To take to the woods in any form or manner and not partake of its free gourmet offerings is to leave a thing half done. When the spring beauty pushes up its lovely flower in April, there in that same swale will be the wild leek to mix in with your morning eggs (and indeed, both the leaves and the tubers of the spring beauty can be eaten). When June unfolds into summer, there will be strawberries and mulberries, raspberries and blueberries, hearkening to the chance sunlight of roads, culverts, power lines, and natural openings. When the striking red bee balm has passed, and now only the wild asters are there to grasp the last rays of summer, the black walnut will drop its pungent green fruit, wherein resides the most exquisite-tasting nut in all the wilds.

So, then, let's talk about goodies you can gather free just that way: season by season. But first, some general precautions.

With more than 20,000 wild plants found in North America north of Mexico, not even a serious botanist is going to know all of them. But whether you can positively identify 50 or 5,000, know this: There are dozens of plants out there that can make you very sick. With some of the most toxic ones, only a handful of vegetation (or other plant part) can make you extremely ill or even kill you.

On the heels of those thoughts, a little specific advice:

1. If you have any questions whatsoever about the plant, don't eat it. Remember: When in doubt, leave it out.
2. If you have only begun to forage for wild edibles, start with the more obvious ones.
3. If you wish to go beyond gathering just the most obvious and best known wild edibles, read everything you can about the subject first. Get several good guide books, at least one of which has color photographs of the plants it describes.
4. Learn from those same guide books or in other ways the most poisonous plants so that you are particularly aware of them.
5. Remember that many edible plants have poisonous look-alikes.
6. Remember that certain parts of a plant may be very edible while other parts of that plant may be poisonous.
7. Some plants or plant parts are edible in certain stages of their growth and poisonous or at least very distasteful in other stages. It's sometimes best to avoid these plants altogether.
8. Never pick plants that are endangered or threatened. Harvest only those that you know to be abundant. Pick wildflowers or parts thereof only with great discretion, since their beauty provides pleasure to all who pass.

While I elected to put this chapter in part 2 of the book, it has equal applicability to campground settings. Wild edibles are found in the remotest forests, in urban lots, and every place in between.

Several recipes in other chapters incorporate wild edibles or name wild edibles as options. You can also use your imagination as to when you can substitute a wild edible for a store-bought ingredient. Although each of these wild succulents is discussed under a particular season, many are available over a longer period than just one season. This is noted where relevant. On the other hand, some wild plants or the stage at which they're edible are very short-lived indeed. This is also noted.

I have purposely not included guidelines for identifying these plants, feeling that it would have been dangerous to list only partial guidelines without accompanying color photographs. The reader is strongly urged to consult and purchase at least two, good, authoritative guide books for identifying wild edibles.

Two early spring treats: wild onions (right) and fiddlehead ferns. In bottom photo are some wild leeks, and the small spade used to dig them up.

Spring

WILD ONIONS *(Allium cernuum* and related species) and WILD LEEKS *(Allium tricoccum).* Onions are staples not only in western cookery but around the planet. In many parts of the country, campers are very fortunate to be able to gather in the wild members of this pungent group of plants (wild garlic, *Allium canadense,* is not discussed here but do look for it).

Pick the young leaves of the wild onion when they are small, preferably soon after they emerge from the ground. Chop them and use them as you would chive. They will not be as subtly pleasing as chives, however. The best part of the wild onion is the bulb. It is best in spring and fall, but the onion plant is most findable in spring. Rinse the bulbs well and simmer for one minute in salted water. This will help to partially remove that bitter edge. Pungency will vary depending on soil and other factors. Now use them as you would regular onions.

WILD ONIONS (OR LEEKS)
BRAISED IN MARSALA

Clean about 1 cup wild onions. A quarter- or half-inch of stem can be left on bulb. Place in small frypan filled with salted water. Blanch for 3 minutes at a light boil. (Leeks are sweeter and do not require this blanching.) Drain water. Add more water, just to cover onions. Cook until water has nearly evaporated. Add 1 T. butter, cook till onions are lightly browned, about 10 minutes. Sprinkle on 3/4 tsp. sugar. Stir to coat onions. Turn heat to medium-high. Add 1/4 cup Marsala, stir quickly. Cook until the liquid in pan is somewhat syrupy. Serve as an appetizer over toast points, or as an accompaniment to red game meat or pork. MAKES 3 APPETIZERS.

Whereas the wild onion favors comparatively high and dry places, the wild leek will usually be found in moist, cool woods of rich soil. The leaves are best harvested when they're still very small in early spring, but the best part is the bulb. Your small backpacker's entrenching tool works fine when collecting either leeks or onions; without such a tool you'll break off too much of the vegetation without extracting the bulbs. Don't expect anything like what you see in the supermarket. Both wild onions and leeks are only about an inch in diameter maximum, and usually smaller. Gather a nice brown bag full, and before you get back to the car or camp, stop at the brook and wash your leeks. Be sure to have a pole in the car in case any wild brook trout are seen darting off at your approach. When you clean the leeks back at camp, cut the bottom off just above where the whitish bulb ends. Reserve a little of the purplish stem and green leaves if you wish.

As with the domestic counterparts, wild leeks are more mellow than wild onions. Wild leeks are excellent in soups. One good example would be the ever popular potato and leek soup. In savory beef or venison stews or pot roasts add them as you would onions. Mash some potatoes, or reconstitute some dry ones, and mix in some finely chopped leeks. Sauté in sweet butter a half-dozen tiny native brook trout or panfish fillets coated with flour, and stir in a few tablespoons of leeks.

For an interesting venison (or lamb chop or beef steak) sauté, brown the steak or chops in a heavy skillet. After five minutes or so, flip the meat and sprinkle on salt and pepper. Dash on a little Worcestershire or steak sauce if you have it. Now toss in ⅛ to ¼ cup of chopped wild onions or leeks (or a combination) which had first been blanched one minute in salted water. Toss the contents around. Raise the heat to very high, and add ⅛ cup of any wine. Cover and quickly reduce heat. The wine, onions, and pan juices will all steam together nicely with the meat. Remove cover after one minute or less. Serve meat atop a slice of thick white bread, with a little of the onion sauce spooned on top.

Looking for a quick, tasty appetizer? Blanch some wild leeks for a minute in boiling salted water. Remove and chop. Melt a little butter in the same pan, and lightly brown the leeks. Spoon them over a slice of toast that has been cut into squares.

FIDDLEHEAD FERNS *(Mattlucia struthionopterus)*. Fiddleheads are part of spring's bounty that you must not miss. A fiddlehead is the unfolded frond of a fern. (Ostrich fern is the one most frequently harvested. Some ferns are inedible—learn which ones.) They are common in the Northeast, the Great Lakes region, and much of Canada. The picking stage is brief. Fiddleheads are now gathered commercially in eastern Canada and are occasionally seen in better supermarkets for a brief time in spring. They prefer rich soil and are often found along river bottoms or at the edges of swamps and swales. They are best when the stalk they are supported on is only eight inches tall or less. To harvest, just grab the curled up fiddlehead with all five fingers and pull it off as if you might be picking a blackberry. Gently scrape off the brown, flaky material, then wash in two or three changes of very cold water, swishing the fiddleheads around vigorously. Bring a good-sized pot of water to the boil, and boil the little green prizes for 12-15 minutes until just fork tender. Serve with butter and salt and pepper and a dash of lemon juice or cider vinegar. They make an excellent accompaniment to most panfried or grilled meats, especially game or lamb. Once cooked, they can be tossed into a cold, green salad. Use a nice, pungent vinaigrette dressing. Recently, I floated some leftover, precooked fiddleheads in a bowl of leftover fish chowder, as a garnish. It was the perfect conclusion to both leftovers.

If you're laid up in camp with good provisions but lousy spring weather, a chilly mist clinging tightly to the woods around you, you might want to try this luscious soup.

CREAM OF FIDDLEHEAD SOUP

2 T. shallots, finely chopped	2 qts. veal, chicken or gamebird
1 T. butter	stock
1/4 cup finely chopped carrots	Salt and pepper
1/4 cup finely chopped leeks (white	2 egg yolks
part only; wild if available)	1 cup heavy cream
1½ cups fiddleheads, picked	1/2 cup fiddleheads for garnish
clean of all brown fuzz	

Sauté shallots in butter in a large heavy pot. If you lack shallots, substitute onion. Add carrots, leeks, and 1½ cups fiddleheads, being careful to keep the heat nice and low. Add stock and salt and pepper to taste. In place of the stock, you can substitute an equal amount of canned chicken broth. This may be salted, though, so don't add any salt until you taste. Simmer 30 minutes. ✦Beat the yolks well and then beat in the cream (use a blender if you've brought your greens back home) until the mixture is very smooth. Add the egg yolk-cream mixture to the soup, and heat the now composed soup to very hot but not boiling. ✦Boil extra fiddleheads in salted water for 6 minutes. Drain them, and use as a floating garnish for your soup.

WILD STRAWBERRIES *(Nagaria virginiana)*. One of the most delicious of all North American wild edibles, the wild strawberry is common across the eastern United States, in southeastern Canada, the upper plains states, and across the northern Rockies. The plant favors moist places; a semiopen flood plain would be a good typical location. Yet I have seen them in quite dry places, too.

The fruit is much smaller than commercially grown strawberries, but if you eat them fresh out of hand you won't believe their sweetness. Generally, but depending on latitude, you can start looking for ripe fruit in early June. Try the fresh berry cobbler in chapter 9. Use them any way you'd use store-bought strawberries but don't add a lot of sugar until you taste. You may need less, or none.

If you've a pint or a half of one of heavy cream sloshing about in your cooler, beat it till it's slightly stiff, adding a little sugar towards the end. This is where it's really important to have that little whisk listed in chapter 1. Take your strawberries and marinate them in a little of whatever sweet cordial is being passed around the campfire. After a time, spoon the red jewels into small, individual serving bowls and top each with a generous glob of the cream.

Now that you've become skillful with your reflector oven, a strawberry short-cake, I'm convinced, is not out of your reach. Use a prepackaged mix, to which you'll probably have to add an egg and perhaps some milk.

Bake the shortcake in your square, eight-inch baking tin in your reflector oven or your stove-top oven, usually about 20 minutes. Remove, cool, and if you wish, split in half horizontally. Spread a little softened butter onto each half. To avoid this admittedly tricky operation, bake two separate times but use less bat-

ter in each so the cake will be thinner. Spread on some sliced and slightly crushed wild strawberries that you earlier had marinated in sugar and a small bit of water or liqueur. Drape on the second layer of shortcake, more strawberries, then some whipped cream. Now is the time to rummage around everyone's food boxes to see what potential toppings might be in the offing: curls off a chocolate bar, any kind of chopped nut (but especially wild hazelnuts, preferably toasted till golden in a hot pan), shredded coconut, and so on.

Wild strawberry leaves make a wonderful, fragrant tea that, like rose hips tea (which we'll get to) is extremely rich in vitamin C. Just steep a couple of loosely packed cups in a quart of gently boiling water. Pure, fresh honey, and nothing but, is essential in this and all other teas worth brewing. Know that the leaves from an overharvest can be dried for later tea making.

Black birch (below), an unmistakable tree with dark twigs. Above, a handful of those twigs are about to be steeped for tea.

SWEET BIRCH *(Betula lenta)*. Another great tea you can make in camp is birch tea. Both sweet birch, also called black birch, and yellow birch *(B. alleghaniensis)* may be used for tea, but the sweet birch will be the more flavorful. Just take a handful of crushed and broken small twigs and steep these in an appropriate amount of barely simmering water. I usually put 8 or 10 broken twigs into two cups of water. Do not boil, or you'll vaporize the volatile wintergreen oils. The resulting tea, like the broken twigs fresh from the tree, will exude a heady aroma of wintergreen. It will have no bitterness, and will be a beautiful amber color. With large birch trees, the usable twigs may be too far from the ground, so I always look for the smaller trees of six inches or less in diameter.

This soothing hot tea is a delight for eastern backpackers since sweet birch grows plentifully along the Appalachians. For some reason I seem to frequently encounter them immediately alongside hiking trails. Using the twigs is easiest, but the inner bark may also be used for tea and in several other ways. Sweet birch twigs can be harvested for tea 12 months a year, but it's best in springtime. Try to take only one or two twigs each from several different trees.

A genuine, delicious birch beer can be made from sweet birch twigs. The process is beyond what campers can do, but for the serious forager it's a make-at-home possibility.

Summer

BERRIES. Depending on where you camp, wild berries start becoming available in late spring. Strawberries are often the first, followed by mulberries, black raspberries, raspberries, wineberries, currants, blueberries, and blackberries. The later elderberries bring down the curtain in late summer and early fall. There are, of course, other wild edible berries, but these are the most popular.

More so than with, say, wild roots and tubers, wild berries can freely be substituted for one another in many recipes. Raspberries, black raspberries, strawberries, mulberries, and blackberries are very much interchangeable. Blueberries are too, in many cases. Elderberries and some currants are much less sweet and so treatment may be different.

The dense, prickly foliage of the black raspberry (top photo). For eating out of hand, they're far less flavorful than raspberries, but for pies and pancakes they're exceptionally good. Left photo, some delicate wild raspberries about to be incorporated into this sourdough pancake batter.

FRUIT AND CHEESE BUTTER
KAREN SHERWOOD

Soften 8 ozs. cream cheese in a bowl. Add 1 T. lemon juice and 1/4 cup maple syrup and mash well. Add 1 cup wild berries, mash and stir well to combine. Serve on muffins, toast or crackers.

If you encounter wild berries near camp or on the trail, don't get hung up on recipes or on the idea of seeing a quart of them all nestled together. Nibble on them as you go along, and they'll be at their sweetest and most nutritious. Just try to avoid eating berries if they are in a location where they may have been exposed

Several umbels of elderberries. I like to eat them right off the stem, though at times the fruit is not sweet enough for that. Elderberry jelly and elderberry wine are of course exceptional treats; in New York's Catskill Mountains, the right picking time is first week of October.

to toxic sprays, for example along some roads, train tracks, power lines. If camp smoke is rising pleasantly on the horizon, gather some of the colorful jewels and fold them into next morning's pancake batter. Include them in sourdough muffins, breads, and cakes. Dust them with sugar and pour over them a little milk or half-and-half, or sweet or sour cream. Top with any nuts, including wild nuts which may possibly be available if you're picking late berries. Partially crush your berries in a glass of pure, spring water and let stand for an hour or more. Drizzle in some honey, stir, and you have a fast, refreshing, healthy drink.

Now let's get a little fancier. First, pies. Above I said that the sweeter berries are largely interchangeable. That is reasonably true, but in pies certain of the basic ingredients and spices are varied. Some of this has to do with relative degree of acidity or water content in the different berries. Some spices also have particular affinity to certain berries. Many cookbooks for the indoor chef get into this in detail. A recipe for pie crust may be found in chapter 9. Tips for baking pies in the reflector oven may also be found in that chapter.

If the fruit is dry, perhaps being a bit unripe, add a small amount of water or fruit cordial. Toss the fruit with this water, as well as the lemon juice and any other liquid ingredients that might be called for. Don't be afraid to crush the berries a little. Mix the dry ingredients, then blend the two mixtures together. Fold into an unbaked pie crust and dot with butter. Cover with a top crust or a lattice, or omit this step. In camp, a plain open pie is fine. No one will complain. If after you've folded the fruit into the pie (before adding the butter) there is too much liquid in the bottom, cant it off or you will have a runny pie. With very ripe berries the pie may be runny no matter what you do. If this is the case, add extra flour or cornstarch. If you use cornstarch, use half as much as you would flour. In a reflector oven, a two-crust pie will probably take 50-80 minutes. Rotate the pan several times to ensure it cooks and glazes all the way around.

If you're near the store, consider using a premade pie shell. They are quite good, and they usually give you an extra top.

WATERCRESS *(Nasturtium officinale)*. Watercress is a widespread aquatic plant found all across the country and beyond. It has been eaten and praised by cultures across the globe for at least several dozen centuries. It prefers the coolness of springs, or any slow-moving, clean water. This lush, green plant will often be found at least partially floating in water, with the roots growing out of the floating stems. It can be harvested nearly the entire year, barring ice on its watery home. Just cut off the brown parts and retain the clean, fresh-looking green stems and leaves.

CHILLED WATERCRESS SOUP

1½ T. butter or oil

2 large potatoes (or substitute
   spring beauty tubers)

6 small wild garlic bulbs, minced
   (or 2 medium cloves regular
   garlic, minced)

1 16-oz. can low-salt chicken broth

1/2 broth can water

Salt and pepper to taste

2 large handfuls watercress, heavi-
   est stems removed

1 broth can low-fat milk

Peel potatoes and boil about 5 minutes. Cool, cut into cubes, and sauté with garlic in butter or oil. Add broth and water to same pot and simmer 10 minutes. Add seasonings and chopped watercress and simmer 5 more minutes. Add milk, adjust seasonings. Chill and serve. A splash of white wine may be added. SERVES 4-5.

Watercress is used widely as a salad ingredient. I love it, and find it to be mild, pleasant, and slightly piquant. My favorite salad is a simple mixture of romaine lettuce and watercress, each cut or chopped into mouth-size pieces. I top it with an equally simple vinaigrette (see p. 139). Almost any simple, freshly made dressing will work. Just please avoid those horrible bottled dressings.

Add the chopped leaves, plus stems if you wish, to most any cream-style soup. Make an egg, tuna fish, or chicken salad sandwich and top it with a little watercress as you would lettuce. Chop up some 'cress and mix it in with your scrambled eggs as you might with wild leeks. Or, chop it up coarsely with some hard-cooked eggs and slather the resulting blend onto some dark pumpernickel. Now you're living.

HAZELNUTS *(Corylus americana* and *C. cornuta)*. Unlike the most popular North American nuts, the wild hazelnut grows on a shrub, not a true tree. Both the American hazelnut *(americana)* and the beaked hazelnut *(cornuta)* may be utilized. In either case, the mature nuts will be ready some time in late summer or early fall. Look for hazelnuts especially in tangled thickets.

After removing the soft husk, crack open the shell and eat the tasty hazelnuts as a trail snack. Back at camp, mix your little prizes into any concoctions where you normally might use nuts. Certainly, add a handful to your zip-locking bag full of gorp to perk it up.

Fall

In September, farm stands spring up all across America, and people flock to them by the millions. This must be testament to the fact that Americans, for all their commercialism, still have an innate yearning to be a part of the miracle of the harvest; to avoid, for the moment, the assembly line food of the neon supermarket; to go right to the source. Fortunately, if it's autumn and you're camped in the outback, you can really go to the source, for wild edibles abound in the early part of the colorful season.

APPLES. You won't even see apples listed in most wild edible guidebooks, since this fruit is perceived to be a domestic. Being a tattered, New England grouse hunter, I can testify to the contrary. On abandoned farms and woodlands around the country, now-wild apples provide earthy good taste and nutrition.

I've found that the redder the wild apple, the greater the chances of it being sweet. While some domestic apples are green even when mature, wild green apples are usually very bitter. If you find some reasonably sweet wild apples, take them to camp and whip them into this delicious and easy mock apple pie. Also look ahead to the recipe under black walnuts.

MOCK APPLE PIE

5 cups thin-sliced wild apples	1/2 cup flour
3/4 cup quick cooking rolled oats	1/2 tsp. cinnamon
1/2 cup brown sugar	1/3 cup butter or margarine

Grease your largest baking tin. Arrange apples in bottom of it. In a separate bowl, combine oats, sugar, flour, and cinnamon. Cut butter into this mixture using two dull knives or your fingertips. Sprinkle this coarse, crumbly mixture over the apples. Bake in a preheated dutch oven or reflector oven. It's not advisable to make this directly on the bottom of a dutch oven without the tin. ✦This recipe can be cut to one-half or even one-third if you lack a large enough baking tin. ✦Peeling makes for mighty big work in camp. If I'm certain the apples were not sprayed, I will not peel them. SERVES 6-7.

HICKORY (Carya genus). There are plenty of plants you can dine on in fall, but during this heady time of gorgeous foliage and Indian summer, wild nuts reign supreme.

There are three hickory nuts that are commonly eaten: big shellbark hickory (Carya laciniosa), shagbark hickory (C. ovata) and mockernut hickory (C. tomentosa). Among the three, the shagbark is preferred because its thinner shell makes for easier nut removal. Easier, but never easy.

The outer husk will often be split when it falls to the ground (shagbark) and so can be quite easily removed. The shell must then be cracked with a hammer, vise, or similar tool. You're apt to wind up with a lot of shell mixed in with the nut meats, so here's a trick to get around that. After you've cracked the shells, place the whole mix into a pot. Cover with water and bring to the boil. Most of the nutmeats will rise to the surface where they can easily be skimmed off.

BLACK WALNUT. I guess every real disciple of Euell Gibbons has his or her own favorite wild edible, and mine is the black walnut. I'm fortunate in that I have a half-dozen walnut trees growing along the grassy trail that passes behind my house. I run or walk along this trail every day, and carefully watch their progress. The locustlike leaves come very late, but the fruit starts to form along about June.

A beautiful, healthy black walnut tree. The late-appearing foliage is very lacy, but identification is never a problem. Scattered nuts, new or last year's, will always be found around the base of the tree.

The first pungent green nuts start to fall about early July, and I love to pick up these immature, grape-sized drop-offs and take them home. The nuts in their protective green husk have a very distinct, pungent smell, and I know that when I first get a whiff of one, summer is moving along quickly. The mature fruits are about two inches in diameter, and start to fall in earnest in early September. Should a strong storm pass through in late September, perhaps a wayward hurricane, the walnuts will come down by the hundreds and I'm right there to gather them. No one else in my neighborhood seems to be interested. I think they're all down at the local McDonalds.

I've discussed black walnuts with other naturalists, all just as entranced with this extraordinary wild food. We tend to agree that the best course of action is to immediately cut off the aromatic green husk. The husk can be removed with an old dull knife. Use thick gloves for protection, and also to prevent staining. Black walnut shells can be used to make a fine dark ink, so just imagine what they can do to your hands. Now place the blackish, furrowed nuts in boxes and set them in a cool, shady place. They will be ready for your Christmas baking, and what a treat if you've so far been deprived of this most exotic tasting nut.

"Musty" is the way my friend and fellow cook Mike describes them, and that's a pretty fair adjective. But you really have to taste them, as black walnuts do not resemble anything else and they surely do not taste like your basic supermarket walnuts. In truth, a lot of people won't like black walnuts. But those with adventurous palates will go wild for them.

One of the most amazing desserts I know of includes black walnuts, and is done beautifully in the dutch oven. My mother, by the way, came up with this recipe. She first made them with regular walnuts, but then she tried black walnuts and what a difference it made.

BAKED APPLES WITH BLACK WALNUTS

Core 3 large apples nearly to the bottom but do not break bottom skin. Peel apples one-third of the way down. Fill the centers with a mixture of black walnuts, brown sugar and raisins. Sprinkle a little lemon juice on top of this. Now drizzle maple syrup and a splash of grenadine on each apple. Bake in a dutch oven for about 40 minutes or until done. Baste tops with pan liquid if possible. ✦A camp-stove oven would be the one viable alternative to a dutch oven. SERVES 3.

I would not say that you should use black walnuts just any place you would use more mundane nuts. They are just too full-flavored and also too special for such casual treatment. Chopped and mixed in with cookies or cakes, they make those baked goods absolutely unbelievable. Thus I cannot resist including here one cookie and one cake recipe. These are not terribly simple, but they'd be doable in many camps. Bake the cookies in your reflector oven. Bake the cake in a dutch oven or camp-stove oven.

KISS-THE-COOK COOKIES

1/2 cup melted butter or margarine
3/8 cup brown sugar, firmly packed
5/8 cup finely ground black
   walnuts, or regular walnuts
1/2 tsp. vanilla
1¼ cups flour
1/2 tsp. baking powder
1/2 cup chocolate bits

Stir together butter, sugar, 3/4 of the walnuts, and vanilla. Sift the flour (if possible) with baking powder and stir into butter mixture; blend well. This is the finished dough. Shape each cookie by pressing some dough lightly between two teaspoons. Bake on an ungreased cookie sheet in reflector oven for about 20 minutes or until light, golden brown. Cool. ✦Melt chocolate over warm water; cool slightly. Dip large end of cooled cookie in melted chocolate and then in the remaining finely ground nuts. ✦Do not attempt to chill the dough. Form cookies and bake right away. MAKES ABOUT 24.

BLACK WALNUT POUND CAKE

Mix the contents of an 18-oz. package of pound cake mix with the required ingredients—usually milk and fresh eggs. Beat the batter the required number of strokes. Towards the end, add 1/2 cup black walnut pieces. Fold into a 9-inch bread pan. Bake in your camp-stove oven for about 1¼ hours at 325° and do not let temperature rise above that. Could also be baked, in the tin, in your dutch oven, a poorer choice for this cake.

CHICORY *(Cidrorium intybus)*. All across America, the wild chicory grows weedlike along roadsides as well as in vacant lots, ditches, fields, and other open, sunny places. Its pretty blue flower is a dead giveaway, and once you've seen it identification will not be a problem. The leaves can be eaten, but the distinctive treat that awaits you lies beneath the ground, not above it. From spring through fall, but especially in fall, dig up the meaty root and roast it in your oven until brown throughout. At home this is a snap. In camp, if a gas range is not available a dutch oven or camp-stove oven will work. When very brown, I take the roots out of the oven and break them into smaller pieces with a mallet. Then I roast them a second time. Now you can grind the roots and brew just like coffee. Admittedly, you'd really have to have along some kind of grinder. If this is not feasible in camp, bring your chicory home where the process will be so much easier.

Freshly-dug chicory roots, shown above. Scrape them with a knife, wash them, and they will look like slender parsnips. Roast them till they're very brown; break them up, roast them again, then grind and brew like coffee.

ROSE HIPS *(Rosa* genus). Roses in the wild never approximate the grandeur of show varieties grown along the patio, but they are pretty in their own more subdued way, and when they bloom in June, many a country road is perfumed with their fragrance. Best of all, the "hips" or fruits of wild roses are powerhouses of nutrition, being one of the richest sources of vitamin C of any known plant. There are some three dozen rose species native to North America, and while quality will vary all have edible parts. Luckily, there are no known poisonous look-alikes.

The hips will ripen in autumn and that's the time to pick them. If you miss your chance in fall, you can often still gather the hips in winter.

Some people make jelly from rose hips, and other things are done, too. For example, an old mountain woman who lived near our hunting camp used to make a soothing salve out of rose hips. One day I picked up a ferocious sunburn, and Gertie's cream saw me through the torment. But the most popular use of rose hips is in tea. Pick the dried flower parts from the top of the plant, split them open, and place them aside to dry for several weeks. Use them to make tea through the winter whenever you feel the need for a shot of vitamin C.

A GRAIN PRIMER

Let's start with the dictionary definition of grain: "A small, hard seed or seedlike fruit, especially that of any cereal plant, as wheat, rice, corn, rye, etc."

Some of the most often used grains are seeds of plants in the grass family, for example wheat, rye, and oats. However, a few commonly used grains come from plants not at all related to the grasses. A good example is buckwheat, which is a member of the family *Polygonaceae* to which rhubarb, dock, and sorrel also belong.

Because grains are so hard, they rarely are eaten whole uncooked although some people will soak grains overnight and then eat them raw. Some are eaten whole after cooking. Many are sprouted. With most, some mechanical processing (milling) is done before you buy them.

Easily the most popular camp grain is oats. Oats are usually rolled flat between large rollers, and so rolled oats is what you usually start with when you set out to make a crowd-pleasing pot of oatmeal. Some grains, like wheat or buckwheat, are mechanically cracked and toasted. With at least a few grains, for example buckwheat, you have a choice as to how finely cracked the grain is: coarse, medium, or fine.

A change of pace from rolled oats is Scotch oats, also called Irish oatmeal. Here, the oat groats are cut into two or three pieces each and not rolled.

For our purposes here, cereal is a grain that has been ground and is thus able to accept water or other liquid freely, reducing cooking time and difficulty of chewing. In cultures around the world, cereal is a staple food, indeed even a life-giving and life-saving food, and it is not served just for breakfast. Highly processed cereals of all types are normally eaten cold out of the box, with milk. The more natural cereals that we'll dwell on here are usually eaten hot, also with milk. Some grains in their cereal form compose wonderfully into desserts (oatmeal cookies, for one).

A "cream" is nothing but a very fine cereal. It accepts liquid more readily and cooks more quickly. It makes for a very fine-textured dish.

Finally, we come to flour, which is grain in its finest common form. White flour, whole wheat flour, corn flour, buckwheat flour: All these are very finely ground grains.

There are three main parts to any grain: The outer layer or bran; the part that will become the plant shoot, or germ; and the starchy bulk of the grain kernel, which is the endosperm (food for the new plant). Centuries ago, industrious but misguided people learned that you could get a whiter, "purer" cereal or flour by removing the darker, coarser bran. Methods also were eventually developed for removing the germ. In medieval times, royalty ate this "purer" white bread and became ill with constipation, hemmorhoids, diverticulitis, and other ills. The peasants ate their darker "peasant bread" (still called that, sometimes) and avoided these medical calamities. While knowledge of nutrition has blossomed, this irony hasn't quite been put to bed yet. Peasants the world over still indulge heavily in whole grains and whole-grain products, often because they carry a lower price tag. Both the bran and germ are important nutritive elements, and health-conscious people today want their grains—regardless of how finely milled—to be whole (as opposed to fragmented), that is, with all parts of the grain kernel present. Many individuals go so far as to demand that their whole grains be organically grown.

A food-processing company will often remove the bran and/or germ and then later add certain minerals and vitamins and call the product enriched. (One Canadian nutritionist quipped, "If that's enrichment, I'd like to know what impoverishment is.") It's also important to note that the degree and method of processing will vary considerably from one grain product to the next.

In the following discussion, I'll talk about all the popular grains and state whether they're normally sold whole or fragmented; virtually all fragmented cereals are enriched. In this book, breakfast, lunch and dinner recipes employing grains are presented, healthy alternatives to the often high-fat dishes that dominated camp cookbooks of yesteryear.

WHEAT. There are, botanically, many varieties of wheat, and we won't get into the distinctions here. Wheat berries can be purchased and eaten whole after cooking. Sold more often cracked, ground into a cereal either whole or fragmented, and ground into a flour also either whole or fragmented. Widely available.

BULGUR WHEAT. You could consider bulgur to be precooked since it has been cracked, steamed, and toasted. Can conceivably be eaten as a cereal, but is usually served later in the day, often in combination with vegetables. Look in natural-food stores, some supermarkets.

BARLEY. Usually eaten whole, cooked. Whole grain barley is available; pearl barley is barley from which the bran has been removed. Like bulgur, not typically a part of the American breakfast. Often used in soups and stews. Widely used for making malts and for feeding livestock. Widely available.

MILLET. Like barley, usually eaten whole, cooked. Also like barley, often added to soups or casseroles. Usually sold in its whole-grain form. Look in natural-food stores.

RICE. Usually eaten whole, cooked. Brown rice is whole grain. White rice has had the bran removed. Polished rice has had deeper layers of bran removed. Rice flour is available both whole grain and fragmented, but is not routinely used in American cooking. White and brown rice widely available.

WILD RICE. Eaten whole, cooked. Often harvested by Native Americans in the Great Lakes region. Can also be found growing wild. Available in most supermarkets as a whole grain. Very expensive, but magnificently good to eat, especially as an accompaniment or stuffing for wild game. Available in larger supermarkets.

BUCKWHEAT. Not related to wheat or any of the above. Usually sold in whole-grain form, normally cracked or ground into a flour. Kasha is cracked and toasted buckwheat kernels, and can be made into a cereal or eaten plain as a side dish. Buckwheat flour makes delicious, hearty pancakes.

Buckwheat is a powerhouse of nutrition. It is one of the best sources of high biological protein in the entire known plant kingdom, coming closer to animal protein in some regards than any other commonly eaten plant. It has 50 percent more vitamin B than wheat. It is no higher in calories than most other grains. Certain health-conscious people who avoid wheat and some other grains due to their high gluten content extoll buckwheat, which is gluten-free. Kasha widely available in larger supermarkets. Look for buckwheat flour in natural-food stores.

CORN. Like wheat and rice, one of the most basic and important foods in the world. Probably sold in more physical forms than any other grain. Whole, dried kernels can be popped over the campfire or in a pot or skillet. Cornstarch, a corn-kernel by-product, is an important thickener. Corn flour is common to Latin American cultures and can be made into tortillas, among many other things. Hominy is puffed kernels of corn that have been soaked in a lye solution and then washed in order to remove the hulls. Grits (which can also refer to wheat) is ground hominy with the germ removed.

There is little nutritional difference between white corn and yellow corn. Either can be whole grain or fragmented. Cornmeal and corn flour are usually whole grain. With fine hominy, both the bran and the germ may have been removed. Some cornmeal has been degerminated and is often labeled as such.

Corn products except flour widely available in supermarkets. Look for corn flour in Spanish stores.

OATS. Usually sold in the whole grain form. Rolled mechanically so that what you buy is rolled oats. Other forms of oats not readily available. Rolled oats can be made into cereal or cookies, and are also widely used in the making of hearty, multigrain breads.

There you have the nine most common grains and a little insight about them. I hope this extra bit of knowledge will inspire you to use them more in your camp cooking, as well as in your home kitchen.

It's not at all out of the question to eat cracked grains raw, and I've been known to munch on kasha or Wheatena right out of the box. Both rolled and steel-cut oats and whole barley can be soaked to soften them—the oats overnight, the barley for a couple of days. Many health advocates claim that cooking destroys essential nutritive elements. That's a good reason to eat some of these whole grains in a raw state. Virtually every nutrition expert in the world believes sprouted grains to be health-giving.

There is a further discussion of grains in chapter 10. Recipes incorporating grains are numerous in this book. See the Index that follows.

SELECT BIBLIOGRAPHY

Angier, Bradford. *Skills for Taming the Wilds: A Handbook of Woodcraft Wisdom.* Harrisburg: Stackpole Books, 1967.

———. *Field Guide to Edible Wild Plants.* Harrisburg: Stackpole Books, 1974.

Axcell, Claudia, Diana Cooke, and Vikki Kinmont. *Simple Foods For the Pack.* San Francisco: Sierra Club Books, 1986.

Balsey, Betsy. "Dutch Treat." *Los Angeles Times* (September 3, 1987) 1, 14-18.

———. "Roughing it Made Easy: A Practical Guide to the Camper's Dutch Oven." *Los Angeles Times* (September 3, 1987) 32.

Barker, Harriett. *The One-Burner Gourmet.* Chicago: Contemporary Books, 1981.

Bashline, Sylvia. *Cleaning & Cooking Fish.* The Hunting & Fishing Library. Minnetonka: Cy De Cosse, 1982.

Bates, Joseph D. *The Outdoor Cook's Bible.* Garden City: Doubleday & Co., Inc., 1963.

Boy Scouts of America. *Scout Field Book.* N.p., n.d.

Brown, Edward Espe. *Tassajara Cooking.* Berkeley/London: Shambhala, 1973.

Carey, Dave. "Dutch Oven Treats." *Outdoor Life* (November, 1986) 88-91.

Child, Julia, Louisette Bertholle, and Simone Beck. *Mastering the Art of French Cooking*. New York: Alfred A. Knopf, 1979.

Davenport, Rita. *Rita Davenport's Sourdough Cookery*. Tucson: H.P. Books, 1977.

De Gouy, L.P. *The Derrydale Cook Book of Fish and Game*. Vol. 1, Game. 1937. Reprint. Wautoma: Willow Creek Press, 1987.

Gilpatrick, Gil. *The Canoe Guide's Handbook*. Yarmouth: DeLorme Publishing Co., 1983.

Elliott, Charles. *Care of Game Meat and Trophies*. New York: Outdoor Life Books; Harrisburg: Stackpole Books, 1975.

Elliot, Rose. *The Complete Vegetarian Cuisine*. New York: Pantheon Books, 1988.

Farmer, Fannie Merritt. *The Boston Cooking School Cook Book*. rev. ed. Boston: Little, Brown and Company, 1933. (Originally published 1896.)

Gibbons, Euell. *Stalking the Wild Aspargus*. 1962. Reprint. Putney: Alan C. Hood, n.d.

Hoffman, Mable. *Crepe Cookery*. Tuscon: H.P. Books, 1976.

Hunter, Beatrice Trum. *The Natural Foods Cookbook*. New York: Pyramid Books, 1967.

Lemlin, Jeanne. "The Nature of Grains." *Country Journal*. (Vol. number not known): 35-39.

Livingston, A.D. *Cast-Iron Cooking: From Johnnycakes to Blackened Redfish*. New York: Lyons & Burford, 1991.

Marshall, Mel. *Complete Book of Outdoor Cookery*. New York: Outdoor Life Books and Van Nostrand Reinhold, 1983.

National Outdoor Leadership School. *The NOLS Cookery: Experience the Art of Outdoor Cooking*. Harrisburg: Stackpole Books, n.d.

North American Hunting Club. *NAHC Wild Game Cookbook*. Hopkins: North American Hunting Club, n.d.

Ragsdale, John G. *Dutch Oven Cooking.* 2d ed. Houston: Lone Star Books, 1988.

Reader's Digest. *Quick, Thrifty Cooking.* Pleasantville/Montreal: The Reader's Digest Association, Inc., 1985.

Ririe, Robert L. *Let's Cook Dutch: A Complete Guide for the Dutch Oven Chef.* Bountiful: Horizon Publishers, 1979.

State of New York, Office of General Services. *Your Commodity Cookbook.* State of New York, Office of General Services. N.p., n.d.

Steindler, Geraldine. *The Game Cookbook.* South Hackensack: Stoeger, 1985.

Tested Recipe Publishers. *Barbecue: The Fine Art of Charcoal, Gas and Hibachi Cooking.* Chicago: Tested Recipe Publishers, 1971; distributed by Doubleday & Co., Inc.

Titterton, Robert J. *North County Gourmet: A Vermont Chef Cooks at Home.* Woodstock: The Countryman Press, 1991.

The University of Chicago Press. *The Chicago Manual of Style.* 13th ed. Chicago/ London: The University of Chicago Press, 1982.

Vegetarian Times magazine. *Vegetarian Times Cookbook.* New York: Macmillan Publishing Co., Collier Books, 1984.

Weiss, John. *Trail Cooking.* New York: Outdoor Life Books and Van Nostrand Reinhold, 1981.

ABOUT THE AUTHOR

Jim Capossela, a native of New York's beautiful Hudson Valley, has been a full-time professional writer for 20 years and a book producer for 12 years. He has fished, hunted, and camped throughout his home state, as well as in many other states and in Canada and Europe.

He developed an early love of the outdoors, which was nurtured by his several active years in the Boy Scouts of America, where he began to learn the lore of outdoor cookery. Besides *Camp & Trail Cooking Techniques,* he has published a booklet of Christmas recipes, and numerous of his other book projects have included extensive recipe sections. Also a serious amateur home cook, he personally compiles and tests all the recipes in his books and articles.

A widely published magazine journalist, Capossela's articles have appeared in dozens of different publications. One piece, "Downstream," was published in *Sports Afield* and was entered in The Orvis Outdoor Writing Contest. It later appeared in *The Orvis Anthology.* His books have received favorable reviews in many prestigious publications, including the Sunday *New York Times.*

An accomplished photographer, Capossela's work has appeared on the covers of two books and several magazines. His drawings have illustrated one full-length book, and partially illustrated several others. He makes all the maps for his outdoor guide books, including the ones in his popular *Good Fishing in New York Series.*

INDEX

For a list of recipes by category, see page xi.
Page numbers in bold face refer to illustrations or photographs.

Books from The Countryman Press

The Countryman Press is well-known for its books on travel, cookery, outdoor recreation, and under the name Foul Play Press, mysteries. Here's just a sampling of what we have to offer.

Nature and Outdoor Recreation

Fly-Fishing with Children: A Guide for Parents, $19.00
Fishwatching: Your Complete Guide to the Underwater World, $18.00
Sketching Outdoors in All Seasons, $20.00
Fifty Hikes in the White Mountains:
   Hikes and Backpacking Trips in the High Peaks Region of New Hampshire, $12.00
Fifty Hikes in Vermont:
   Walks, Hikes, and Overnights in the Green Mountain State, $12.00
Fifty Hikes in Massachusetts:
   Hikes and Walks from the Top of the Berkshires to the Tip of Cape Cod, $13.00
Fifty Hikes in Northern Virginia:
   Walks, Hikes, and Backpacks from the Allegheny Mountains to the Chesapeake Bay, $13.00
Walk to Your Heart's Content: The Way to Fitness, Health, and Adventure, $14.95
25 Bicycle Tours in and around Washington, D.C.: From the Capitol Steps to Country Roads, $10.00
25 Bicycle Tours in Maine: Coastal and Inland Rides from Kittery to Caribou, $10.00
25 Bicycle Tours in Maryland: From the Allegheny Mountains to the Atlantic Ocean, $11.00
30 Bicycle Tours in Wisconsin: Lakes, Forests, and Glacier-carved Countryside, $13.00
Waterfalls of the White Mountains: 30 Trips to 100 Waterfalls, $15.00
Canoeing and Kayaking Ohio's Streams: An Access Guide for Paddlers and Anglers, $17.00
Backwoods Ethics: Environmental Issues for Hikers and Campers, $13.00
Wilderness Ethics: Preserving the Spirit of Wildness, $13.00

Travel

Maine: An Explorer's Guide, sixth edition, $17.00
The Hudson Valley and Catskill Mountains: An Explorer's Guide, $15.00
Vermont: An Explorer's Guide, sixth edition, $17.00
New Hampshire: An Explorer's Guide, second edition, $17.00
Food Festival:
   The Guidebook to America's Best Regional Food Celebrations, second edition, revised & expanded, $16.00
New Jersey's Special Places:
   Scenic, Historic and Cultural Treasures in the Garden State, second edition, revised & expanded $14.00

Cookery

The Best from Libby Hillman's Kitchen: Treasured Recipes from 50 Years of Cooking and Teaching, $25.00
The King Arthur Flour 200th Anniversary Cookbook, $21.00
Wild Game Cookery: The Hunter's Home Companion, $13.00

We offer many more books on hiking, travel, biking, walking, fishing, and canoeing in the Midwest, New England, New York, and the Mid-Atlantic states—plus our mysteries, history, gardening, and how-to. For a free catalog of books from The Countryman Press, please call us toll-free 800/245-4151.

Our titles are available in bookshops and in many sporting goods shops, or they may be ordered directly from the publisher. When ordering from the publisher, please add $2.50 shipping and handling for the first book, $.50 for each additional book. To order by mail, write
The Countryman Press • PO Box 175 • Woodstock, VT 05091